THE *Bent World*

The world is charged with the grandeur of God.
  It will flame out, like shining from shook foil;
  It gathers to a greatness, like the ooze of oil
Crushed. Why do men then now not reck his rod?
Generations have trod, have trod, have trod;
  And all is seared with trade; bleared, smeared with toil;
  And wears man's smudge and shares man's smell: the soil
Is bare now, nor can foot feel, being shod.

And for all this, nature is never spent;
  There lives the dearest freshness deep down things;
And though the last lights off the black West went
  Oh, morning, at the brown brink eastward, springs—
Because the Holy Ghost over the bent
  World broods with warm breast and with ah! bright wings.

—*Gerard Manley Hopkins*

J. V. LANGMEAD CASSERLEY

THE *Bent World*

GREENWOOD PRESS, PUBLISHERS
NEW YORK

First Greenwood Reprinting 1969

Library of Congress Catalogue Card Number 76-90480

SBN 8371-2214-7

PRINTED IN UNITED STATES OF AMERICA

TO

my elder son, Richard,
who is old enough to read his father's books
and may just as well start with this one.

Preface

Of the making of many books about Christianity, communism, and Western civilization there is apparently no end. It is useless to make a show of apologizing for having written a new one. If the book itself will not serve as my apology, then I have no apology. I can only say that although I have read many excellent books on this particular subject, all of them seem to me to have overlooked important things which I have tried to look at here, and to have omitted some vitally relevant matters which I have endeavored to incorporate in these pages. This book attempts a kind of completeness which can be achieved only by a certain degree of superficiality. The attempt to discuss everything that is relevant to a question inevitably means that insufficient space is allocated to any particular discussion, but in my view the kind of book that is an essay in synthesis — an attempt to assemble together things that really belong together, but in more acute and erudite discussions are usually taken apart — has its own particular function and may perhaps succeed in performing a valuable service.

Some of the chapters in this book were in their original form addresses delivered to various audiences on special occasions. The three chapters which compose part one of the book, on Marxism in Theory and Practice, are based on a series of addresses given to a large Rotary audience in Devonshire, England. The chapter on Christianity and Democracy was in its first form an address given at a George Washington breakfast in Manhasset, Long Island. It was subsequently published in the quarterly magazine, *Cross Currents*. The chapter on technics contains the substance of an address given at Jesus College, Oxford, to the Church Union Summer School of Sociology. But in every case these discourses were considerably enlarged and revised in order to incorporate them into the general structure and pattern of this book, so that it cannot be regarded simply as a collection of essays and addresses composed for numerous and distinct occasions.

J.V.L.C.

New York
March 1955

Contents

THE *Bent World*

Introduction

IN RECENT YEARS we have increasingly lapsed into the misleading habit of using the word 'communism' with reference only to one particular type of communism, which we may call the Russo-Marxist variety. This linguistic habit causes some people to forget that there are other varieties of communism besides the Russo-Marxist, or, if we are careful to remember that these other varieties exist, it leaves us without any clear and unambiguous set of terms with which to distinguish between them. Broadly speaking, we may separate three strands in the tangle of recent and contemporary communist belief, and we may differentiate between various groups of communists in accordance with the different ways in which they combine them. These three beliefs are as follows:

1. The belief that the communist way of life and scheme of social relationships has a special moral beauty, that it is a desirable thing which righteous people may well band together to practice, commend, and create.

2. The belief that a communist society, whether desirable or not, is rendered inevitable by the laws of history, so that intelligent people who understand the laws of history

will accept its necessity, and not squander their lives and energies in a vain attempt to resist it.

3. The belief that a communist society is now in process of being created in Soviet Russia, and in the countries which have fallen under its influence or accepted its leadership, and that in all these countries it will finally be established in a relatively short time.

The essence of Marxism is to insist on the second of these three beliefs. It is true that Marx, and most Marxists, also held that the communist society is desirable as well as inevitable, but such a belief in the ethical value and desirability of a communist society is not essential to the Marxist philosophy. The Russo-Marxists combine the second of these beliefs with the third, but by no means all Marxists are Russo-Marxists. Thus, for example, the Marxist regime in Yugoslavia is not Russo-Marxist. On the contrary it holds, like many Marxists in other parts of the world, that Soviet Russia has corrupted and abused the Marxist cause by turning Marxism into a sinister ideology which conceals and furthers its imperialistic designs and is no more than a mere instrument of the expansion of Russian national power. There is nothing paradoxical about an anti-Russian Marxism. Marx himself detested the Slav peoples, and believed that it was the destiny of the German nation to lead the world into communism, which, in his view, would be established first of all not in the predominantly peasant countries of Slav Europe and Asia but in the primarily industrial countries of the Western world. Thus Marx himself was anything but a Russo-Marxist.

The ethical or voluntary communists who turn up again and again in the long history of our civilization do not rely at all on the second and third of these three beliefs, but place their whole emphasis on the first of them. Nowadays some of them entertain a sentimental, and often rather unrealistic, affection for Soviet Russia, but they have no use at all for the particular philosophy of history which teaches the inevitability, as distinct from the desirability, of a communist social order.

Marxist and Russo-Marxist communism are obviously phenomena which have emerged only during the last hundred years or so. There were, after all, no Russo-Marxists as we now know them before 1917. Ethical communism, however, goes right back through our history and finally disappears into the mists of antiquity. It has even been supposed by some anthropologists — and this was also the belief of Marx and his friend Engels — that the most primitive forms of human society were communist in their economic organization. Private property was supposed to have developed much later, to have undermined the solidarity of primitive society and set men against each other. This was almost certainly a mistaken belief, but the mistake was not a mere surface mistake about the facts, it was a more subtle mistake about the way in which the facts must be interpreted. From our contemporary point of view, we are likely to suppose that private property and communism are the antithesis of each other, so that a society is based either on private ownership and use or on collective ownership and use. But we misunderstand the nature of primitive society if we interpret its economic institutions in terms of this modern antithesis. Even in contemporary society we are quite familiar with one particular form of communism — the family. In the united and happy family we find both private property and the collective use of the family's possessions happily and harmoniously combined. Usually the family property is in strict legal theory regarded as the private possession of one particular member of the family, the father or the mother or perhaps both combined, but in actual social practice all the members of the family share in the use and enjoyment of the family property. Thus the children will speak of *our* house or *our* automobile, and the food at the family dinner table, though the father may pay for it, is in fact shared among the members of the family in accordance with their needs. Each member of the family contributes to the prosperity of the whole according to his ability, or perhaps does not contribute according to his lack of ability, and receives his share of the family wealth according to his need. Thus, if there is a shortage of milk, the infant members of the family will get most of what little of it there is, despite the fact that they make no contribution to the family fund out of which the price of the milk is paid. Thus the property of the family is private from the point of view of the wider society to which the family belongs, but collective from the point of view of the family itself. Primitive society, so far as we can tell, was organized on a very small scale and consisted of families or small groups of kindred families, often interpreting themselves as one large family, called clans or tribes. These families and clans practiced the collective ownership and use of their resources, but they very much resented any taking over of these resources by other families and clans. The point is that it is quite possible for wealth to be at the same time corporately owned from one point of view and privately owned from another. Thus in primitive society communism and private property are not different or antithetical institutions; rather they are two different aspects of the same institution; and wherever the family survives, and so long as the family survives, the same thing is to some extent true of modern society.

During the long period when the young Western civilization was flourishing and developing under predominantly — although never exclusively — Christian influences, the most familiar and enduring form of communism proved to be the monastery. But here also we see that property which is collectively owned from one point of view — from the point of view, that is, of the members of the group which possesses it — is at the same time privately owned from another point of view — from the point of view of the wider society in which that group exists. Thus monks have no property and they live together a communistic existence; but although the monks themselves do not own any property, monasteries and monastic orders do, and from the point of view of society as a whole monastic property is private property. A whole legal theory has been developed, the theory of trusts and corporations, for the express purpose of assimilating these forms of collective ownership to the pattern and structure of a society which bases itself primarily on the assumptions of private property.

The great difference between the kind of communism practiced by families and monastic groups and the kind of communism nowadays advocated by the political communists may now be very simply defined. The former kind of communism is voluntary and spontaneous and it bands together only small, self-generating local groups in communistic practice. Political communism, on the other hand, advocates transforming whole nations into collective ownership groups, and this can be done only by compulsion. Political communism is thus quite a different thing from the voluntary, spontaneous communism of the family and the monastery, and would in fact destroy it altogether. From the point of view of political communism, the common property of a group of monks or nuns is private property which would be expropriated and transferred to the entire community like any other kind of private property. Similarly, the tendency of political communism is to be hostile to or at least suspicious of the family. Even where it tolerates or encourages the survival of the family, it turns it into a kind of pensioner existing in a state of total dependence on the wider community, and in order to fulfill such tasks and functions as the wider community thinks desirable to entrust to its care. Thus modern political communism is in no sense a revival of primitive communism. On the contrary, it is a totally new development which would effectively destroy all the forms of communism which society has known, tolerated, and even honored hitherto. Political communism not only menaces private property; it also menaces real communism, as well as the delicate but precious balance between legal private property and community and fellowship in the use of it which civilization has so artfully contrived and preserved. Part of the objection of Christian civilization to political communism is to be found precisely here. Political communism would destroy the very real social communism of the family which has done so much to bring sweetness and unselfishness to the world.

This leads us to a brief consideration of another very prevelant error of interpretation. It is commonly supposed that the true answer to communism, indeed our own characteristically Western and democratic answer to communism, is to be found in what is called 'individualism.' I seriously doubt whether this is at all true. Our society indeed professes to be individualistic, but this is only because most of us do not understand what real individualism means and would involve. In fact our society is to an overwhelming degree, even now, one in which men are grouped together in families, one which in everyday social practice presupposes that men are not solitary individuals but people who need each other, whose happiness is bound up with each other, so that apart from fellowship with other people human existence would be an empty thing.

But of our error in supposing that ours is in fact an individualistic society I shall write in a later chapter. The point that I want to make here is the extent to which political communism is in fact individualistic in its assumptions. For political communism the primary and most significant way in which men are grouped together is in the proletarian state. The other ways in which men group themselves, in families, in neighborhood units, in associations of friends and like-minded people, in churches, and the like, are either undervalued by political communism or disliked and distrusted and viewed as objects of suspicion. The communist state is essentially a chaos of individuals, welded together by their common subjection to the political regime, which is taken to be the sole creator of true social order. From this point of view men do not create society spontaneously by living together in free association; rather society has to be created for them and forced upon them by the political state. Thus at the very basis of political communism is to be found an individualistic interpretation of human existence. Society, from this point of view, is created by the state. From our Western, democratic point of view society is natural to man; it is created by men, who out of their own living together produce the state as the agent and servant of the common purposes. Thus at this deep level of analysis it is political communism that is individualistic rather than our own form of modern Western civilization. We shall return to this distinction at a later stage.

The important point to be emphasized here in this introductory chapter is this: the contemporary struggle of Western civilization is not a struggle, as the language in which we conventionally express it seems to suggest, against communism in general. Nor is it necessarily a struggle against non-Russian forms of Marxism. It is essentially a struggle with the Russo-Marxist form of communism. Some forms of voluntary and spontaneous communism are actually to be found in our own tradition of civilization. With non-Russian Marxism, as we find it, for example, in Yugoslavia, we may indeed differ and differ profoundly on the philosophical and religious level, but these philosophical and religious differences need not necessarily involve us in a political or military struggle. With Russo-Marxism, however, in which Marxism is inextricably intertwined with Russian imperialism, the Western world is now at war politically, and may conceivably be one day at war in the military sense. This conflict with Russo-Marxism is taking place on several distinct levels. There is at the time of writing no actual military conflict, but both Russia and the West are employing a high proportion of their economic resources in such a way as to insure that they will be fully prepared should a military conflict suddenly erupt. There are certainly areas of acute military tension and sensitiveness. There is, on the other hand, a violent and embittered diplomatic and political conflict. Indeed it is only because of the terrible scope and the unimaginable destructive potential of modern weapons that this political and diplomatic conflict has not yet produced an outbreak of war on a vast international scale. Perhaps never before in world history has it been possible for diplomatic relations to be so strained for such a prolonged period without either side venturing to resort to general war. But beneath this diplomatic and political conflict there is also a profounder but not less — indeed perhaps more — significant conflict on the philosophical and religious level. Is Marxism a true or perhaps *the* true philosophy? Even if Marxism is false, may it not still be true that some of the Marxist criticisms of our civilization are valid? Marxism thus challenges us to think clearly and to probe our own hearts and consciences to the very depths.

The main preoccupation of this book is with the conflict between Russo-Marxism and Western civilization on this third and deepest level. Merely to reject Marxism is not enough. Too many of us reject it without understanding it, and too often for the wrong reasons. In any case what we reject and deny in life is never so important as what we accept and affirm. Healthy denial is a kind of by-product of affirmation. When a man rejects a theory or philosophy with any conviction he does so because he believes in another theory or philosophy which he regards as better than and incompatible with what he rejects. One of the weaknesses of anti-Marxist propaganda in the contemporary Western world is our failure to combine it with and base it upon really deep and worth-while affirmations of the positive philosophy which is the basis of our anti-Marxist position. Any anti-Marxist propaganda that does not really take the trouble to understand Marxism will certainly fail to convince mankind. Similarly any anti-Marxist propaganda that does not affirm a religion and philosophy which it clearly sees and can show to be superior to Marxism will in the long run prove almost equally futile and ineffective.

It seems to me that a great deal of anti-Marxist propaganda in the Western world is futile and ineffective. Too often the anti-Marxist propagandists have not taken the trouble to achieve any deep understanding of what Marxism teaches, and of the source of the fascination it exercises over many contemporary minds. Too often, also, they repeat old shibboleths about freedom and individual rights without understanding them any better than they understand Marxism itself. Too often they fail to give any clear and cogent account of a possible alternative to Marxism in the name of which Marxism is and must be decisively rejected. Too often, to put it briefly, the answer to the challenge of Marxism is given by Western thinkers who represent our civilization only in its humanistic and secularized phase and who are almost, perhaps quite, as much estranged from its Christian roots and its Christian values as the Marxists themselves. I believe that although these propagandists may convince many of us in this country, they are in fact losing the ideological struggle in the world as a whole.

The really powerful alternative to Marxism is not a pagan and secularized individualistic democracy but the Christian interpretation of human existence in society and history, which transcends the conflict between Marxism and humanistic democracy in a new and deeper understanding of what both these contending forces are searching for. The essential basis of the West's answer to the Marxist challenge must be a new understanding of Christianity, and a new understanding of itself in terms of Christianity. When we achieve that we shall see that the challenge of our own Christianity to the present condition of our own Western civilization is profounder and more crucial than the challenge of Marxism can ever be.

For Marxism does not challenge Western civilization in its present form all along the line; what it proposes in effect is a reorientation of our paganism, a new program for implementing and fulfilling our materialism, a different technique for carrying out our humanistic purposes and ambitions. The real reason that Western civilization, in its neo-paganism, its economic materialism, its purblind humanism, in its all-pervading secularity, cannot answer the Marxist criticism of Western civilization effectively is this: *Western civilization in its secular phase is half-Marxist already.* Marxism is indeed itself a product of Western civilization in this secular phase, and it claims that it alone can fulfill the secular ambitions of modern Western man and make full use of those things on which modern Western secular man most characteristically and unhesitatingly relies. The Marxist will often argue that Marxism is not really a challenge or a menace to the West after all, but rather the fulfillment of the whole dialectic of Western civilization. It is possible for him to argue this because he interprets the essence of Western civilization in a secular and anti-Christian fashion. We shall find it difficult to evade the Marxist conclusion, however, if in the area of our deepest convictions and attitudes toward life we ourselves accept the premise on which it is based.

The shape of this book is already clearly envisaged in this brief introductory chapter. First of all we shall have to consider, in brief summary fashion, precisely what Russo-Marxism amounts to, and try to understand the secret of its appeal to so many of our contemporaries. After that we must examine the characteristic weakness and inaptitudes of the kind of secularized thinking that attempts to answer the Marxist challenge. Finally we shall take into account the central role of the Christian Church and its theology in this historic and tragic controversy, for underlying this whole book is the conviction that if the defense of Western civilization against the Marxist attack is left to the mind and outlook of that civilization in its secular phase, then the defense of the West is a doomed enterprise which will be undertaken in vain.

PART I *Marxism in Theory and Practic*

ONE

The Teachings of Karl Marx

It cannot be pretended that Marx was a pleasant person. He was loyal and affectionate to his family and, after an early period of vacillation and opportunism, consistent and sincere in his beliefs. There must have been something in him, too, capable of inspiring and sustaining the lifelong, unselfish devotion of Engels, his only real friend. But his human sympathies were narrow. He was intolerant of criticism and opposition, and one after the other his colleagues of a stature comparable with his were hounded out of that section of the working-class movement of which he was the acknowledged *Führer* — Proudhon, Bakunin, and Lassalle, for example. But whether or not he was a pleasant person he was clearly one of the most important and influential of all modern thinkers and the communists are not the only people who may profit from his teaching.

Indeed, the orthodox Marxist tradition has not even preserved all that we find in Marx himself. There were elements of his philosophy that his followers failed to assimilate — for example, the almost existentialist subtlety of his analysis of the paradoxical relationship between man and the things which man makes, and which subsequently go far toward remaking him. Here, however, it is the more familiar aspects of his teaching, which still dominate the contemporary Marxist preaching and apologetic, with which we must be concerned.

MARXIST ECONOMICS. Contrary to the general impression, Marx was not a creative or original economist. He was a brilliant analyst of the economic aspects, and impacts, of contemporary events, and he had a genius for grouping ideas together in a coherent system, but he added few novel economic ideas or discoveries of his own. His chief economic doctrines were in fact derived from the classical economists of the early capitalist epoch. Thus a first sketch of the labor theory of value can be found in Adam Smith, and some kind of 'iron law' theory of wages — which implied that the working-class standard of living can never rise above the minimum level essential to bare subsistence — was an integral part of economic orthodoxy for at least half a century after Malthus. Most economists would now hold that the former of these theories is almost certainly, and the latter quite certainly, false, but at least it must be conceded that when Marx interpreted capitalism in terms of expropriation and exploitation, and prophesied that under capitalism the physical burdens of the workers could not be eased, he was drawing not on his own imagination but on the writings of recognized and celebrated, indeed the classical, expositors of the institutions of the capitalist epoch.

THE ECONOMIC INTERPRETATION OF HISTORY. It is important to emphasize that the economic interpretation of history is not itself economics. Just as a metaphysical theory such as Bergson's 'creative evolution' cannot be reckoned as biology simply because it makes use of a biological concept in a metaphysical argument, so Marx's economic materialism is just one more speculative philosophy of history, and its use of economic concepts in no way implies that it belongs to or possesses the authority, such as it is, of economic science.

Certainly Marx's emphasis on the fundamental importance of the influence of economic factors and processes on social development and change has taught the non-Marxists quite as much as it has inspired the Marxists. But is it true that the economic factor is the only, or even necessarily the sovereign, factor in the determination of social change? It is not even clear that Marx himself ever really supposed that it was. Engels says in one of his letters that both he and Marx always realized that there were other fundamental factors, but lacked the time and opportunity in which to study them. But in practice all Marxist propaganda seems to proceed on the assumption that economic factors alone are ultimately decisive, and that all other social and cultural forms only reflect on their own levels and in their own contexts the contemporary conditions of production.

We have barely space here to enumerate the objections to this theory. We find very different social systems and types of cultural activity flourishing in very similar economic circumstances. There may be vigorous cultural developments in periods during which the conditions of production remain relatively static. In a time of swift economic development like our own, economic change may be much more rapid than social change, and the vogue of any one particular set of economic circumstances may be too brief to permit it to exert its maximum influence on social and cultural institutions. It is this factor that often gives the cultural conservative a sporting chance of success. Economic and material change tends to establish itself most securely, and most of all to succeed in transforming society to its very depths, when it takes place relatively slowly and has ample time in which to make its full impact on fundamental human attitudes and social institutions. Again, many changes in the conditions of production are themselves due to developments in the cultural field. It is more plausible, for example, to interpret modern technological developments as the consequence of the progress of scientific thought and research than to interpret the latter as the reflection of the former. Marx himself remarks that it is the function of philosophy not to understand reality but to change it — which certainly implies that it does not merely passively reflect it.

The modern sociologists, who have replaced the older and more speculative philosophers of history, generally agree that there is no one sovereign concept in terms of which all social phenomena can be interpreted and unified. On the contrary, in sociology we have to do with a plurality of independent but interacting functions, which reflect the richness and variety of man's natural endowment. Marxism is by no means the only example of what we may call the sociological fallacy of illicit simplification, but it is perhaps the most striking and important.

The Paradox of a 'Dialectical' Materialism. Behind the readily comprehensible economic interpretation of history loom the vague, cloudy outlines of Marxist metaphysics — a materialism that is quite unlike the kind of doctrine we usually associate with the word. This materialism is *dialectical.* It attributes to matter the kind of behavior which the great idealist-philosopher, Hegel, who was Marx's chief mentor, attributed to mind.

What does the word 'dialectic' mean? It is a broad term used to describe the methods by which reason proceeds in and through discussion toward a resolution of its problems.

Hegel analyzes the process along the following lines: in a discussion one of the participants advances an initial proposition A, called the *thesis,* to which the other replies with a proposition B, the *antithesis,* which is apparently incompatible with A. If the discussion is on both sides a sincere search for truth, and not a mere argument in which the antagonists desire no more than to score debating points off each other, they then proceed to a further proposition, the *synthesis,* which contains and reconciles all that was true in both A and B. The conversation may be represented like this: 'Clearly A is true.' 'But, surely, the fact is that B is true.' 'There is something in what you say, but I am not altogether wrong about A either. I have the solution! C makes sense of all that really attracted us to A and B, while avoiding their narrowness and transcending their limitations.' The same process can be observed in our private thought, for reflection is only a kind of internal conversation which a man holds with himself. The conception of a dialectic of reason is not, of course, peculiar to Hegel. Ancient Greek philosophers such as Plato and Aristotle were greatly preoccupied with analyzing the dialectical process, and medieval philosophers, such as St. Thomas Aquinas, habitually employed a method of thought and exposition substantially identical with Hegel's dialectic.

Thought thus advances through and by means of a kind of creative opposition and strife. But Hegel believed that the laws of thought were also the laws of reality. Thought is only able to operate fruitfully in this dialectical fashion because reality itself is rational, and therefore behaves in the same dialectical way. Because reality thus behaves in accordance with the laws of thought, Hegel concluded that reality itself is of a mental or spiritual character. 'The real is the rational.' Whether we agree with him or not, this certainly gives us a coherent philosophical system. We can tell how the mind behaves by scrutinizing carefully how our own minds behave when we are thinking fruitfully and to some purpose. But if such thought helps us, as we see it does, to discover the truth about reality, it can do so only if reality itself behaves in the same dialectical fashion. But to say that reality behaves as thought behaves is another way of saying that reality is akin to thought, that they both belong to the same order of being. All reality, for the Hegelian philosopher, is therefore of a mental character.

Now Marx accepted Hegel's account of the dialectic of thought, and he agreed that since we find thought worth while and fruitful we are driven to the conclusion that thought and reality are fundamentally akin to each other, that the dialectic of the one must be the dialectic of the other. Where he differed from Hegel was in the further conclusion which he drew from these premises. Whereas Hegel argued that since thought and reality are akin, and since thought is certainly mental, reality must be mental too, Marx 'stood Hegel on his head' and contended that if thought and reality are akin, then, since reality is certainly material, it follows that thought must be material also.

And so he conceived this strange speculative materialism which attributes to matter the kind of behavior which was first discovered and analyzed not in the sciences that deal with obviously material realities but in the philosopher's abstruse study of his own abstract mental processes. Of course, Marx holds that some form of dialectical opposition turns up everywhere if we look for it. Thus we have the class struggle in history and the struggle for existence in evolutionary biology. In the physical sciences the process is more difficult to trace, but the Marxists are emphatic that it must be there, and the tendency of the communist governments to interfere from time to time with scientific thought and research, recently relaxed a little for purely pragmatic reasons, is partly to be explained by the importance they attach to its discovery, and by their impatience with scientists who show little disposition or capacity to discover it.

Nevertheless, the whole theory is profoundly paradoxical and self-contradictory. It is, indeed, one of the curiosities of philosophy. The laws of dialectic are declared to be the laws of material reality but they are discovered, observed, and analyzed not by scientists, who make it their business to discover such laws, but by 'airy-fairy' metaphysicians like Plato and St. Thomas Aquinas and Hegel. The Marxist theory is in no sense scientific. Dialectical materialism cannot be verified or demonstrated by scientific research. No doubt the theory can be reconciled with the results of scientific research by ingenious people who think such an operation worth the effort and trouble entailed, but the concept of the dialectic remains itself the product of that extremely speculative and abstract kind of metaphysical theorizing which, if materialism is true, ought to be dismissed and abandoned as a mere waste of time.

The word 'idealistic' was one of Marx's favorite abusive epithets — and Marx was a specialist in the not very gentle art of abuse, as are most of his disciples to this day — and yet he himself had borrowed the key conception of his whole philosophy from the greatest of all modern idealistic thinkers. It is a profoundly paradoxical situation. The independent reality of mind is denied and yet mind's most characteristic forms of behavior are attributed to matter, so that the ultimate and basic laws of material behavior have been discovered not by the natural scientists but by the speculative idealistic metaphysicians. We are led to the conclusion that Marx had little aptitude for metaphysics. If his reputation rested on the theory of dialectical materialism alone he would have been forgotten long ago.

Nevertheless, although the doctrine is confused and paradoxical, it is important to observe that the Marxist brand of materialism is quite unlike any other form of materialism to be found in non-Marxist philosophy. Conventionally the word materialism is used to indicate and identify the naïve doctrine that material particles in motion constitute the only reality, and that all processes whatsoever can finally be understood in the light of the laws of physics and chemistry, as these have been ascertained by the accepted and appropriate methods of scientific analysis and research. It is very clear that the materialism of Marx is not a materialism of this simple and naïve character. For Marx all reality is material, but what he calls matter suspiciously resembles in its mode of behavior what other philosophers call mind, and the basic laws of material behavior are discovered not by scientific thought and research but by metaphysical analysis and speculation. Some writers hold that Marx insisted on the material character of all reality, and on using the word materialism to describe his philosophy, for emotional rather than intellectual reasons. For him the words materialism and materialist had the virtue of indicating in a rather confused way that he was a good, respectable, up-to-date, mid-nineteenth-century positivist philosopher who was against religion, as religion was understood in the nineteenth century by the theologians and anti-Christians alike, and in favor of science. Actually, however, his choice of the word was unfortunate, for in the conventional and everyday sense Marx cannot be described with complete accuracy as a materialist.

There is, however, another sense of the words materialism and materialist which describes Marx much more appropriately and accurately. There is a philosophical or metaphysical materialism, which teaches that matter in motion, as science defines and analyzes the laws of motion, is the only reality. But there is also an ethical or practical materialism, which teaches that the only truly human satisfactions are material satisfactions and that, in consequence, only material satisfactions are worth working for. This belief is the very essence of secularism in all its forms. For such a philosophy man is a purely temporal being and the rational man will devote his energy to the pursuit of purely temporal ends. It is a radical this-worldly philosophy. Clearly Marx and the Marxists are materialists in this sense, but so, we must add, are a great number of non-Marxist Western philosophers, some of whom at least have been venerated in recent times as important philosophical interpreters of the spirit of democracy. In this sense of the word, for example, Dewey and many of the pragmatists are quite as materialistic as Marx himself, so that we must acknowledge that many of the anti-communists are as materialistic in their philosophy as the communists are.

Nor can we say, from the Christian point of view, that materialism is totally false. It is woefully inadequate as a philosophy of life and interpretation of human existence. But Christianity must agree that materialism is at least right to take seriously what is usually called material reality and life in this world. Christianity cannot have anything to do with the kind of introverted religious thinking which bids men turn their backs on the world and the problems of life in order to concentrate on the spiritual world. For Christianity there are not two worlds, one material and one spiritual, but one world in which both material and spiritual realities are inextricably intertwined with each other. Properly understood the word 'spiritual' does not mean merely the non-material, and the primacy of the spiritual does not mean simply that the spiritual world is higher and more important than the material world. Certainly for Christianity it is an utterly false spirituality which proceeds by neglecting and ignoring the reality of the material world. The meaning of Christian existence is not to turn our backs on the material in order to cultivate the spiritual, but rather to make the material the instrument of the spiritual, so that spiritual purposes predominate even in a material world, for in Christian doctrine matter is just as much the creation of God as spirit. The late Archbishop Temple was fond of remarking, 'Christianity is the most materialistic of all the great religions.' If to take matter seriously as a work of God which embodies a divine purpose is to be materialistic then Dr. Temple was undoubtedly right. The Christian will not criticize the materialist for taking matter seriously and believing that material satisfactions are of real importance to men. The Christian will be critical not of what the materialists affirm but of what they ignore and deny. Matter is real, but it is not the only reality. Material satisfactions are important, but they are not the only satisfactions necessary to human well-being. A narrow materialism that ignores spiritual reality is as bad as, but not worse than, a narrow spirituality that ignores material reality. Christianity can have nothing to do with either of these heresies. Man cannot live by bread alone does not mean that man can live without any bread at all. We see the Christian synthesis most clearly worked out in the sacraments, in which material realities of water, bread, and wine become the channels of the deepest and profoundest spiritual experiences of the Christian Church. Christianity believes in and embraces a spirituality that knows how to make material reality the instrument of its spiritual reality and self-expression. It believes in and reverences a material reality which was created for that very purpose, that it might serve the spiritual ends and purposes of God and man.

THE CONCEPT OF IDEOLOGY. But whatever we may think of dialectical materialism as metaphysics, and of the economic interpretation of history as sociology, it remains true that the economic factor in social development is clearly of an importance second to none. That is why we must examine carefully the Marxist conception of ideology, for it is in the theory of the ideology that Marx tries to show us how in fact economic tendencies do influence and sometimes determine cultural behavior. According to strict Marxism all religious beliefs, philosophical theories, and artistic forms reflect, justify, and embellish existing economic interests. There can be no doubt that this is often true. Thus the saintly Hannah More remarked, sometime about the beginning of the nineteenth century, on the wisdom and graciousness of divine providence in creating both the rich and the poor. There are few virtues so sweetening in their influence on social life as generosity and gratitude. And so God in His wisdom has given us the rich to be generous and the poor to be grateful. Admirable contrivance! Now this good Christian woman, as indeed she was, sincerely supposed herself to be uttering a beautiful and spiritual thought. Whomever else she deceived, she certainly began by deceiving herself. But it is important to notice that, although she exploits the theological ideas of creation and divine providence, and the ethical belief in the goodness of generosity and gratitude, in order to reconcile us to the social context in which she found herself, she did not *invent* any of those ideas for that purpose. The system of ideas to which she gives her own ideological twist had in fact a quite independent origin and appeal of its own. This example suggests that Marx was mistaken in supposing that ideas are created for purely ideological purposes. On the contrary, when we use ideas ideologically our purposes will be more efficiently served if we employ only such conceptions as we find already possessing a prestige and authority of their own independently of our ideological needs. In other words, the genesis of an idea can hardly ever be ideologically explained. It is only in the use to which we put our ideas that we can often trace what we may call the ideologizing process. So understood, the Marxist conception is of invaluable aid to Christians even in the discipline of their private spiritual lives. 'Have I exploited Christian ideas for ideological purposes?' is a question that might well be included in every devotional manual and guide to self-examination.

But is Marxism itself an ideology? Quite clearly it serves to justify and express the economic exasperation and interests of the proletarian classes, and to strengthen their morale by convincing them that the whole process of historical development is moving by inevitable stages toward a final and dramatic vindication of their claims. Some Marxists argue, however, that Marxism is non-ideological because it is science, and that science, unlike philosophy and religion, deals not with ideas but only with objective facts. Now is it quite clear that Marxism is not science in this sense, but highly speculative philosophy. But it is more important to observe that the Marxists are not by any means agreed that even science is in fact non-ideological. On the contrary, the Lysenko incident, now apparently drawing to its close, and the similar attacks on the quantum theory and the indeterminacy principle as degenerate bourgeois doctrines seem to imply that, in the Marxist view, modern science can be put to ideological uses just as efficiently as religious beliefs and philosophical theories. And this is clearly true. Consider, for example, the way in which certain German thinkers have used the Darwinian notions of natural selection and the struggle for existence to justify and even glorify war. Sumner employed the same doctrine in his apologetic for an economic society based on ruthless competition. Nevertheless, here as elsewhere it remains true that to detect the ideological motives that sometimes prompt and determine the use we make of our ideas is never the same as to expose and refute the ideas themselves.

It is this confusion between ideological exposure and rational refutation that has done so much to bring about the marked decline in the art of rational discussion in the modern world. In the old days the object of argument was to refute the reasoning of one's opponent. Now we labor only to expose his motives. 'Yah! you only believe in property because you've got some.' 'Yah! you only disbelieve in property because you haven't any.' From such depths of rational ineptitude it is but a short step to crying out, 'Fascist hyena,' or 'Bolshevist beast,' and reaching for a gun. But provided we are careful to remember that ideology exploits ideas but never invents them, so that to expose a man's unconscious and self-interested motives is never the same thing as to refute his explicit rationalizations, we can safely accept the conception of ideology as a profoundly important contribution to the sociology of knowledge and culture.

The theory of the ideology is in my view Marx's most important contribution to modern thought. It may even be seriously considered as a contribution to Christian theology. The belief that man is a fallen creature would appear to imply that the fall injures and corrupts man's rational thinking just as much as it distorts every other human activity from its true purpose. The theory of the ideology shows us one of the ways in which even the rational thinking of fallen man can be corrupted, robbed of its honesty and integrity, even without the thinker himself being conscious of the fact. All ideology is sin and man's tendency toward ideological thinking is one of the consequences of his fallen condition. Nevertheless the Marxists are mistaken in supposing that only economic motives and class interests lead to and produce the formulation of ideologies. In the modern world we know of many ideologies that are not primarily economic in their original motivation. Thus we have theories that employ an elaborate pseudo-biological and pseudo-psychological apparatus in order to prove to the satisfaction of one racial group that scientific methods can show that it is naturally superior to all other racial groups. Thus, for example, an elaborate Nazi biology was developed in the German universities during the period of the Nazi domination of Germany. Intensely color-conscious groups will often elaborate quite imposing ideological structures in order to prove the innate superiority, mental, moral, and physical, of white men over Negroes. Feminism has produced a sex ideology which will often go to quite ridiculous lengths in reducing the differences between men and women to nothing. Similarly what we may call 'generation consciousness' may produce ideologies. We are told in some societies that the old must be wiser than the young because of their greater experience, or conversely that the young must be more energetic than the aged for all sorts of rather questionable physiological reasons. Whenever thought devotes itself to demonstrating the inherent superiority of one human group, to which the thinker himself usually belongs, the sin of ideology must always be suspected. The validity of such arguments is always subject to the gravest doubt, and the intellectual honesty of those who put them forward must be scrutinized with the deepest suspicion.

MARX AND THE CLASS STRUCTURE. Fundamental to the Marxist thesis and the Marxist hope is a sociological analysis which purports to show that we have now reached a point in history at which for all practical purposes only two contending classes remain — the bourgeoisie and the proletariat. All history so far has been the history of class struggles. But with the triumph of the proletariat and the liquidation of the bourgeoisie a new kind of history will begin in which the class struggle can have no place. Indeed, in a fine eschatological passage, recalling somewhat the Hebrew prophets, particularly Isaiah, Marx tells us that in that hour of victory real history will at last begin. But all this unbounded proletarian optimism is precariously based on the two-class analysis of capitalist society. Can we really believe in it?

First, who, according to Marx, constitute the bourgeoisie? This is clearly a portmanteau term which includes the decaying remnants of the old aristocracy; an idle *rentier* class living on the proceeds of invested capital; an economically active property-owning class which controls the means of credit, production, and distribution; professional groups such as doctors and lawyers; and, in Marx's time, a relatively small company of white-collar workers engaged in various types of administrative occupations, the germ of our modern bureaucracy. The proletariat includes the great mass of industrial wage earners. There are two major problems, the white-collar, wage-earning bureaucracy and the rural workers or peasants. For the moment I have included the former among the bourgeoisie, but Marx himself believed that this white-collar proletariat would in the long run realize the solidarity of its interests and those of other wage earners and merge with the industrial proletariat. The problem of the peasant is more difficult. A recent communist prime minister of Hungary informed the world that, in the technical Marxist sense, of course, the peasant is not a worker; and Lenin, it may be remembered, declared that he 'is the principal enemy of our Bolshevism.' More often, however, he is interpreted by Marxist writers as a mentally backward and unprogressive type of worker. One of the aims of the collective-farming system is to provide the peasant with the kind of environment that will foster in his mind something more like the industrial workers' corporate consciousness of mass solidarity. For the moment, however, the peasant would seem to be neither proletarian nor bourgeois, an enigmatical social factor which the two-class analysis cannot assimilate.

Equally out of line with the Marxist interpretation of the class situation is the fact that during the century since the publication of the *Communist Manifesto* the bureaucracy has increased enormously in numbers and power and evinced little or no disposition to merge itself in thought, feeling, and aspiration with the proletariat. In the modern highly industrialized, heavily administered democracies of the new Western welfare type, the bureaucracy to all intents and purposes is the bourgeoisie. Indeed, with the increasing rationalization of industry and the growing organizational complexity of the welfare state, the tendency is for society to require fewer proletarians and more and more bureaucrats. The twentieth century has even showed us how, in certain circumstances which depress and exasperate this new middle class, it may become a revolutionary class and stage a kind of revolution very different from any Marx foresaw.

Marx understood well enough that a man's outlook and social aspirations are very largely determined by the way in which he earns his living, but he paid too much attention to the pure economic form of occupations and too little to their concrete details. Thus he supposed, at all events for the purposes of his analysis, that all forms of wage earning are fundamentally of a similar character. But in fact an occupation is much more than a livelihood. It is also a way of life. Veblen, the American sociologist, comprehended the depths of the Marxist insight here much more profoundly than Marx himself did. Earning a wage in an office is a very different thing from earning a wage in a factory, and both differ again from earning a wage on a farm. In the same way owning a shop differs from owning a factory, both differ from owning land, and all three are different from merely passive shareholding.

The two-class analysis is thus a gross over-simplification which entirely fails to comprehend the psychologies of different groups of workers. It is this fundamental sociological error which very largely explains the failure of the communist revolution to proceed even from the outset according to the Marxist plan.

THE MYSTICISM OF MARX. But the attraction of Marxism today is not to be found in the real or imagined illumination and cogency of these somewhat precarious and very abstract metaphysical and sociological speculations. First and foremost, Marxism is a mystical substitute for religion, not a mystique of transcendent deity but a dynamic mystique of history. (Christianity, it will be noticed, is both of these things at the same time, a kind of synthesis of Marxist and Eastern mysticism.) The essential difference between Marxism and other forms of socialism is that whereas the latter treat the equalitarian society as ethically desirable the Marxists regard it as historically inevitable. Hence whereas socialist exhortation is moralistic, Marxist preaching, like Christian preaching, is mystical, and, in a peculiar way, theological, concerned not with moral ideals and imperatives but with the realities that preside over man's destiny. The Marxist consciously co-operates with what he believes to be the forces of history. Rational, purposeful living means, according to him, life which reconciles itself to reality and does not struggle vainly against it. We are reminded of Peter's stinging cry to the Jerusalem Jews, 'God has made Him both Lord and Christ, this Jesus Whom you crucified.' The point is that to live against or without this death-conquering Christ is not so much wickedness as vanity. Even so for the Marxists true freedom is to be found not in sheer arbitrary self-determination but in understanding and willing the inevitable, 'whose service is perfect freedom.'

Even the Marxist scheme of history runs precisely parallel to the Biblical scheme, of which indeed it is only a secularized version. First we have the long period of history dominated by the ubiquitous class struggle (corresponding to the history of a fallen world B.C.); then the revolution (the Marxist parallel to the redemption of mankind in Christ); then the dictatorship of the proletariat (a secularized version of the history of a fallen-redeemed world A.D., knowing its King and waiting for the fullness of the Kingdom); lastly the coming of the classless society and the 'withering away' of the state (the earthly counterpart of the Christian belief in the end of the world and the final establishment of the Kingdom of God). For myself I accept the

Christian scheme wholeheartedly and find the Marxist version of it self-contradictory and incredible, but that is only because I am one of those whose thought and imagination are not chained up and restricted by the narrow presuppositions of the secular outlook. But there are millions of people today who are still subconsciously and spiritually attracted and enthralled by the Biblical account of life and history, but who, because of their secular presuppositions, can express and believe it only in its secularized Marxist form. In this sense Marxism is a Christian heresy rather than a system of downright unbelief. The truth is that Marx himself was always a Jew at heart, and stands in the tradition of the Old Testament prophets — a kind of atheistical Amos, paradoxically denying God's existence and yet at the same time still finding a way of asserting the sovereignty in history of his righteous will.

MARX AS A PROPHET. Nevertheless, Marx's essays in prophetic prediction were not conspicuously successful. His analysis of the internal contradictions of capitalism was profound and important, but even now — perhaps with the aid of moderate socialist, welfare economics, and Keynesian financial techniques, perhaps in some other way — it may well prove possible to overcome them. He supposed that the revolution would come about first of all in advanced industrial countries, whereas it has in fact broken out in backward, mainly peasant countries, which have not yet developed a large and powerful middle class. He entirely failed to foresee that the white-collar wage earners would not merge with the proletariat but, on the contrary, when sufficiently exasperated, they would stage a new kind of revolution of their own. (In 1933, 44 per cent of the Nazi party membership was drawn from this social stratum.) Because Marx failed to foresee fascism the Marxists to this day have proved quite incapable of interpreting it, and they are usually reduced to the feeble pretense that it is only a form of violent capitalist reaction. Even in the officially Marxist countries, the course of events, as we shall see, still obstinately refuses to conform to the proper Marxist pattern. Marx's failure as a prophet and interpreter of events is vitally relevant to our discussion. Marxism, like Christianity and all forms of prophecy, takes the risk of appealing to history, and must therefore accept the consequences.

TWO

The Russian Revolution

CONTRARY TO Marx's own expectations the revolution began in Russia. He was himself imbued with a characteristically German dislike of Slavs, and would not have taken kindly to the notion that the great east European empire should become the beloved fatherland of the revolution. Yet so it has come about, and his own gospel has been transformed into an ideology which ministers to Russia's expansion, along lines of which the Czars often dreamed but were never able to advance successfully.

WHY RUSSIA? For centuries Russian society has been distinguished from that of western Europe primarily by its reception and assimilation of Christianity in a non-prophetic form, a Christianity with an ingrained habit of conforming loyally to state directives. The conflict between Church and State, so characteristic of Western history, does not appear in Russian history. In the West the tendency is always to build up two parallel and sometimes competing systems of ecclesiastical and secular loyalty. This is not peculiar to Roman Catholics but common to almost all Western Christians. The Calvinists were always ready to resist the State from the first. The shallowness of the Anglican profession of passive obedience was exposed by the seven bishops who resisted the fiat of James II. Even the Lutherans — the most Eastern in spirit of Western confessional groups — turned on Hitler at last, and with very considerable effect. Now, a non-prophetic Christianity inevitably encourages non-Christian forms of prophecy, and is ill-equipped to resist them when they appear.

In modern times east European society has been distinguished from west European society by its comparative industrial backwardness. In the Eastern countries a large and ill-organized peasantry predominates, and the urban-dwelling proletarians are a small but easily united minority. Even more significant, the bureaucratic class is small and relatively unimportant. Recent history shows that a peasant majority can be won over by large and exciting promises at the time of the revolution and later crushed by a well-organized proletarian minority. More difficult for the communists to overcome — perhaps impossible — is the opposition of the large and politically and socially conscious urban bourgeois groups characteristic of states more developed organizationally and industrially. In such circumstances it would appear to be impossible for even large and well-organized communist parties, such as the French and the Italian, to establish themselves by revolution. At present their only hope of attaining power appears to be through the armed conquest of their countries by the Red Army.

THE PERSISTENCE OF THE PEASANT. The Russian Revolution of 1917 was really a well-contrived coincidence of two revolutions — a socialist revolution in the towns, collectivizing the means of industrial production, and a distributist revolution in the countryside, dividing up the old estates among the peasants. But the substance of political power remained inevitably with the urban revolutionaries. At a later stage came the inevitable clash between the two. The urban workers wanted an assured and inexpensive food supply — this type of conflict between urban and rural workers recurs repeatedly throughout all civilized history — and their political interests and human outlooks were too sharply opposed for peasant proprietors and urban socialists to settle down side by side indefinitely.

From the point of view of a proletarian government the collective-farming policy has a twofold aim. In the first place it reduces the rural workers to a condition of inferiority and servitude. It gives the proletarians control of their food supply and food prices, banishing all fear of a peasant strike or any tendency on the part of the rural producer to refuse to dispose of his products in an unattractive market. In the second place it represents a genuine effort to assimilate the conditions of agricultural production to those of industrial production so that through such a new way of life and environment the peasants may be psychologically transformed into good proletarians at last. It is only fair to add that the collective farm also holds out the possibility of a greater volume of agricultural production, although whether it will necessarily increase yields in the long run is still a question open to some doubt. It has two characteristic defects: it fails to secure the enthusiastic cooperation of the peasants themselves, and its primarily urban inspiration and direction may easily produce a 'soil mining' policy in the interests of higher production which will lead at last to the erosion of the fertile earth.

In Russia itself the main attack on the peasants was delayed until thirteen years after the Revolution — although the satellite postwar communist states have not all, it seems, been so patient — and raged from 1929 to 1936. At times ruthless force was employed, at others more peaceful methods of persuasion were attempted. Nevertheless, the total number of casualties, from famine and disease as well as through fighting and executions, was, although variously estimated, by common consent horrifyingly large. By the end of 1936, however, the Nazi menace was beginning to modify Russian plans, and a policy of conciliation was embarked upon. Since 1932, individual peasants had been permitted to own, to a very small extent, their own cattle within the general framework of the collectives, and later individual families were permitted to have their own allotments and to sell their produce in a free market. The collective thus came to resemble a medieval manor, with the peasants dividing their working time between the collectively owned land and animals and their own. The latter of these two functions was understandably enough discharged more enthusiastically and effectively than the former. According to official complaints and decrees issued during 1938 and 1939 the privately owned animals bred more rapidly than those collectively owned and the size of the private allotments displayed a strange capacity for spontaneous increase. 'Steps have to be taken to stop this kind of thing,' declared a government decree in 1938, 'as it leads to the development of bourgeois tendencies.'

There is thus plenty of evidence of the survival of the peasant spirit. It is perhaps significant that it was precisely in the areas which had witnessed the collectivization struggle ten years before that Hitler found it easiest to secure the military services of disaffected Soviet citizens.

THE SURVIVAL OF THE BOURGEOISIE. More than thirty years after the Revolution it is still necessary for the watchdogs of the proletarian culture to remain vigilantly on guard against the expression of bourgeois cultural tendencies. Soviet composers display a lamentable tendency to create bourgeois music. The poets are equally unreliable. Professors of literature cannot be depended upon. Physicists must be warned, and biologists even denounced, for they are responsible for a scandalous situation in which Soviet science is not recognizably different from the reactionary science of capitalist countries. Even the more popular aspects of cultural life must be carefully scrutinized. Circus clowns are guilty of bourgeois forms of humor, and there are good proletarians, it seems, who enjoy reading translations of the exploits of that counter-revolutionary sleuth, Sherlock Holmes. To the Western mind these experiments in the political control of culture may seem too ludicrous to be taken seriously. But from the Marxist point of view they are really important. They signal the failure of the Revolution to produce what the faithful were quite sure it would produce, a new kind of culture and a new kind of man.

The Soviet system has produced no new incentives to hard work. It has to bribe men with higher wages and bonuses. It weakens the workers by breaking all free trade unions, and even bullies them with threats of physical violence and death. Not even Hitler's Germany during World War II made such a lavish use of forced labor. It has reinstituted social honors of a most elaborate character. There is no trace of either a new culture or a new psychology.

On the contrary, Russia is probably more bourgeois now than ever before, because she now has more bourgeoisie than ever before. Before the Revolution the Russian bourgeoisie was relatively small, for Czarist absolutism was never so highly organized as the dictatorship of the proletariat. But socialist and collective welfare institutions have a paradoxical tendency to increase the numbers and power of the bourgeoisie. More social organization requires more white-collar workers in administrative occupations; better health services demand more doctors, dentists, nurses, and so on; improved education calls into being a new army of school teachers and university professors. These inherently bourgeois occupations have an inevitable tendency to create bourgeois outlooks. The more thoroughly Marxist we are in our understanding of the impact of occupational factors on social outlooks and aspirations, the less surprised we shall be by these developments. Whatever men profess and desire, the fact is that the collectivized welfare state must inevitably become a bourgeois managerial state. The aggressive proletarianism of revolutionary socialism and communism becomes with the passage of time more and more recognizably a hollow sham, a strategic pretense that must be maintained in countries in which the revolution has yet to take place, and at home the cause of increasing concern to sincere devotees and doctrinaire interpreters of the original principles of the Revolution.

THE PERSISTENCE OF THE STATE. Yet, discrepant and untimely factor though it may be, to dwell upon the extent and persistence of the bourgeois mentality in Russia is an essential element in the present strategy of Marxist propaganda. For that propaganda has the responsibility of explaining to good Marxists why it is that the Russian state shows not the slightest symptoms of 'withering away.' Toward the end of his life Stalin several times hinted that this 'far off divine event' must now be regarded as indefinitely postponed, but the long and unlooked-for survival of the dictatorship of the proletariat can be explained and defended only by reiterated assertions that the regime established by the Revolution is still in danger. There are two ways of doing this. One is to dwell on the external menace of the hostility of a powerful capitalist world, the other to emphasize the persistence of bourgeois disaffection within. The world is not yet a communist world and Russia itself is not yet a truly classless society, and therefore there is still plenty of work for the dictatorial proletarian state to perform. There we have the bare elements of an ideological interpretation of the international and domestic situation which may serve the class interests of many generations of Russian power-politicians yet to come.

THE UNATTAINABLE CLASSLESS SOCIETY. The truth is that the Russian ideal of the classless society is not only very 'unideal' but also incapable of achievement. The classless society, as the Marxists conceive it, rests not on any moral transcendence of class feeling but on the complete victory of the highly class-conscious proletarians followed by the elimination of all other classes. It is not really a classless society at all, but a very class-conscious society in which one class has completely triumphed. It is a fallacy to suppose that we have attained a 'classless society' because we have set up by violence a 'one-class' society. A class imperialism of this kind is in no way superior to the older and more familiar racial imperialism. The Soviet treatment of the kulaks, for example, is just as immoral and inexcusable as Hitler's treatment of the Jews. The proletarians are no more a *herrenvolk* than the Germans.

But our criticism of the Marxist two-class analysis suggests that, whether desirable or not, the classless society is unattainable. The proletarians cannot be fed, organized, and cared for in the welfare state without the services of peasant food producers and bourgeois administrators and members of professions. So long as there are people earning their living and getting their experience of life in peasant and bourgeois occupations there will continue to be peasants and bourgeoisie, irritated and exasperated, no doubt, by the cant and hypocrisy of the self-consciously proletarian state, in which it must at least be pretended that the proletariat is the triumphant ruling class.

A primitive society in which the whole community engages in a single occupation — for example, a tribe of food gatherers — is, of course, a classless society by nature, but any community based on the division and specialization of labor is bound to comprehend a variety of social outlooks and aspirations. Again, where an organized state exists there will also be the fundamental distinction between the governors and the governed, and where the state is a 'one-party' state there is the additional inequality between the privileged minority of party members and the great majority not admitted to its ranks. Theoretically, of course, and to some extent in practice, entry to the political and other professions, and to the party itself, is open to all who can show themselves to possess the requisite abilities. But so long as family ties and feeling survive, there will also be a hereditary element in this kind of social stratification. In many non-communist countries we are familiar with the way in which the sons of members of respected and prosperous professions — e.g. medicine and law — tend to follow in their fathers' footsteps. Similarly in Russia it has often been noticed that the sons of party members frequently become party members in their turn. The purist may regard such tendencies as corrupt, but the true humanist will probably welcome the re-emergence of warm, natural human feelings of this kind out of the cold-blooded equalitarianism with which the Revolution began. But nevertheless such signs indicate clearly enough that the classless society will not in fact put in its long-heralded and much advertised appearance, either in Russia or anywhere else.

But is this necessarily a bad thing? Surely, a stratified society, honeycombed with different outlooks, aspirations, and human backgrounds, each free to express its own point of view and follow its own traditions, is likely to be a richer cultural unity than a classless society created by the imperialistic triumph of one class over all others. It is probably true also that what the masses desire is not a rigid classless society but a class society in which there is real fraternity and mobility between the component classes, a society with class barriers low enough to be climbed and high enough to be worth climbing. It is this kind of society which we still have a chance to create in the West, whereas the rigid classless society must remain an impossible dream, in the East or anywhere else.

THREE

The Communist Challenge to the West

THE EVENTS OF the postwar period have added one totally new element to the orthodox conception of Marxist strategy. They have shown that the internal social revolution is not an absolute necessity. There is in fact an alternative to revolution: conquest and occupation by the Red Army, under the shadow of whose power the dictatorship of the proletariat may be securely established. Conventional communist propaganda has even invented a cant phrase to describe this happy event. The Red Army will never invade any country in the old imperialistic way, but it may perhaps enter a foreign territory 'in pursuit of an aggressor.' In such circumstances, of course, it must not be resisted by the faithful.

This is the real danger with which the West now feels itself to be confronted. It is clear enough that in most Western countries, with their large and energetic bourgeoisie, the communist parties have little chance of achieving power by their own strength and initiative. Will Russia accept her political defeat in the West as decisive? Or will it goad her into an appeal to armed force? I have recently met many Continental observers who fear communism — or even fatalistically accept its coming as inevitable — but they no longer, except perhaps in Italy, fear their own internal communist parties as they did for a short time after the end of the war. What haunts their minds is the possibility that communism will be imposed on the West by military force. In such circumstances the internal communist parties would come into their own, for, as Mr. Eden has remarked, they would constitute a fifth column in comparison with which Hitler's once vaunted fifth column would appear more like a troop of boy scouts. This situation must be faced seriously and realistically. Every communist leader is a potential quisling, every party member a potential fifth columnist, every fellow traveler or intellectual sympathizer a potential collaborator.

All that is true, and it is always a good thing to face the truth fairly and squarely. On the other hand there is one insidious danger which we must be careful to avoid. The contemporary communist party, as it is presently constituted on its rigid Marxist and authoritarian foundations, is, from one point of view, just one more political party like any other, and as such it would appear that a democracy ought to tolerate it, not because the democracy has any tenderness for communism, but in order to be true to its own ideals and traditions. From another point of view, however, the communist party is seen to be quite unlike any other political party, except perhaps in those countries where some kind of fascist party still exists or is quietly waiting for the right moment to re-emerge from the darkness in which its postwar collapse enveloped it. The communist and fascist parties, in fact, despite their violent opposition to each other, resemble each other very closely. So the communist party, like the fascist party, is not only a party. It is also a conspiracy. Every democratic social order ought to tolerate all genuine political parties, even those with which the mass of its citizens violently disagree. But no organized community, whether democratic or not, can reasonably be expected to tolerate conspiracy. There is a grave danger, however, that when a democratic nation knows itself to be confronted with a conspiracy, it may react to the situation with so much violence and hate as to be led into a betrayal of that very spirit of democracy which it seeks to defend. The trouble with so many of the anti-communist zealots who are seeking to defend democracy against the communist menace is that they know not of what spirit they are. We cannot in the long run defend democracy by means that outrage the spirit of democracy, for the resort to such means voids democracy of its essential content even in the very act of defending it. This is perhaps the most subtle way in which communism menaces our democracy, threatening it with a slow spiritual erosion from within. If this is true, it is necessary to watch the emotional, sometimes almost hysterical, anti-communists as vigilantly and critically as we must watch the communists themselves. Democracy must learn coolly and calmly to walk the tightrope without losing its balance. Otherwise we may well awake to find that we have murdered the West in a desperate effort to forestall and thwart its murderers.

It is possible that Russia may during the next few years pursue an alternative policy to further her advances in the West. She may well react to political frustration and stalemate in the West by withdrawing into herself for a season, during which she might seek to consolidate and extend her great gains in the East. At the time of writing — and I say at the time of writing because Russian policy is subject to violent spasms and changes which we in the West cannot predict, because we do not know enough about their causes, and by the time this book reaches the reader the situation may well have been completely transformed — however, at the time of writing it does seem as though the Russian government of the post-Stalin epoch, without changing the ultimate communist aims, has embarked upon a policy of speaking more reasonably and reassuringly to the West while exploiting the more favorable and inviting Eastern situation to the fullest possible extent. But would such a shift of emphasis in Russian policy altogether remove or merely postpone, or even do no more than transform, the present world crisis?

It might even be that the postponement brought about by such a trend of Russian policy would be only a very brief one. For all the present straws in the wind indicate that Russia would find her objectives opposed, and perhaps frustrated, in the East by precisely the same powers that have opposed and frustrated her expansion in the West. If Russia seeks expansion in Asia, we have no reason whatever for entertaining the slightest hope or confidence that the newly independent countries of southeast Asia could oppose her with any chance of success. If the independence of southeast Asia is to be preserved, then it must be the role of the Western alliance to preserve it. Thus in the East as in the West, Russian expansionism brings her into collision with the Western powers. This only serves to illustrate the world-wide dimensions of the present conflict.

Some people believe that our best chance of avoiding outright war lies with the consciousness of both sides of the vast and unparalleled horror of the weapons that would almost certainly be employed. To use atomic and hydrogen bombs in an age in which both sides possess them and both are well equipped to deliver them is inevitably to invite, and almost certainly to receive, retaliation. May it not be, some people are wistfully asking themselves, that both sides will be too fearful of the extent of such a retaliation to dare to invite it? Certainly the past experience of the human race gives little ground for expecting to find such a high degree of intelligence and self-restraint in angry men. On the other hand, past experience provides us with no parallel to this new and all-comprehensive horror. It is safe to prophesy that even the winning of a war fought with such terrible weapons of destruction — whatever victory could mean in such a context — would be a more terrible experience than losing any previous one. Fear is a poor counselor and an unreliable ally, but it is just conceivable that the universal fear of such a warfare as the next one promises to be may help the human race to avoid it. We have already remarked that never before, not even at the height of the Nazi crisis before 1939, have diplomatic relations between great powers been so strained and embittered without any one of them daring to resort to the sword as the only solution of its difficulties.

THE APPEAL OF MARXISM. We have already seen that the heart of the appeal of Marxism lies in its mystique of history. Before everything else it is a substitute for Christianity — a dogmatic scheme in terms of which those who are prevented by the presuppositions of the secular outlook from believing in Christianity can nevertheless accept and express something like the Biblical philosophy of life and history, giving them a sense of purpose and direction and self-transcending worth, an experience of generous emotions and moral ideals akin to those which Christianity inspires. Against a fundamentally religious propaganda of this kind, a merely secular liberalism must inevitably prove powerless in the last resort. The wave of secular and skeptical liberalism that has swept across the Western world since the eighteenth century has created a tragic void in the Western soul. For great multitudes it has emptied the religious dimension of life of all content. The merely secular liberals in effect desire that this spiritual vacuum should continue as such indefinitely, but that is impossible. If Christianity is gone something must take its place, and that something is more likely to be communism than anything else. On the intellectual and spiritual plane, therefore, the most important way of opposing communism is to level an unceasing attack against the secular outlook on life, an attack that aims at exposing the hollowness and unreality of its presuppositions and characteristic modes of existence. There would be very little temptation to believe in Marxism if modern men and women could only be delivered from the misleading — and, logically speaking, quite unnecessary — prejudices and attitudes that make it impossible for them to believe in Christianity. Who would relish the insipid substitute if he was capable of digesting the natural food? Thus Christian preachers, poets, novelists, journalists, and philosophers are in the very front line of the anti-communist struggle, whether they care for the situation or not, because their existence and witness is a living demonstration that the secular point of view is not, as has been widely supposed, the only outlook possible for modern men.

But the Christianity we have now in mind is the downright dogmatic and institutional Christianity, a Christianity equipped, so to speak, to survive the rough and tumble of human history, a revealed and proclaimed gospel, not an idealistic aspiration. A merely moralistic, liberal Christianity of noble purposes and high ideals of personal integrity cannot help or sustain us at such a time as this. We have to recover the power to believe in the genuine Biblical and credal Christianity, a Christianity that is as much a dogma about history as Marxism itself, a revelation of the power and purpose of the forces that preside over human destiny. To me, quite frankly, this seems the only kind of Christianity worth having, the only kind worth the infinite mental and moral strain and effort exacted by the process of living it, and the endless expenditure of time and breath and words and paper and ink consumed in the process of propagating it. Some such dogma about life and history men must have, and also some institutional channels through which it can find expression. These the communists provide. The West will strive against them in vain unless it knows and resorts to better ones.

Nevertheless, we must not generalize too easily about the appeal of communism to important dissident groups within the structure of Western civilization. For each of such groups it has a particular appeal about which it is possible to be specific.

THE APPEAL OF MARXISM TO THE WORKERS. The primary appeal of Marxism is, of course, to the proletarians themselves. Nevertheless, the tendency in the West is for this appeal to fall on a surprisingly high proportion of deaf ears. The great improvement in the physical lot of the workers which has resulted from the industrial activities of the trade unions, the political activities of the parliamentary socialist parties, the invention of the social-security institutions of the welfare state, and the development of more responsible forms of capitalist management have falsified Marx's gloomy prophecies of the increasing misery of the workers with the development of capitalism, and seem to indicate that they may hope to attain their natural economic objectives without the violence and suffering of revolution. A new depression of sufficient dimensions to exhaust the resources of the welfare state might well drive them to the opposite conclusion, but if that can be avoided the Western

Marxists will be effectively deprived of one of the most obvious themes of their propaganda. Again, it is clear that in fact a communist regime would destroy the social institutions which the workers have labored so long to create and which express all that is most characteristic of their psychology and outlook. Even here and now, for example, Marxist activities weaken the trade unions, and a communist state would in effect transform them into something quite different from what they have been hitherto. Pride in the achievements of the working class itself serves to inoculate many Western workers against the infection of communist propaganda.

But still, for many others, the communist party seems to represent in the contemporary world the hallowed tradition of revolutionary action which has claimed the reverence of many Western spirits ever since 1789. The very success of the trade unions and the constitutional working-class parties makes them appear 'respectable' and moderate, and estranges their leaders from the traditional left-wing emotions. Leadership of prosperous and socially accepted labor movements tends persistently to become a bourgeois occupation, so that those who are emotionally, and almost religiously, in love with the revolutionary legend and tradition for its own sake move farther and farther to the left. For such hardy spirits revolution is not a means to an end, an unpleasant medicine sweetened by the hope that it will remedy an intolerable situation, but a form of action to be valued for its own sake, because it liberates pent-up energies and releases the deep-seated tensions and complexes that seem to be an unavoidable by-product of our kind of civilization. But such chronic revolutionary sympathies are by no means peculiar to the proletarian class. They are not even characteristic of it. We in the twentieth century have witnessed a new kind of non-proletarian revolution — quite as horrible in its own way as the Bolshevist revolution — fascism.

THE APPEAL OF MARXISM TO THE YOUNG. This revolutionary complex has been in our society particularly characteristic of the young. I say 'in our society' because there can be no doubt that the 'youth problem' as we know it is peculiar to our kind of civilization. We know of many other societies in which the social devices employed for transmitting the reigning social traditions from generation to generation operate with almost perfect efficiency. Whether what Freud called the 'Oedipus complex' — the jealous revolt of the son against the father — is a universal human characteristic or not, it is certainly a peculiarity of our society that it has developed the trick of releasing and externalizing itself in moral delinquency, irreligion, and revolutionary politics, the suppressed hostility toward the father expressing itself in a rejection of the accepted moral, religious, and social values with which he is associated. Either other civilizations did not produce and foster the Oedipus complex or with them it found some other channel of expression. In our society Marxism is excellently adapted to the requirements of the Oedipus complex, and is frequently the visible symptom of its hidden presence.

THE APPEAL OF MARXISM TO INTELLECTUALS. This is a more complex phenomenon. Sometimes pro-Soviet sympathies, like pro-Nazi sympathies before the war, express the instinctive pacifism of the intellectual. He clings to the hope of preserving peace by trying to co-operate with the new challenger, perhaps even by passively submitting to him, and shrinks from the certain conflict which it seems must be the consequence of resisting and opposing him. But for the kind of intellectual who is concerned with the techniques of socially useful operations, or their scientific basis, Marxism has a less disinterested appeal. Such men may well calculate that in a highly organized, technological, and authoritarian society they could themselves aspire to membership of the ruling class. Under capitalism the thoughtful technician may well feel himself the paid servant of private interests. Nor has he sufficient voice, he may be tempted to believe, in the choice of the purposes which his technical activities subserve. With both his egotism and his idealism thwarted by existing social conditions, he may be tempted to see in the communist state the possibility of a truly technical social order, created and directed by technicians for the physical welfare and benefit of the great mass of non-technicians, who cannot be expected to take thought for themselves in a complex and scientific social order but ought nevertheless to profit by its achievements. Both attitudes betray a state of mind which learns little from experience. Marxists show not the least tendency to feel any sense of gratitude toward intellectuals who have sympathized and co-operated with them during the period of their struggle for power. The communist state has little regard for the scientists' intellectual freedom, and reduces the technician to the status of a paid servant, without any voice in the selection of social policies, and does it quite as effectively as capitalist private interests.

THE APPEAL OF MARXISM TO CHRISTIANS. Christian sympathy for Marxism has been much more widespread than is generally supposed. When we consider the professed atheism of the Marxists this may appear somewhat surprising. But the fundamentally religious character of Marxism goes far toward explaining it. There is a real affinity between Christianity and Marxism. Both, as we have seen, are rooted in the Biblical philosophy of life and history. The Church leader may well feel, in certain moods of frustration which he inevitably experiences during the course of a ministry in a more or less indifferent secular society, that he has more in common with the Marxist, with his strangely inverted and transmuted but obviously Biblical eschatology, than with the secular liberals and humanists with whom he must range himself for the moment in an attempt to confront and out-face the communist challenge to the West.

European Christians have little or no tenderness for the prevailing outlook and presuppositions of capitalist society, which, as they have experienced it, has accompanied, tolerated, and perhaps prompted and fostered an indifference to spiritual reality almost without parallel in Western history. In addition, many contemporary Christians feel, with some justice, that a century ago Churchmen were too little inclined to rise up in prophetic judgment against capitalist society, precisely in the age in which it was most of all inflicting suffering on its victims. Nowadays the denunciation of capitalism is in Europe a rather tame and pointless occupation, but it was once urgently necessary and tragically neglected.

Still less, in the present circumstances, are European Christians anxious even to appear to be concerned with the defense and propagation of what is usually rather vaguely referred to as 'the American way of life.' Most of them know very little about the social realities which this phrase purports to describe. They cannot get the dollars to visit America, and they obtain most of their confused notions about it from visits to the movies and from hostile anti-American propaganda, of which there is enough and to spare. The widespread European ignorance of America and the misleading impressions of American life provided by Hollywood are a serious embarrassment to the efforts of those Europeans who see clearly the tremendous political and cultural importance of the Atlantic Alliance and labor to communicate their convictions to their fellow countrymen.

To many observers on this side of the Atlantic the existence in Europe of even a small minority of communist sympathizers in the European Churches seems an inexplicable problem. 'How,' they ask, 'can any sincere and committed servants of the Church of Jesus Christ consort and collaborate with such declared enemies of Christianity and the Church as the communists undoubtedly are?' If we understand the situation in which such men find themselves we may find it easier to understand and be in charity with them, however strongly we may feel compelled to reject their point of view. All over Europe the major evangelistic problem which confronts the Church is the almost complete estrangement of the great majority of the working classes from the Christian Church. Into the causes of this tragic estrangement it is not necessary for us to inquire at present. But anyone who knows Europe well will realize that the fact of this estrangement is quite undeniable. Hence none of the tasks which confront the European Churches is so vital and imperative as that of the evangelization of the working classes.

It is among European Christians particularly concerned with the evangelization of the working classes that extreme, left-wing attitudes are most prevalent. Missionaries everywhere tend to develop a deep and comprehending sympathy with the dominant point of view characteristic of the groups to which they are sent. Indeed, unless they shared to some extent the natural social aspirations of their people they would be almost useless as missionaries. For example, what good could come of sending a man who was convinced of the necessity of maintaining white supremacy, and of the importance of upholding a rigid color bar, to run a Negro mission? His lack of sympathy with the traditional and almost inevitable point of view of his parishioners would frustrate his work almost completely. Among the European working classes the tradition of being politically left wing is so deep-seated as to be almost ineradicable. Hence it comes about that those who are particularly concerned to take the gospel of Jesus Christ to the working man where he is, to speak in the name of Jesus Christ to the working masses in a manner which they can understand and to which they can respond, tend to share the traditional political sympathies of the European workers. The point of view of such men may appear to us illogical and untimely, but we cannot deny it every shred of sympathy and understanding. On the other hand, we cannot altogether accept the view that the Christian mission to the workers may not and cannot do something to deliver the workers from some of their illusions, and seek to counteract the insidious influence of those demagogues and false shepherds who would exploit the frustration and resentment of such large sections of the European working class in order to create a tyrannical social order in which they themselves would be the masters, and enjoy not only prosperity but also the even greater and more enticing prize of supreme power.

What our missionaries to the workers too easily forget is that there still survives among us an authentic tradition of Western civilization, overlaid by its more recently acquired veneer of materialism and secularism, but still living beneath, at once spiritual and humane, which Christians can understand and recognize because they contributed so lavishly to its creation. This tradition of Western civilization is at the same time the real hope of the workers and the basis of the unity of the West. Hence it is not surprising that most Christians agree in sharing a common concern that it should be preserved and defended. It is notable that at both the Amsterdam Conference of the World Council of Churches and the Lambeth Conference of the bishops of the Anglican Communion in 1948 the condemnation of Soviet totalitarianism was coupled with equally severe strictures on the past record of Western capitalism. In other words the Russo-communist menace to the West was exposed and denounced, not in the name of Western civilization in its recent and contemporary form, but in the name of the more permanent and underlying Christian tradition of Western civilization. The Christian Churches must be as much concerned that there should be a resurrection of this tradition in the West itself as they are concerned that the West should defend itself effectively against communist aggression. In opposing the challenge of Marxism the Christian Church must make it quite clear that it is defending not a particular economic system, however much there is to be said for as well as against it, but that conception of the dignity and responsibility of the human spirit which the Christian Gospel has revealed and which the Christian Church cannot cease to proclaim without betraying itself and its mission.

THE APPEAL OF MARXISM TO THE ORIENT. But the greatest victories of Marxism since the Russian Revolution have been won not in the West but in the East, not in Europe and the New World but in Asia. The impact of Marxist-communism on the peasant populations of the Orient, and the source of its appeal, must be clearly distinguished from its impact on the minds of Western intellectuals and proletarians. In the first place there is no question here of any repudiation of democracy and Western capitalism in favor of Marxism. The great majority of Eastern peasants have never experienced the Western way of life, either at its best or at its worst. Those of them who have lived under colonial regimes have some acquaintance with Western government, leadership, and technical efficiency, but their relation to these things is quite distinct from ours as citizens of a democratic country. In any case, colonial regimes have for the most part ruled the subject peoples, and even brought them many undeniable blessings in the process without in any way destroying their basic way of life. This is particularly true of the peasants, who so enormously predominate in most Oriental cultures. They have lived under the colonial regimes very much as they lived for centuries before and very much as they would continue to live, if left to themselves, for centuries after these regimes have vanished. It is useless to reproach such peoples for abandoning democracy; they have never known it. It is unjust to criticize them for accepting communist domination, for domination by one regime or another has been their lot throughout almost all their recorded history. Communism promises them a new kind of domination which may easily appear to them less undesirable than any previous form of domination with which they have been acquainted. For instance, communism would apparently overthrow the present forms of colonialism and provide them with at least the outward trappings of national independence. They may also be convinced by propaganda that it will abolish landlordism and the remnants of feudal servitude, and vest in them the proprietorship of their own land. We have every reason to expect that such a promise will ultimately be broken, but if the more advanced peasant peoples of eastern Europe have been lured and trapped by propaganda of this kind, we must not be too surprised if Oriental peasants are in their turn deceived in the same way. Meanwhile communist domination may apparently give them some of the advantages of colonialism, a reasonable degree of law and order, Western technical efficiency, and so on, without at least the outward name of colony and the outward appearance of colonial government. Such peoples are almost certainly not attracted and deceived by the subtleties of communist philosophy. It is the communist promise of a better and fuller way of life — of introducing into the East the fabulous industrial revolution that has given the West its strength — which acts as the bait that draws them into the Marxist net. It is in this part of the world that Russia has made its greatest advances and it is here that it is most important to undertake some kind of counter-attack, and at the same time most bewilderingly difficult to decide how best to do so. For here so many of the forces upon which we can rely, and to which we can appeal, when we are seeking to combat communist propaganda in the Western world, are entirely, or almost entirely, absent, and the long experience of Western colonialism has left its inevitable legacy of suspicion and distrust. Thus even Oriental anti-communism, as we see it, for example, at its strongest and best in India, tends to be neutralist in its attitude toward the tensions and conflicts between Russian and Western civilization. The West will be wise if it adopts an attitude of great patience and forbearance in this situation. There are deep-seated historical reasons for the present touchiness of independent India about any form of Western policy which seems to threaten in any way a resurrection of Western leadership in the Eastern world. These reasons are readily comprehensible and should be met with sympathetic understanding. The friendship and collaboration of India in the present struggle are so essential to our purposes and so richly worth having that we should be willing to embark upon a long and patient wooing in order to get them. The wooing will almost certainly have to be very long, and will thus exact from us a very high degree of patience indeed.

PART II *The West in Practice and Theory*

FOUR

The Deification of Democracy

FEW TWENTIETH-CENTURY tendencies have been more surprising, disappointing, and shocking to the modern Western secular liberal mind — its convictions shaped by the eighteenth- and nineteenth-century phases of our culture — than the marked disposition of peoples and nations during the last thirty years or so to withdraw from and go back upon the basic tenets of democracy. I can well remember the consternation and perplexity of my father during the 'twenties and the 'thirties. For him the movement toward and into democracy was an example of irreversible progress. No people who had once made this journey could be prevailed upon or even tempted to retrace their steps. Anti-democratic trends and propagandas he could only interpret in terms of downright wickedness or pathetic insanity. Since his generous, optimistic humanism made it difficult for him to think in terms of human wickedness, he preferred on the whole the category of insanity, with occasional lapses into the category of wickedness whenever he felt more than usually angry and frustrated. His was not an uncommon state of mind. It is difficult indeed to react to and interpret the more horrific and demonic events of our time without some employment of the categories of wickedness and sin. We may say in theory that we do not believe in sin, but it is almost impossible in practice to deny the reality of sinners and sinful actions when we see them before our eyes. It is wiser, perhaps, to take reality seriously and to search for the causes and reasons of the things of which we disapprove rather than merely to deplore and denounce them as irrational perversions.

What, then, are the most prevalent causes of the alienation of so much Western thought and energy from democratic institutions and ideals? No doubt it is impossible for any one thinker to perceive and enumerate them all, but there are at least four tendencies at work which seem to me of the profoundest importance. I list them here not because they provide a complete account of the whole phenomenon but as my own contribution to the discussion.

1. THE DEMOCRATIC MOVEMENT HAS CEASED TO BE A REVOLUTIONARY MOVEMENT. In most of the great and leading countries of the Western world, democratic institutions, in one form or another, were more or less securely established by 1914. Germany was perhaps the only significant exception, and even she possessed at least a plausible façade of democratic institutions. The democratic struggle after 1918 was thus in most Western countries a struggle to preserve rather than to attain and establish democracy. Nowadays we talk about defending our democracy, not creating it. In other words, in countries like America, Britain, and France, enthusiasm for political democracy is an essentially conservative attitude.

There is nothing surprising about this. Every brand of revolutionism is transubstantiated into a form of conservativism once its goals have been attained. Nor is such a transition in itself a morally reprehensible one, for the conservative attitude has its proper place in a mature and balanced social outlook. Any community in which anything worth doing has been done and achieved is a community which embodies values worthy of preservation. A community in which nothing is worth conserving would be a very poor community indeed. What is worth doing in the first place is worth conserving in the second place. Nevertheless we must face the fact that a conservative emphasis finds it difficult to stimulate and sustain the zeal and devotion which revolutionary movements so easily arouse. A conservativism, however valid, is nearly always less exciting than a revolutionary propaganda, however mistimed and inappropriate. Ever since the French Revolution there has been abroad and at work in the world a certain mystique of revolution, and many of the most gifted and energetic of modern men and women feel intellectually, emotionally, and morally uncomfortable if they cannot tell themselves that they are on the revolutionary side. This is an undesirable social phenomenon, but it is a real phenomenon all the same. Revolution for revolution's sake is a poor and unconvincing kind of gospel when we put it in so many words, but people who live their lives on the basis of such a conviction very rarely put it into words. It is the excitement of it all, the sense of living dangerously, the conviction that they are on the side of the future against the past and the present, which warm their hearts and gladden their minds and give them a sense of purpose and validity in life which they otherwise could not find in our modern secular world. In short, the sort of people who once fought for democracy, precisely because it was not, tend now to react against it, precisely because it is.

The greatest handicap of democracy in the modern Western world is the fact that it has arrived. It cannot be said that it has fulfilled all the hope and idealism of those who created it. In real history social and political programs never do that. Society is still confronted by grave problems; masses of men are still frustrated and unhappy; if many old wrongs have been righted, many new wrongs have been swift to take their place. The utopian dreamers are always disappointed in the event. If we would avoid disillusion at the last, it is better not to cherish any illusions at the first. Yet if democracy has not brought with it social and moral perfection and the dawning of a golden age, it has solid achievements to its credit and it is churlish and ungrateful not to acknowledge the achievements simply because men once hoped for too much. Still the disappointments and the disillusions are real factors which our strategy for the defense of democracy must take into serious account.

2. AT LEAST IN OUR WESTERN WORLD DEMOCRACY AND NATIONALISM HAVE NOW PARTED COMPANY. During the great period of the advance toward democracy in the nineteenth and early twentieth centuries the cause of national independence and national unity often went hand in hand with the cause of democratic progress. To many thinkers and idealists they appeared to be but twin aspects of the same thing, for both were spontaneous uprisings of the people demanding at the same time democratic freedom for themselves and independence and unity for the nation to which they belonged. It is true that even in this period they did not always walk together. Thus, for example, Germany achieved its unity under the leadership of Bismarck's authoritarian Prussia, and the German liberals and democrats lost prestige precisely because they were not the party who succeeded in creating modern Germany. Normally, however, it was democracy that liberated dependent peoples and united divided peoples.

At a later stage, however, nationalism and democracy

tended to come into conflict. For the genuinely democratic mind the achievement of democracy and the rule of law within nations is usually interpreted as the necessary prelude to the achievement of democracy and the rule of law among the nations; national order is thought of as the foundation of international order. But nationalism, which is quite distinct from patriotism, usually rejects this second movement of the democratic mind and becomes the enemy of democracy in this later phase of democratic development. Nationalism can take either of two forms. It can think in terms of conquest and domination or in terms of proud isolation and self-sufficiency. Sometimes the nationalist mind will oscillate bewilderingly between the two. Thus Nazi Germany tended to be isolationist and autarchic in its economic policy, and at the same time nationalistic and imperialistic in its military and political policy. Similarly we find that not a few American nationalists alternate bewilderingly between a desire to cut themselves off from and take no responsibility for international situations — e.g. in the Far East — and a desire to dominate them. But whatever the form contemporary nationalism takes, its genius tends to be hostile to democracy. Nationalists regard the independence, security, and greatness of their nation as prior to and more important than its integrity as a democracy, and so they tend to become impatient with the strict observance of democratic forms, so essential to the survival and preservation of democracy, whenever they feel that higher and more important national aims are at stake.

3. MUCH OF WESTERN DEMOCRATIC THOUGHT AND POLICY HAS FAILED TO PRESERVE THE ESSENTIAL FOUNDATIONS OF HUMAN HAPPINESS. In the most advanced Western democratic countries the most marked and characteristic failure

of a rather superficial humanistic and individualistic secular democracy has been its misinterpretation of the role of marriage and the family as one of the basic factors in human happiness. The two nations that most of all embody the democratic ideals and champion the democratic cause, America and Britain, are both of them areas of culture in which the unity and stability of the family are in greater danger than in any other part of the civilized world, except perhaps Scandinavia. They must be described as societies given to the intemperate practice of divorce, with all the unhappiness, frustration, and neurosis which invariably accompany a gravely disordered sexuality. Few things are more essential to human happiness, and to a rational and satisfying social order, than a cohesive, coherent, and secure family life, and this is one of the great blessings which the most advanced democratic societies have most singularly failed to confer upon their peoples. The weakness and failure of the family under democratic conditions is like a malignant cancer gnawing at the very vitals of democracy. We shall have to ask ourselves, in a later chapter, whether the so-called 'democratic family' is really essential to democracy, or whether it is not, on the contrary, a tragic misinterpretation of democracy, rooted and grounded not in democracy itself but in the false understanding of democracy which has become widely current in its secular phase.

4. THE PREVAILING SECULAR TONE OF SO MUCH DEMOCRATIC THOUGHT, IDEALISM, AND POLICY HAS TENDED TO ESTRANGE MODERN DEMOCRACY FROM THE RELIGIOUS MOTIVATIONS AND IMPULSES THAT LIE AT THE HEART OF WESTERN CIVILIZATION. When we find, as we do again and again in certain areas of Western civilization, Christian men dabbling and flirting with anti-democratic politics, this is almost always the root

cause of the trouble. From their own point of view such men are rejecting not a democratic political order which represents and fulfills in political terms important elements in the Christian conception of man as a free person made in the image of God, and for the eternal service of God rather than the temporal service of the state, but, as they see it, a godless liberalism, a secular regime, which, although it may make a show of tolerating Christianity, is either fundamentally hostile to it or contemptuously writes it off as a second-class issue aside from the really serious business of life.

There is in fact a real conflict not between Christian faith and democracy but between Christian faith and the purely secular state, whether democratic or not. The widespread assumption that a democratic state must be secular, the tendency of not a few democratic thinkers and idealists to put forward democracy and what they call the 'democratic way of life' as though it were in itself a kind of religious absolute standing over against Christianity, or possibly including a drastically reinterpreted and liberalized Christianity, or even as something higher or more valuable than Christianity, is clearly an assumption which no Christian can conceivably accept. When democracy presents itself to the world and seeks to justify itself as a merely humanistic secularism, it cannot expect to secure the allegiance and support of a Christianity worthy of the name, of a Christianity reawakened, as modern Christendom tends more and more to be, to a new consciousness of its own essential point of view and a renascent faith in the power and necessity of the Gospel. For such a Christianity nothing in life is really secular, and the doctrine of the secular state is something it cannot accept. The re-emergence on the twentieth-century scene of a purged and disentangled

Christianity, once more conscious of its Gospel and its own unique point of view about everything in God's creation, is one of those factors which we cannot conceivably exclude from our attention when we are discussing the whole question of the strategy to be adopted in the defense of democracy. Democracy must make its peace with the religious forces at work in the Western world if it is to succeed in uniting all its friends in its defense, and this means that the aggressively secular phase in democratic thought and policy must be brought to an end. It belongs to the eighteenth century, not the twentieth. It survives only as an outmoded anachronism.

The main concern of this chapter is with this last aspect of the contemporary predicament of democracy — its ambiguous relationship to Christianity. We must remember that this book is written by a member of the Christian Church. For me it is Christianity, not democracy, which is absolute, and democracy, not Christianity, which lies under the judgment. The question before us is not: How democratic is Christianity?, or, How can Christianity be so modified and interpreted as to make it compatible with the spirit of democracy?, but, How Christian is democracy? or, How can democracy be so conceived and formulated as to keep it in touch with the spirit of Christianity?

I am aware, of course, that there are some Christians, particularly in Britain and America, who can see no problem here. For them apparently Christianity is the religion of which democracy is the practice; Christianity is the cause of democracy and democracy the fulfillment of Christianity. I mean no disrespect to democracy when I say that I cannot accept such formulas of concord as these. I do not believe that any proposition of the form, 'Christianity is the religion of which democracy — or whatever you will

— is the practice,' can ever be valid. Christianity is the religion of which Christianity is the practice. It may very well be that social forms and institutions desperately need and require the inspiration, counsel, and spiritual force of Christianity to give them the strength and the will to survive, but to Christianity nothing is absolutely essential but Christianity itself. We must find some other way of establishing the importance and validity of democracy, which does not commit the error of identifying it with Christianity.

On the other hand, we do not wish to separate democracy from Christianity altogether, for that would be to secularize democracy. Modern democracy has a Christian theological sanction, and to trace the history of modern democracy is to perceive its Christian origins. My contention will be that although we cannot properly say that Christianity needs democracy, we may say that our Western democracy needs Christianity. We may also validly say that among the various alternative forms of political order between which we have to chose in a fallen world it is democracy which should be selected by the Christian mind as the best and most commendable type of political order here below, precisely because it has a theological sanction which no other set of political arrangements can claim to possess.

I propose to arrange the argument under two heads: What can Christianity *not* say or do with or about democracy? and, What *can* Christianity say or do with or about democracy? I begin with two claims or affirmations concerning democracy which, in my view, Christianity ought not to make and cannot make.

1. CHRISTIANITY CANNOT AFFIRM DEMOCRACY AS HIGHER THAN ITSELF. By this I mean that Christianity cannot conceivably accept the prevalent view that democracy has

clearly grasped and put into practice truths and values to which Christianity was clumsily pointing throughout the pre-democratic ages, without quite knowing precisely what it was doing. Some writers almost seem to suggest that Christianity is related to modern democracy rather as the Hebrew prophets were related to the coming of Christ. Christianity is much more than merely the prophecy which points toward a future fulfillment of its hopes in a democratic age.

We must remind ourselves again and again that democracy is after all no more than an important and valuable set of political arrangements. It is a way of carrying on the government of a group. Its greatness lies in the fact that if its forms and values are steadfastly respected, social change, even social changes of a very fundamental and revolutionary character, can take place without violence. In the same way the shifting of power from party to party and from group to group within the body politic, which, apart from democracy, usually involves a certain amount of fighting and bloodshed, can be achieved by democratic means without any violations of public peace. The advantages of such a system are manifest.

Unfortunately, however, many people are not satisfied with democracy merely as a desirable and advantageous type of political machinery. They want to turn it into a moral ideal, almost an absolute religion. They desire to get out of democracy more than democracy properly understood can possibly contain. Such an idealization of democracy is doomed to frustration. We cannot get a quart out of a pint pot. When we insist on using the adjective 'democratic' to qualify social realities which lie deeper than the political level of human relationships we usually find that it does not fit this kind of reality at all well. Thus many enthusiasts have labored to describe what they call the 'democratic family.' But, in fact, as we shall see later on, the 'democratic family' is simply a name used to describe the inefficient family, the kind of family that is always breaking down and persistently failing to fulfill its functions both as the nursery of human character and as the architect of human happiness. The so-called 'democratic family' means a matrimonial system in which divorce is almost as common as marriage, a family system in which children are continually and unjustly deprived of their human right to two parents; it means irresponsible parents and untrained children; it means the enthronement of insecurity and frustration in the very heart of the social life of the people. Such a radically unsuccessful way of conducting our domestic life does not merit such a high-sounding adjective as democratic. Our contemporary family system is just an inefficient and insecure one. It is much better to call a spade a spade.

The truth is that there is no 'democratic way of life.' Most of the basic ways of human life antedate democracy. The function of democracy is not to overturn and transform the basic types of human order which preceded democracy in time, but rather to defend and uphold them. Similarly it is a mistake to suppose that there are any characteristically democratic ethical virtues or moral values. Of course, we cannot maintain democracy or any other form of social order without the great ethical virtues and moral values, but there are no ethical virtues and moral values which are peculiar to democracy and which simply do not exist elsewhere. Thus some people, for example, regard tolerance as a democratic virtue. Many non-democratic governments and societies in the past have believed in and practiced tolerance, and some democratic societies, it must be confessed, have at times lapsed into intolerance. I would agree that a democratic society is more likely to be tolerant than any other, but it cannot be said that tolerance is impossible without democracy or that democracy automatically achieves tolerance. The great ethical virtues must be practiced and the great moral values must be reverenced whether our society is democratic or not. To appropriate some great universal virtue on behalf of some particular form of political order is as foolish and misleading as to appropriate some great virtue as though it were the peculiar possession of one particular nation. A phrase like democratic tolerance or democratic kindliness is quite as absurd as talking about British courage, Canadian honesty, or German self-discipline. The virtues and the values are not bounded and possessed in this exclusive way.

Democracy is primarily a political word, a word used to describe a particular technique for arriving at decisions which bind the group that makes them. Of course, the democratic group need not be a nation. It may, for example, be a church or a tennis club or a ladies' sewing guild. But whatever kind of group it is, it will be a democratic one if it believes in arriving at group decisions by way of open discussion, and perhaps by some technique that involves voting, the whole process being conducted in accordance with either a written constitution or some more flexible set of conventions and traditions which are accepted as binding by the whole group.

It should be noticed that no democratic group exists merely or primarily for the sake of behaving democratically. The primary purpose of a tennis club is playing tennis; the primary purpose of a ladies' sewing guild is presumably sewing in a ladylike manner. They are democratic in so far as they are doing what they have gathered together to do in a democratic way. Similarly, the primary purpose of a democratic nation is not to be a democracy but to be a nation. The democratic nation is democratic because it is convinced that the best and most successful way of being a nation is to be a nation in the democratic way. In a sense the primary purposes of democratic and non-democratic nations are the same. Contemporary Russia wants to be Russia, just as America is determined to be America. It is their political techniques, their ways of implementing their kindred purposes, which differentiate them so sharply from each other.

Democracy is thus essentially a method of group behavior. It does not usually dictate the primary purposes of the group, although it may, indeed must, restrain it from pursuing purposes and objectives — for example, the domination of other nations by conquest and military power — which in the nature of the case cannot be pursued in a democratic way. But the positive purposes of a group stem from deeper levels of human existence than those on which we are politically organized together. It is this fact which makes it necessary to say that democracy cannot amount to, must not pretend to be, a complete system of social ethics and social purposes. There is no democratic way of life. There is only a way of common life which employs democratic techniques for regulating group relationships and arriving at group decisions. Democracy, even for the democratic man, indeed above all for the democratic man and the democratic society, is neither the highest nor the deepest thing in life. To absolutize and worship democracy, as some modern liberal thinkers would seem to do, is to absolutize and worship a technique, a process as ridiculous intellectually as it is unsatisfying existentially.

It is important that the reader should not misunderstand me at this point. In saying all this I am not decrying or criticizing democracy. I am only trying to ascertain what democracy really is, so that we can clearly understand wherein lies its real value and importance. Democratic philosophers who make false and inflated claims about democracy are not democracy's true friends. The false and inflated claims can be exposed, and those who expose them may easily be deluded into thinking that because they have refuted prevalent misinterpretations of democracy they have refuted democracy itself. So it is that I have set about the task of finding out what democracy is by saying in the first place as clearly as I can what democracy most certainly is not. It is not a complete ethic or a total way of life.

But a total way of life is precisely what Christianity is, and hence Christianity is both a higher thing and a deeper thing than democracy. What we really need in order to display to the world democracy at its best is a Christian society that practices and employs the techniques of democracy with sincerity and integrity. But to suppose that a society can survive and amount to anything merely by concentrating on being a democracy and nothing else would be like supposing that a man can become and be a real person and develop a rounded and balanced character simply by scrupulously observing all the ordinances of statute law, or that a teacher can become a good teacher simply by learning the best educational techniques and without having any idea of what it is that must be taught. (This second example is not really so fantastic as might be supposed, for not a few modern teachers do seem to have embarked on their life's vocation with a merely technical preparation of this kind. But the result has not tended to increase the efficiency or the health of the educational system!)

Thus the essential first step in what I might call a Christian reinterpretation of democracy is this salutory assertion that democracy is a good and useful social technique, and neither a rather feeble and unsatisfying humanistic religion without worship nor a cold and unconvincing social ethic without God. We shall value democracy more highly if we value it for what it is. To hymn the glories of democracy while ascribing to it heights and qualities that it does not in fact possess is not to cherish democracy at all. It is simply a way of cherishing our own illusions.

2. CHRISTIANITY CANNOT AFFIRM DEMOCRACY AS ESSENTIAL TO ITSELF. This is so obviously true that the point seems hardly worth laboring. Democracy cannot be essential to the profession of Christianity and the survival of the Christian Church for the very obvious reason that the Christian Church succeeded in existing and maintaining itself for many centuries before the first modern democratic state came into being. It is true, of course, that from the days of the Roman Empire onward the Christian Church found itself again and again at war with the kind of totalitarian state which is apt to demand that men should in some form or other worship the state itself and acknowledge their temporal, secular loyalty to the state as the highest and supreme obligation of their lives. The struggle between the prophetic religion of the living God and the doctrine of loyalty to the state as the highest of all loyalties, before which every other loyalty must give way, is clearly and unforgettably set out in the great myths that constitute the narrative portions of the Book of Daniel. The principle laid down in that book is clear: those who know that the supreme loyalty and moral obligation of man is to be found in the sphere of his relationship to the living God, and that to this loyalty every secular loyalty whatsoever must defer, cannot conceivably worship any

emperor or state or temporal political reality. Loyalty to God in and through the life of the Church takes precedence of any possible loyalty to state and nation.

But we must not suppose that all non-democratic states, simply because they are non-democratic, necessarily come into conflict with and oppress the conscience of the Christian man in this way. It is quite possible for a state not democratically constituted and ordered to respect and even share the conviction of its Christian citizens that their primary duty and loyalty are to God alone. It is equally possible, alas, for a democratic state so to mistake and misinterpret its own nature as to put loyalty to itself above the loyalty of the awakened religious consciousness to the God who makes Himself known to men in the Christian Gospel. Indeed, when democracy interprets itself in a purely secular way this is what tends to happen again and again. Sometimes loyalty to God in and through the life of the Church is even represented as incompatible with the duties of a democratic citizen. This seems to be the main point, for example, of the anti-Catholic writings of Mr. Paul Blanshard. By the adroit strategy of concentrating his fire on the Roman Church, Mr. Blanshard has succeeded in gaining for himself a fair measure of misguided Protestant sympathy, but in reality his point of view calls in question the legitimacy in a democracy of any church or supernatural loyalty whatsoever. He does not really believe that the democratic system ought to entertain and cherish any loyalty higher than the citizen's loyalty to the democratic state.

In fact it is precisely this doctrine that the highest loyalty of man is his loyalty to the state, however constituted, which is the real essence of totalitarianism, for the totalitarian conception of the state is that the state holds unquestioned sway over the total area of human existence. We should avoid confusing the adjective 'totalitarian' with the adjective 'authoritarian.' All states, even the most democratic ones, claim and exercise some measure of authority. It is essential to the very nature of the state that it must do so. A state is authoritarian in the bad sense when it exercises its authority in a totalitarian way. 'Totalitarian' is thus a profounder and more significant word than 'authoritarian.' A totalitarian democracy, a democratically organized state which claims and proceeds on the assumption that the total life of man falls within the sphere of its responsibilities, is at least a possibility, but it is a paradoxical possibility, for such a claim would contradict something that lies at the very heart of democracy. Democracy is essentially a way of organizing the group life of a community which frankly acknowledges that there is much that is important and significant in the lives of the members of the community which does not fall within the scope of its authority.

'Man was not made for the state, but the state for man,' we often say, boldly adapting a Gospel phrase for our own purposes. Do we pause as often as we should to consider what this means? If man was not made for the state, for what or for whom was he made? In what dimension of his existence does man transcend the sphere of the state's responsibility? Can we possibly say that man was made for himself? This, I suppose, is what a sheer individualistic humanism would have to say. But consider the enormity of such an utterance. It would mean that man transcends the sphere of the state in the dimension of his egocentricity, that his duty and loyalty to himself are somehow a higher thing than his duty and loyalty to the community in which he truly, in the deep sense of the word, *finds* himself, which he needs in order to become and fulfill himself. It is surely impossible to hold that our selfhood is a reality prior to, independent of, and higher than the reality of the community in which we find ourselves. No, the various forms of collectivism, totalitarianism, and communalism seem to me at least nearer to the truth than sheer individualism. (This is a subject to which we shall have to return at a later stage.) Surely we cannot say with real conviction that man was not made for the state, but that on the contrary the state is made for the service of man, unless we first of all believe that God created man for Himself, that the human being is a being with an eternal destiny and an eternal significance, whereas the temporal state is no more than the servant of his destiny, a means in and through which he journeys onward through time toward his final and eternal end. Such a doctrine as this clearly rules all totalitarianism out of court as, and this is the important point, no other doctrine of man succeeds in doing.

We have already pointed out that individualism and totalitarianism go together. If men left to themselves are no more than a chaos of self-regarding, mutually independent individuals, then, since for the sake of their own peace men have got to be united and welded together for common action somehow or other, it seems plausible to suppose that the state is the best agency for bringing about this desirable result. The state from the point of view of sheer individualism thus becomes the creator and master instead of the servant of the community. All this was very clearly brought out by a great English political philosopher of the seventeenth century, Thomas Hobbes. Hobbes was at the same time a completely individualistic philosopher and a preacher and defender of political absolutism. I believe he was utterly wrong, but I cannot deny that he was rigidly logical. It is not in the dimension of his selfhood but in the dimension of his duty to God that man transcends the state and is clearly seen to be more important than the state.

And this great truth, to return to our original point, can conceivably be realized and recognized in a non-democratic order, just as it may unfortunately be forgotten in a democratic one. What makes a political and social order Christian in the last resort is the extent to which it knows and recognizes itself as a temporal order of being which is all the time transcended by the eternal destiny of each one of its members. It admits that it exists only to serve the temporal needs of the children of God. Thus, in certain favorable circumstances, a non-democratic social order may be a Christian one, just as, in unfavorable circumstances, a democracy may become a non-Christian, or even an anti-Christian, society.

But there is another and deeper reason why Christianity cannot conceivably concur in the view that democracy is essential to Christianity itself. The Church as we know it now in the world, the empirical Church which acts upon the stage of human history, 'the Church Militant here on earth,' as it describes itself in its liturgical phraseology, does not contain or make manifest the whole reality of the Church. The prevalent habit of using the word 'Church' in general conversation to mean simply the empirical Church as we know it on earth is a misleading one. The theologian, when he talks of the Church, refers to the death-transcending, time-transcending Body of Christ, of which the Church Militant here on earth is simply one phase or aspect, and not the most vital one at that. The full reality of the Church, its latent promise and inward yearning, will be achieved and made manifest only in the Kingdom of God.

It is there that we shall see the Church as God intends it to be. The Church, in other words, is an *eschatological reality.*

Theological terms like this only cloud and mystify the issue so long as we are ignorant of their meaning; if and when we know what they mean, they clarify the discussion enormously. To say that a reality is eschatological means that it must be interpreted not in terms of what it is or has been but in terms of what it is becoming and what it is destined to be. Such a reality here and now only hints darkly at what it will be, and be seen to be, at the point of its ultimate consummation. So it is that the poet Wordsworth tells us that 'the child is father of the man'; the young growing human being is not merely what he seems to be at the present moment but, more truly and profoundly understood, he *is* what he is to become. Even so the latent promise of the being of the Church, as yet unfulfilled, will be realized only in the Kingdom of God.

Now the Kingdom of God, and this is the important point, cannot conceivably be described as a democracy. It is indeed a *theocracy,* in which the kingdom, the power, and the glory belong to God alone. The best earthly analogy to employ when we attempt to grasp and illustrate the nature of the Kingdom of God in human images is not the democratic state but a serenely happy family, presided over and cared for by a loving and responsible father who is trusted and loved by his wife and children. No other consideration makes so clear to us the reason why Christianity, in so far as it appreciates and affirms the value and importance of democracy, is compelled by its own nature to interpret democracy not as an absolute and ultimate value but as an essentially transitional, this-worldly phenomenon which is useful and perhaps even necessary in our present imperfect state of development, yet is at the same time an institution that must wither away and be no more seen when man is made perfect in the Kingdom of God.

But now, having briefly considered what Christianity cannot say about democracy, however much many enthusiastic devotees of democracy would like to have Christianity say it, let us turn to the more positive side of the picture. What claims can Christianity make for democracy in conformity with its own traditions and in complete loyalty to its own essential message?

1. CHRISTIANITY CAN UNDERSTAND DEMOCRACY AND THUS PROVIDE IT WITH A TENABLE PHILOSOPHICAL FOUNDATION. The great difference between the interpretations of democracy provided by secular humanists and the interpretation of democracy put forward by the Christian theologian is this: the secular humanist tends to understand and defend democracy in terms of a romantic belief in human perfectibility, whereas the Christian theologian prefers to understand and defend democracy in terms of one of his basic Biblical conceptions, the doctrine of original sin.

The romantic belief in human perfectibility is usually closely associated with ideas, more or less clearly articulated, about a law of moral progress for mankind which became almost an article of faith in the secular humanism of the eighteenth and nineteenth centuries. In this twentieth century the notion has had to withstand many hard knocks but it is not quite dead yet. The notion is optimistic about man as he is; it supposes that he is already visibly better than he was in even the comparatively recent past, and that he will be better still very shortly. There are many different ways of formulating this doctrine, of which Marxism itself is perhaps the clearest and most cogent. (That is why we remarked in the introductory chapter of this book that the secular humanist is often a poor defender of democracy against Marxism because he is already half-Marxist himself.)

As a basis for the defense of the democratic idea, this optimistic doctrine of man has two serious defects. In the first place, as it seems to me and to most realistic interpreters of the human situation in the twentieth century, it is so plainly untrue. There never was very much to be said in its favor, and unless we are intellectual Bourbons, completely imprisoned behind the cozy walls of our optimism, incapable of either forgetting or learning anything, there is nothing to be said for it now. Man is not morally improved by the mere passage of time.

The second mistake of those who use a notion of this kind as the foundation of a democratic philosophy is that it does not really or necessarily point in the direction of democracy at all. If men really are perfectible, and in fact are moving rapidly toward perfection, is there any real reason why we should not trust administrative and technical experts to carry on the work of government on our behalf? An optimistic view of the moral potentialities of mankind in general should surely include an optimistic view of the moral potentialities of statesmen, administrators, and technicians.

If we reject the view of human existence which teaches us that men are corruptible, and that above all men are corrupted again and again by power, then there is much to be said for interpreting government as a task for experts, for men of particular gifts heightened and concentrated by a specialized training, and for consigning the burden and responsibilities of government to them alone, just as we leave science to the scientists, art to the artists, and so on. Optimism about men in general surely implies and includes optimism about the experts. There is, indeed, more to be said for this point of view than most of us care to admit. If we are to take the notion of progress seriously, then plainly the most obvious form of progress is technical progress. It is often said, in a trite cliché, that the moral progress of mankind has not kept pace with the technical progress of mankind. This is an understatement. Technical progress is not only a reality, but it has been carried very far indeed, whereas it is, to say the least, doubtful whether there has been any moral progress at all. Civilized man is certainly as sinful, perhaps even more sinful, than the savage. Now one consequence of the technical progress of mankind — and this is one of the most acute problems which modern democracy has to face — is that more and more aspects of government have become highly technical matters. Whether we like it or not this is an age in which we are compelled increasingly to trust experts to do more and more of the things we want done because they alone understand the process by which they are done. Thus we are compelled to trust the physicist to create our military power, to turn to the economists for guidance in matters involving commercial and fiscal policy, to managerial experts to control and organize the vast bureaucracy that carries on the day-to-day business of the modern state. The plain fact is that we cannot exist without such men. Simple societies no doubt could get along without the assistance of such people but to a complex society like our own they are absolutely essential. The 'apeheads' may furiously rage together and imagine many vain things, but they need the 'eggheads' all the same. That is why it is foolish of the apeheads to devote so much of their time to the criticism of the eggheads, for what would happen to the apeheads if the eggheads suddenly sickened of serving them and decided to seek more sympathetic and understanding masters, or even to become the masters themselves? A democracy that cannot understand and respect its experts, and provide an honored place for them, is in mortal danger of being abandoned or even overthrown by its experts. The problem for democracy is the problem of retaining the services of the expert within a democratic framework. Part, at least, of the solution to the problem will be discovered by the democracy that learns to understand the expert and make him happy in its service. Yet although a modern democracy has learned to trust and respect the expert, it can never worship him and trust itself completely to him without ceasing to be a democracy, and this is because the expert also is a fallen man. The uncommon man is a corruptible and corrupted sinner just as much as the common man. But the moment we see and say that this is true we are drawing attention to the fact of original sin.

The classical theological term 'original sin' is a somewhat misleading one now that we have acquired the habit of using the word 'original' to mean new, unusual, or unique. Original sin certainly does not mean a new kind of sin that has never been sinned before. On the contrary, it refers to the spiritual sickness, the underlying sinfulness, which afflicts man from the very point of his origin, so that man is a sinner even when he is not sinning in any overt or particular fashion. We do not say that man is a sinner merely because he is observed to sin with regrettable frequency. It is certain that the observation that man is sinful is not an empirical one based on a broad study of behavioristic data, though no doubt such a generalization would be a valid and well-founded one. Man is not a sinner because he sins; he sins because he is a sinner. The particular sins are facts which we observe; the doctrine of man's original sinfulness is a theological or philosophical category in terms of which we understand and account for what we observe. It answers for us the question, why is it that man is observed to sin again and again in this rather dull, repetitive fashion? Why is it that even when a man is not sinning in any overt, recognizable way we have always to bear in mind the possibility that he may begin sinning in some overt, recognizable fashion at the next moment? Why, in other words, is eternal vigilance the necessary price of freedom? Why is limiting and dividing earthly power and balancing the various forms of earthly power over against each other, and subjecting earthly power to the rule of law, the only way in the long run to avoid being overwhelmed by earthly power? The answer can only be in terms of the doctrine of original sin.

It is because men are everywhere corruptible and always corrupted that no single man or group of men can be trusted with too much power, indeed with any power at all that is not in some way balanced and checked by the power of other men. For the same reason a social situation that leaves any particular man without any power, influence, status, or rights whatsoever is one that leaves him at the mercy of the power of his neighbors. The wisdom of democracy is to divide and disperse, to limit and balance power, to reserve some tiny minimum of power for each citizen as his inalienable right, to create traditions, institutions, and written constitutional documents which insistently remind power of its responsibilities and its inherently limited character. But why is all this necessary and important? The answer is now clear: because this is a fallen world and because in a fallen world the problem of government and the consigning of power to particular persons and groups is the most hazardous problem of all. If men were morally perfect, or perfectible and rapidly approaching perfection, the case for democracy would not be so strong. But because this is not so the case for democracy is overwhelmingly strong.

To understand and interpret democracy in the light of the doctrine of original sin has the twofold advantage of reminding us at the same time of both the strength and the limitations of democracy. To say that democracy consists of a series of socio-political arrangements and techniques designed to avoid unhealthy concentrations of power, which will certainly be abused in a fallen world, is to put it in its proper place and see it in its correct perspective. The liberal humanist tendency toward an idolatrous absolutizing of democracy, which transforms it into an ultimate ethic or even a higher religion, is, of course, from such a point of view as this, a ridiculous illusion. I believe that Sir Winston Churchill once remarked, although I have not been able to check the reference, that a democracy is the least unsatisfactory way of arranging our political affairs that we poor mortals have yet stumbled upon in this sinful world. To say this is to make a very great and important claim for democracy, but it is at the same time to reject entirely any ethical or religious absolutizing of democracy. Now we can see clearly why it is that the Kingdom of God is not a democracy, and why Christianity cannot conceivably affirm democracy as something necessary to itself or higher than itself. Democracy is appropriate and valuable in the context of a fallen world Outside such a context it cannot conceivably have any meaning or relevance. But it so happens that our world is a fallen world. This world of ours is the context in which democracy is appropriate and valuable. The Christian doctrine that defines the limitations of democracy at the same time perceives and diagnoses its essential value and strength. To perceive the limitations of democracy is to state the case for democracy within its limitations. We know of no alternative to democracy that has anything like the efficiency and validity of democracy here in this fallen world. It is the best and most effective way we have yet devised for ordering the process in and through which sinners govern each other and themselves.

In both the American and the British forms of democracy the influence of this particular theological element has been historically very strong, for both of them were profoundly influenced by puritan thought during the seventeenth and eighteenth centuries. Of course, the belief in original sin is not peculiar to the puritans. On the contrary, it is a dogma universally received among Christians. But it must be said, on the other hand, that the belief in original sin belongs to that part of the general Christian tradition which the puritans not only maintained and transmitted but to which also they gave a peculiar emphasis of their own. It is a great mistake to suppose that the American Constitution and democracy are simply a product of the eighteenth-century enlightenment, exclusively the work of deists and unitarians. The puritan impact upon them also is strongly marked. And even the characteristic social philosophy of the eighteenth-century enlightenment is in fact Christian in its origins. The characteristic social philosophy of the eighteenth-century thinkers, skeptical, deist, and unitarian though they were, has a demonstrable Christian ancestry. Their emphasis on the idea of universal natural law, their insistence on the rule of law in human affairs, is inherited directly from the scholastic theologians of the Middle Ages, particularly St. Thomas Aquinas. But did St. Thomas Aquinas influence the eighteenth century? Strangely enough, yes.

The Thomistic philosophy of law was re-created for and represented to the modern English-speaking world by Richard Hooker, an Anglican theologian writing at the end of the reign of Queen Elizabeth. Book One of his celebrated *Ecclesiastical Polity* is a superbly written treatise on the nature of law directly dependent on the writings of St. Thomas Aquinas. Indeed it is little more than St. Thomas Aquinas turned into beautiful Elizabethan prose. This book had a tremendous influence on English thought during the seventeenth century, and John Locke in his *Second Essay on Civil Government* quotes it with strong approval again and again. The influence of the political philosophy of John Locke was as predominant in the secular thought of the eighteenth century as Hooker's was in the Anglican theological thinking of the seventeenth century. There can be no doubt whatever that the founders and architects of American democracy were deeply versed in the writings of John Locke. The theological pedigree of the American Constitution is thus one that can be traced without any great difficulty. St. Thomas Aquinas — Richard Hooker — John Locke — the founding fathers. Of course nobody would suggest that this pedigree tells the whole story. Many other and very different elements can be found in the ancestry of modern American democracy, but at least this theological strain exerted a major and formative influence.

In democracy as we know it now we can in fact trace two quite distinct elements: a 'rule of law' element, which is theological and medieval in its origins, and a 'sovereignty of the people' element, which is much more recent. In some forms of democracy the sovereignty-of-the-people element is completely triumphant over the rule-of-law element. Thus when Soviet Russia claims to be a democracy she is thinking entirely in terms of a system in which those national leaders who, as the theory supposes, somehow incarnate the real will of the people enjoy a supreme and unchecked sovereignty against which no rule of law can prevail. Occasionally Nazi writers during the Hitler regime claimed that Germany was a democracy in this sense. This type of democracy, which thinks solely in terms of the sovereignty of the people, is indeed a purely modern, eighteenth-century invention. Its founding father is the French social philosopher Rousseau, who taught a doctrine of the sovereignty of the general will of the whole people, but was very careful to distinguish between this general will of the whole people and the private personal will of individual people, over which the general will must, if necessary, be made to prevail by force. It is possible that his intentions were democratic in our modern Western sense, but he overestimated the underlying unity of the general will of the people and attributed too much authority to this general will.

In a modern Western nation as we know it there is no general will of the people as a whole, except perhaps during war and in times of grave national danger. Thus it comes about that those who think in terms of the sovereignty of the general will of the people are reduced in practice to some kind of belief in particular human beings who are, so to speak, the incarnations and interpreters of the general will, so that the sovereignty of the people is in practice attributed to national leaders and dictators. Thus

Rousseau, contrary certainly to all his original intentions, is the father of modern totalitarianism rather than the father of democracy.

The democracy of the English-speaking world, by contrast, makes a serious effort toward a synthesis of the much older rule-of-law idea and the modern sovereignty-of-the-people idea. Thus the democratic systems of America and the British countries are essentially 'constitutional democracies' rather than 'sovereign democracies,' in which the sovereign people must exercise their sovereignty in accordance with basic forms of law and can change these basic forms of law only by imposing some new form of law upon themselves. In our tradition the sovereignty of the people is never a lawless sovereignty. Of course, a Soviet legal thinker, such as the late Mr. Vishinsky, will probably comment on this that we do not really accept the doctrine of the sovereignty of the people at all, for how can a real sovereign be subject to law? From his own point of view he would probably be right, for sovereignty is in its essence a lawless conception. Those who talk of the sovereignty of the people are in fact transferring to the people as a whole the conception of the powers of the monarchy which grew up during the Renaissance period, when men were reacting strongly against the medieval conception of the sovereignty of the state or rule of law. Thus one famous Renaissance writer [1] declared that the king, being sovereign, is *legibus absolutus* (absolute in relation to all law). This contrasts strikingly with the medieval Christian notion that the king reigns *sub deo et sub legi* (under God and the law). Even as early as the fifth century A.D. a Christian writer [2] can declare, *Dicitur enim rex a bene regendo*

1. Jean Bodin.

2. Isidore of Seville.

et non a regendo (The king is so called because he rules well and not because he rules). What this early Christian writer means by ruling well is made clear by another author. *Attribuat igitur rex legi, quod lex attribuat ei, videlicet dominationem et potestatem. Non est enim rex ubi dominatum voluntas et non lex* (The king attributes to the law, what the law attributes to him, that is to say, dominion and power. For there is no king where will is dominant and not law).[3] All this makes it plain that our modern constitutional democracy in the West has more in common with Isidore of Seville than with Jean Jacques Rousseau, a fact which is not perhaps so generally realized as it ought to be. For in our Western democracy the notion of the rule of the law predominates over the idea of the sovereignty of the people, vastly so in practice and to a lesser extent in theory. So long as this continues to be the case, the Christian and theological origins of our democracy will continue to be plain to the eye of the careful observer.

Perhaps we should say just a little more about the notion of human perfectibility. Christianity does not necessarily deny that man is perfectible, although some forms of Christian theology do come very near to doing so. For them the great problem is not so much the elimination of sin, the setting free of men from the power of evil which holds them enthralled, but the problem of the forgiveness of sins, so that even in eternity and the Kingdom of God men will be a community of forgiven sinners rather than a community of unjust men made perfect. But the majority of Christian theologians, and this is certainly the Biblical view, think in terms not merely of the forgiveness of sins but also of an ultimate conquest of sin. Sin is not

3. Bracton.

merely forgiven by the loving Christ; its power is broken by the victory of the sinless Christ. For Christianity man is not merely perfectible; he will, in the Kingdom of God, actually be perfected.

The real difference between Christianity and secular humanism is that the latter believes not merely in the perfectibility of man but in the *self-perfectibility* of man. According to secular humanism, man will be perfected either through his own efforts or by the mysterious semi-divine force called progress, which may be no more than the apathetic doctrine that man will be perfected by mere lapse of time, or which may more positively interpret man's own efforts to perfect himself as an essential part of the process. According to Christianity man will be perfected neither by mere lapse of time nor by his own efforts but by the power of the grace of God. Of course, the Christian may say that man will not be perfected without some co-operative effort on his part, nor, since man is a temporal being, will the process be an all-at-once process without any temporal aspect. Nevertheless, for Christianity the primary and central agent of the process is God, and both human effort and the lapse of time will be utterly in vain apart from the grace of God. So long as this world order and the course of human history continue there can be no secure and abiding victory over the forces of evil, and we shall continue to be men struggling against the forces of evil, within us and without, that bedevil a fallen world. So long as this world order and history continue, therefore, democracy will always be a valuable and effective device appropriate to man's sinful condition, and necessary to his temporal and political well-being.

To state the case for democracy in these terms is to state it realistically and effectively. We endanger the cause of democracy by claiming too much for it, because there is always the danger that men who have attached themselves to democracy because they have accepted the inflated claims for democracy put forward by undiscriminatingly democratic philosophers will react against it and reject it at last in a mood of disappointment and disillusion. When we expect too much of anything we are sometimes so frustrated when it fails to live up to our expectations that we fail to recognize its real though limited achievement. Democracy is not a recipe for the speedy production of the millennium; it is simply a way of securing a reasonable degree of decency and order in the conduct of human affairs in a fallen world. Man will not escape by way of democracy from his basic problems or his ultimate spiritual predicament. Even democracy will always be corruptible and sometimes corrupt, and it offers us no salvation from the sins that beset us. But a really democratic nation may hope to avoid the evils of tyranny and gross injustice, and a really democratic world order might even conceivably hope to avoid, or at least minimize, the evils of war. Surely to claim this for democracy is sufficient. It is quite unnecessary to try to present the kind of political arrangements and techniques that we call democratic as though they were an absolute ethic or an ultimate religion.

2. THE CHURCH CAN USE DEMOCRATIC TECHNIQUES IN ITS OWN SELF-GOVERNMENT AND IN THE ADMINISTRATION OF ITS OWN AFFAIRS. The Church itself is not and cannot be a democracy. It is, on the contrary, essentially a theocracy, the outlying earthly province of the Kingdom of God. Nevertheless the Church can employ democratic techniques in the carrying on of its earthly business and in fact has done and does so. In our Western civilization the first parliamentary gatherings were in fact the councils of the Church, and

during the Middle Ages the first parliamentary gatherings —the Cortes in Spain, for example, the States General in France, and the early parliaments convoked by Edward I and other monarchs in England — borrowed their rules of procedure, and their way of conducting their business, very largely from the much older experience of the Church in the conduct of its synods and councils. And still today the bulk of church business is conducted in this way. Thus we see in a church such as the Episcopal Church of the United States a large number of gatherings of elected representatives, parochial vestries, diocesan and national conventions, and so on, which carry on the day-to-day business of the Church despite the fact that the Church itself is not and cannot be a democracy.

The employment of democratic techniques in carrying on the business of what is fundamentally not a democratic society is quite a feasible and workable project. Thus a diocese may elect its bishop, yet the Church does not pretend that it is the election as such which makes a bishop a bishop. He becomes a bishop not when he is elected by the diocesan convention but at the moment when he is consecrated and raised to the rank and office of a bishop by other bishops. If all the other bishops refused to consecrate him, then he could never become a bishop though he were elected ten times over. The process of electing a bishop is thus democratic, while the process of consecrating a bishop remains hierarchic. This is a very clear example of the way in which democratic techniques can be used effectively and wholesomely in what nevertheless remains a non-democratic society.

Nor is this really a departure from what we might call the norm of democracy, for the truth is that no society is democratic through and through. There is, as we have already seen, nothing which in fact corresponds to what is sometimes called the democratic way of life, nor is there any really democratic society. What we call a democratic society is only a human society resolved to employ democratic techniques as far as possible in the carrying on of its social business. But the business itself which a democratic society carries on in its democratic way would have to be carried on in some way or other whether the society was democratic or not. The fact is that our basic social arrangment and necessities are pre-democratic, and most of what makes up the common business of this life is in itself neither democratic nor undemocratic but simply human. For example, the family and the necessity of carrying on economic activities to support life are found in every form of human society. They are not in themselves democratic or undemocratic, though sometimes it may be possible to carry them on and protect them in a democratic manner. It is not necessary in a so-called democratic society that everything should be done democratically. Thus there is nothing peculiarly undemocratic in a father spanking his gravely disobedient son, nor is there any particularly democratic way of administering such a punishment. It may be important, indeed I think it is, that in a democracy fathers should occasionally chastise their sons, but the process itself is just a universally human one. It is equally necessary that fathers should chastise their sons even under a dictatorship. The family that does not discipline its children is neither democratic nor undemocratic; it is simply inefficient. Conversely it is a great mistake to suppose that everything done in a democracy must be democratic.

Even in a very democratic society most of the characteristic social customs are completely neutral so far as democracy is concerned. The clothes we wear, the code of manners we observe, our way of arranging our economic and matrimonial affairs will most certainly include certain customary elements that neither affirm democracy nor call it in question. There is a widespread idea that any characteristically British or American customs must necessarily be democratic social customs simply because Britain and America are democracies. This is a great illusion which may do harm, for it leads us to suppose that other peoples can become democratic only by adopting the whole round of our social customs, music, fashions, matrimonial and economic arrangements, and so on. Now quite possibly many peoples who would like to become democratic do not wish to adopt the entire cultural and social system of the English-speaking world. We have no right to insist that they should do so, and it may be unwise even to propose such a thing. The important thing to tell the swiftly developing peoples of Africa, Asia, and eastern Europe is that they can become democratic and remain themselves, that they can adopt democratic government and social techniques without aping the cultural conventions and habits of the English-speaking parts of the Western world. We must beware of turning the democratic philosophy into an ideology that cloaks and conceals what we may call a kind of cultural imperialism. The suspicion that when we talk about democratizing the world we really mean Westernizing or even Americanizing the world does perhaps more harm than anything else to the cause of democracy. I repeat, not everything in a democracy need be democratic, nor is everything that is done in the existing democratic societies essential to the democratic idea.

The essential contention of this chapter has been that we can assert the case for democracy with greater effectiveness and more valid conviction if we are aware of its limitations. The best way of doing this in a democratic world is to base the case for democracy fairly and squarely on a Christian philosophy of life. The Christian is unlikely to overstate the case for democracy because he can never forget that 'Behold a greater than democracy is here.' But once he has observed the limitations of democracy he is in a position to perceive great strength within its limitations, for democracy has the priceless advantage among theories and methods of social organization of taking the doctrine of original sin seriously, and the doctrine of original sin, as has often been remarked, is the most obviously true of all the Christian doctrines, perhaps the only one that can be verified and proved to the hilt beyond all question by a mere inspection and experience of the facts of life.

FIVE

The Obsession with Technics

AMONG NON-WESTERN peoples the most prevalent interpretation of Western civilization is one that understands and evaluates it in terms of its great technical achievement. It is written off, sometimes admiringly and sometimes critically, as materialist and efficient but radically unspiritual. Even in the West itself not a few romantic thinkers are greatly given to contrasting the materialist technical efficiency of the West with the alleged higher spirituality of the great Oriental nations.

Even superficially considered this is a highly misleading comparison. The contemporary East in fact contains many people who admire Western civilization's technical efficiency to the point of extravagance, and would like to adopt it as an alternative to their own spirituality. Conversely, in the West we find as many again who are critical of the contemporary West's apparent reliance on technics, and plead strongly that it should strengthen its hold on its traditional spiritual values. If we insist upon the technical materialism of the West and the traditional spirituality of the East as their primary distinguishing characteristics, then we shall be faced with the embarrassing fact that a great many Easterners are, so to speak, Westerners under their skins, and a great many Westerners are spiritually more akin to the East. A method of distinguishing Western from Eastern civilization whose implications are so paradoxical as this is clearly an invalid one.

In fact the historical achievement of Western civilization in what we may call the non-technical sphere of existence, in religion, art, and philosophy, is in no way inferior to that of the Eastern world. The Western man who is deeply rooted in the traditions of his own civilization will not in fact find his spirituality greatly enriched by what Western sentimentalists about the East are wont to call 'new light from the ancient East.' Of course, some new light certainly will be afforded him if he cares to cast his eyes in that direction, but with most of what is richest in Eastern religious philosophy and mysticism he is already familiar from within his own tradition.

This is not to deny, of course, that from the Middle Ages onward Western civilization has displayed a continuous and cumulative genius for the invention and imaginative use of new technical devices. It is incorrect to suppose that this disposition to invent new and more efficient means for the carrying out of old and familiar ends and purposes is a consequence or aftermath of the advent of modern science. On the contrary, this technical creativeness was a characteristic of Western civilization for several centuries before the emergence of what we should regard as the characteristically modern form of scientific thought and research. Thus the Middle Ages was a period in which there was considerable technical development.

From about the tenth century . . . there was a gradual improvement of technical knowledge in Western Christendom. This was brought about partly by learning from the practices and writings . . . of the Byzantine and Arabic world, and partly by a slow but increasing activity of invention and innovation within Western Christendom itself. The gains thus made during the Middle Ages were never lost and it is characteristic of medieval Christendom that it put to industrial use technical devices which in classical society had been known but left unused or regarded simply as toys. The result was that, as early as 1300, Western Christendom was using many techniques either unknown or undeveloped in the Roman Empire. By the year 1500 the most advanced countries of the West were in most aspects of techniques distinctly superior to any earlier society.[1]

Elsewhere the same writer notes that what he calls the 'active, practical interest of educated people' was 'one reason why the Middle Ages was a period of technical innovation, though most of the advances were probably made by unlettered craftsmen.' [2] 'It has often been pointed out,' remarks Mr. Crombie again, 'that science develops best when the speculative reasoning of the philosopher and mathematician is in closest touch with the manual skill of the craftsman.' [3] Indeed it is part of Mr. Crombie's thesis in this most interesting and valuable work that what we may call the non-scientific phase of technics in the Middle Ages is one of the main causes of the great outburst of scientific thought and research which we date roughly from the close of the Middle Ages. Even then, however, we do not find that a new kind of technics based on scientific research and discovery suddenly and immediately replaces the type of technical innovation which is the fruit of the inventive genius of the non-scientific practical craftsman. On the contrary, the practical craftsman continued to make important contributions to technics until comparatively recently.

1. A. C. Crombie, *Augustine to Galileo,* Harvard University Press, Cambridge, Mass., 1953, page 157.

2. Ibid. p. 143.

3. Ibid. p. 143.

As time went on, of course, the craftsman acquired and employed an increasing stock of empirical scientific knowledge, but it is only during the last century or so that we have come to look upon scientific thought and research as the natural father of technical development, so that for many people today the chief aim of science is no longer to discover, observe, and interpret natural processes but rather to produce technical devices. It is questionable whether this popular attitude toward science is really in the best interests of science itself. If the desire *to do* should at last replace the desire *to know* as the chief motive which inspires and fosters scientific work, it is at least conceivable that the essential spirit of science will go into a rapid decline. For modern science, as we have known it in its moments of greatest achievement, has always been animated by a theoretical rather than a practical interest.

We may thus distinguish between two overlapping phases of Western technical development, a craft phase and a scientific phase. A more important point to insist upon, however, is this: in whatever phase of technical development a society may be and however great the range of its technical efficiency, technics can never be the soul or substance of a civilization or compensate for the lack of one. The essence of a civilization is a set of purposes and values which determines what shall be done in that civilization, or at least what shall be attempted. The technical equipment of a civilization determines not what will be done or attempted, but in what way and with what degree of efficiency our purposes will be carried out and our values translated into actuality. Thus we may say that technics is always peripheral to civilization. It exists on the edge of civilization, rather than at its center. This is not to say that technics is unimportant. Rather it is a way of saying specifically and precisely what the importance of technics is and wherein its value lies. Since it is in the nature of technics to be instrumental to purposes that technics itself cannot supply, its proper and appropriate kind of value is what is called instrumental value.

Now there is nothing wrong with the concept of instrumental value in itself. The mistake lies in the kind of instrumentalist philosophy which supposes, or supposes that it supposes — for this supposition is really an impossible and irrational one — that instrumental values are the only values. I say this supposition is impossible and irrational because instrumental values — which more concretely means valuable instruments, technical devices that are valuable and useful precisely because they are efficient — would be useless to us unless they served purposes that transcend them. The instrumental value implies the absolute value. In a world without absolute values, that is, in a world where nothing is worth doing or achieving for its own sake, instrumental values would be inconceivable. We cannot dissociate the category of means from the category of ends, or even subordinate the category of ends to the category of means. Means are, as the very word implies, means to ends, and the one conception necessitates and requires the other. If we can imagine a community of men who knew how to do everything but did not know that anything was worth doing, presumably the human condition under a regime of absolute instrumentalism, then nothing would be done and the human know-how would rust unused because of the total absence of any human know-what. It would be rather like the fabled situation in which we are all dressed up with nowhere to go. Thus there is in fact no technical civilization: there are only civilizations that employ technics in the service of their civilized purposes.

Of course we are discussing here things as we see them in what we may call the order of reason, not as we see them in what we may call the order of fact. For there is a grave danger that we may indeed become an instrumentalist society, not so much by denying the validity of absolute values and purposes as by rather apathetically ignoring their reality. We may so concentrate the intellectualism and genius of civilization on solving the instrumental problem of means that we have no time left in which to concentrate upon and consider the more ultimate problems of purpose and value. Worse than that, the heady excitement that comes with the sense of possessing new and more and more powerful instruments of human action may lead to the very prevalent idea that anything which *can* be done ipso facto *ought* to be done, or even *must* be done. For an increasing number of modern men and women the observation of any potentiality whatsoever arouses an overmastering desire to translate it into actuality. Sometimes this mood breeds a kind of technological fatalism. We see theoretically that something or other could happen, and therefore we assume that it is bound to happen, that nothing can stop it happening, however undesirable it may be. This fatal tendency, if carried far enough, means the end of rational personality, for the essence of rational personality is the possession and use of the strange power of rational, self-conscious beings to select among alternative possibilities. Where there are rational persons at work many things that could happen do not happen. Indeed, the things that could happen and do not happen greatly outnumber the things that both can and do happen.

So it is that rational freedom intervenes between potentiality and actuality. So it is, from the theological point of view, that the absolute rational freedom of God is the real cause and explanation of the fact that this world in which we now find ourselves exists in actuality, and that the many alternative different worlds which in theory might equally well have existed have never been called into being. Even so, in human existence we display our freedom and manifest the form of being which is called personal by transcending and contemplating the world of many possibilities and bringing out of it the world of actuality. To suppose that in civilization everything that can be done must be done would ultimately destroy man. It would ultimately destroy him not only physically, although that is one of the possibilities implicit in our modern technical advance, but it would destroy him metaphysically and spiritually by violating the deepest law of personal being, and so dispersing the essential human energies that they could no longer cohere together in free and self-directing personal wholes. In such a situation we should not only be all dressed up with nowhere to go, we should also have a vast wardrobe of attractive clothes with no bodies on which to drape them.

To return, however, to the main line of our argument: it must, of course, be admitted that as a matter of historical fact the origins of modern science as we now know it, and of the kind of technics that emerged out of that scientific tradition at a later date, are undeniably Western and even Christian. Behind the great scientific outburst of the fifteenth, sixteenth, and seventeenth centuries lies the Biblical and Christian way of experiencing and interpreting the world as an order of being created by God, an order of being called into existence out of nothing by His sovereign Word. The world is not from this point of view something that exists in its own right, or carries within itself the ground and reason of its own existence. Hence it is that in order to know the world we must subject our minds to the discipline of careful observation and experiment. We cannot know the kind of world that Christian theology declares the world to be other than through the painstaking and piecemeal discovery of what in fact it contains. This is called the empirical way of knowing. There is another possible way of knowing that is quite inappropriate in the kind of world which Christian theology declares this world to be, and that is the way of pure speculative reason, which attempts to establish what the world *must* be like by a process of deduction from alleged first principles.

But although science as we know it belongs to Western Christian civilization in the sense that only within such a context as Western Christian civilization provided could it have been born, it is not peculiarly Western in the sense that only in the Western Christian context can it continue to flourish. On the contrary, it is very clearly to be numbered among our exportable goods.

Nor is it correct to say that a non-Western society which adopts our Western techniques, commercial, industrial, domestic, and military, is thereby Westernized in any deeper sense. This was once a very prevalent error. Thus it used to be customary to describe the great cultural revolution in Japan, in and through which it adopted Western methods and Western means of doing things, as the 'Westernization of Japan.' We can now see more clearly, however, that in fact Japan never was Westernized. It adopted Western techniques, but its basic stock of values and purposes remained all the time inherently Japanese. The superficially Westernized Japan was a more effective and therefore more menacing Japan, but it was still Japan. To say that non-Western man is Westernized merely because he can drive a truck or an airplane, construct a suspension bridge or a steel plant, plan an empire, and drop a bomb is not merely to misunderstand the soul and mental processes of the non-Western man concerned, but it is also to do a great injustice to the meaning of Western civilization. It is like describing an African Negro as Westernized — and I have heard people descend even to such absurdities as this — merely because he has learned to encase his legs in trousers. Being Western is an emancipation of the soul rather than a confinement of the body. I have remarked already that our technical equipment is in its very nature peripheral to our civilization, and no consideration reinforces that verdict so strongly as this one: that it is possible for non-Western man to acquire and use Western technics without transforming himself into Western man.

But if it is incorrect to say that modern technics is essentially Western, except in the sense that it undoubtedly had a purely Western origin, it is even more misleading to suppose that there is anything peculiarly democratic about the scientific phase of technical development. Communist Russia, and other modern totalitarian states for that matter, have been quite as efficient in the development and employment of technics as the democratic nations. It is a great mistake, indeed a vulgar prejudice, to underestimate the technical creativeness and efficiency of contemporary Soviet society. On the contrary, all the evidence that we have at our disposal attests the reality and importance of the tremendous concentration of the contemporary Russian mind on technical development and the utilitarian aspects of scientific discovery. Even granted that Russia has been considerably assisted by spies in her development of atomic and hydrogen bombs, the fact remains that the speed with which she has utilized this assistance has left Western democratic observers almost breathless with surprise. Indeed, in some ways, the contemporary intellectual situation in Soviet society is almost bound to produce a concentration of intellect and genius on technical problems.

Not only is such a concentration encouraged and richly endowed by the government, but the conditions prevailing in other spheres of thought and research are hardly calculated to attract the best minds. In philosophy there is little to be done apart from inventing new ways of saying over and over again that dialectical materialism is the true philosophy and that all other forms of philosophy are outworn and perhaps degenerate bourgeois ideologies. History and literary criticism are almost equally stereotyped and conventionalized. Even pure science has its dangers. But in applied science the field is wide open to originality and new achievement, and the prizes to be won are rich and numerous. To underestimate the technical efficiency of Soviet society may even be something of a political blunder also, for it might easily render us complacent and overconfident about the ultimate issue of the present struggle.

Just as science and technics are not at the moment in any way peculiar to democratic society, so we may notice in looking back over the history of the development of our own civilization that in fact the emergence of science and modern technics precedes in time — at all events in most Western countries — the emergence of a democratic political order. It is clear that science and the kind of technics that it inspires and makes possible are in no way peculiar to or uniquely characteristic of democracy.

There is one possible objection to this thesis so obvious and prevalent that we had better consider it at once. Surely, some will argue, scientific development requires an atmosphere of intellectual freedom and tolerance. Such an atmosphere is provided by a democratic state, and is by contrast most emphatically not to be found in the totalitarian states. Surely this must mean that in the long run science and scientific technics will be more creative and successful in the former than in the latter. This is a plausible argument and it may well contain a grain of truth, but hardly more than that. We should perhaps expect the freer intellectual atmosphere of the democratic states to be more productive of original developments in the realm of pure science. Since, however, it is of the very essence of the scientific process that original developments in the realm of pure science should be made public and open to the criticism and investigation of the whole scientific world — and there is no way of evading this consequence of the manner in which scientific thought and research are and must be carried on — new developments in pure science are as much at the disposal of the applied scientists and technicians in the totalitarian states as they are at the disposal of their opposite numbers in the democratic states. Thus, even granted that the democratic atmosphere may favor the cause of pure science, it does not therefore follow that the totalitarian states will necessarily be in any way behind in the technical application of such new developments to industrial and military problems.

Apart from this recognition of the grain of truth which such an argument may contain, however, there are many reasons for calling the main contention in question. It is a mistake to suppose that totalitarian states are necessarily equally intolerant in all spheres of thought and research. No society is equally intolerant of any and every novelty. Totalitarian states may be very intolerant of philosophical and religious criticism of the basic ideas and orthodoxies upon which the regime is based, and yet at the same time notably tolerant in other spheres of thought and research. They may even, under the possibly mistaken impression that the conclusions of pure science have religious and philosophical consequences, be somewhat suspicious of pure science. But whether or not pure science has or can have philosophical or religious consequences, it is quite clear that applied science or technics can have no such consequences or implications. It is at least arguable that scientific development does not require an atmosphere of intellectual freedom and tolerance to anything like the extent that philosophy and art, for example, require them. In point of fact the great scientific revolution took place in what was probably the most intolerant phase in the development of Western civilization. Men such as Copernicus, Kepler, and Galileo were not exactly approved by everybody, but at least they succeeded in dying peacefully in their beds in an age in which many heretics, often quite insignificant and foolish ones, were being burned at the stake. In the fifteenth and sixteenth centuries an intolerant civilization was tough in its attitude toward philosophical and theological novelty, and by comparison relatively mild in its disapproval of scientific novelty. The same thing is very largely true in totalitarian states today. It is in fact easy to pursue scientific inquiries — and this is even more obviously true in the realm of applied science than in the realm of pure science — without in any way threatening or criticizing accepted philosophical and religious ideas. There is nothing reprehensible or timid about such a procedure, for it is probably more rational and in the best interests of science itself to recognize that the scientific form of thought is essentially one which neither has nor can have any philosophical or religious consequences, except in so far as the study of the scientific form of thought itself may greatly deepen, enrich, and expand our understanding of the logical processes employed by the human mind. The so-called conflict between science and religion, characteristic of the eighteenth and nineteenth centuries, was always something of a futile and even frivolous mistake, an unfortunate confusion of categories that did little good and reflected little credit upon science, theology, and philosophy alike.

And if it is true that totalitarian states are not necessarily intolerant of novelty in the scientific and technical sphere, we must also confess with some shame that it is quite possible for democratic states to display considerable intolerance of novelty, or sometimes even of a revival of orthodoxy, in the philosophical and theological sphere. Fortunately it is not constitutionally possible in most democracies for intolerance to work its will upon the objects of its hostility. Thus intolerance can no longer burn heretics or put them to death in any other way. But it may nevertheless sometimes condemn them to public isolation and obloquy, or perhaps to an unemployment which not only impoverishes them, and their dependent families, but also denies them the means of pursuing their researches or teaching and proclaiming their conclusions.

Science, particularly applied science, is thus not in such desperate need of an atmosphere of tolerance as are the many other forms of thought and inquiry, nor does it usually meet with intolerance in anything like so extreme and harsh a form. It may well be, as I have conceded, that the totalitarian states are less likely to produce some epoch-making giant of pure science — a Galileo, a Newton, a Darwin, or an Einstein — than the democratic states, but there is no reason at all to suppose that they are not now and will not continue to be fully our equals in the world of applied science and technics.

THE INTELLECTUAL CONSEQUENCES OF OUR PREOCCUPATION WITH TECHNICS. All societies and civilizations, even the simplest, employ technics of some kind or other. Nevertheless, important differences may be observed between societies whose technical equipment is modest in its dimensions and small in its scale, and societies, like our own, whose technical apparatus is tremendous in its efficiency, vast in its scope, and exciting and imposing in its detail. In this second type of society we have to consider the problem of the impact of technics on the prevailing spirituality and mental attitudes of the people.

We have already referred to the fact that a system of technics, however magnificent in its scope and design and however effective in operation, is always peripheral to the essential substance of civilization. This fact is very clear in my mind, and I have endeavored to make it as clear as I can to the reader. But it must be admitted that in our society this is very far from being the generally received view. Large numbers of people now somewhat naïvely suppose that technical efficiency is of the essence of Western civilization, and constitutes its supreme and most important contribution to the welfare of mankind. It is paradoxical that such a judgment, passed on the West by so many Westerners, in effect agrees with and supports the prevalent criticism and rejection of the West to be found among so many non-Western observers. Indeed, such a judgment is, in my view, a kind of horrible treason against Western civilization, which is something far greater than a mere plethora of effective gadgets and techniques. Nevertheless, the very prevalence of such an unjust misinterpretation of its own values and achievements within Western civilization is itself one of the psychological consequences of the technical age. It is as though a man were so delighted and obsessed with the magnificence of his new suit as to identify it with his essential being, and thus forget what manner of man he is, and must, even beneath the splendor of his apparel, continue to be. The glory of what we have, of what has only lately come into our possession, may estrange us from the glory of what we have been and still are. Thus it is that a civilization may lose its soul in the contemplation of its wardrobe.

The contemporary danger is that Western civilization, precisely at the moment when, abstractly considered, it has a greater opportunity of achieving its historic purposes and embodying its characteristic values more effectively than ever before, may be lured and deceived into neglecting and forgetting precisely what those purposes and values are. It may concentrate to such an extent on learning how to do what it wants to do more effectively that it will lose all consciousness of what it is that it wants to do. That the West is merely materialist, activist, and technical we may describe as the great lie about the West, yet it cannot be denied that the great splendor of its technics is the main cause of the strange fact that even Westerners, proud of their own civilization, can be persuaded to entertain and repeat the lie. And the lie itself has a cumulative, self-perpetuating quality. It is caused by an obsessive preoccupation with technics, and one of its consequences is an even greater obsession with technics. This failure to realize that a system of technics does not make or compose a civilization leads to an increasing disinclination, even incapacity, among our intellectuals and in our educational system, to concentrate and devote the mind to the problem of what makes a civilization what it is and what preserves it in being.

In the context of the present discussion I have thought it sufficient to describe a civilization as a set of purposes and values. It is also a kind of preoccupation with the nature of its purposes and values, for a civilization reverences its characteristic purposes and enjoys its characteristic values. We may say that a civilization can persist only in so far as, in the most literal sense of the words, it continues to enjoy itself. If a civilization can no longer enjoy itself, then its time is certainly much later than most of its citizens will care to think. If technics is peripheral to a civilization, the contemplation and consideration of its ultimate purposes and values are central to its very being.

We are discussing here more than the prevailing shape of our intellectualism. It is certainly true that our preoccupation with technics, with means rather than ends, is already producing, among Western intellectuals, a new kind of philosophy, a kind of philosophy that resolutely refuses to think in terms of any ultimate purposes and values at all. But it is also true that the same preoccupation, on less intellectually rarified levels, is producing a new kind of popular culture and a new kind of common man, living on the mere surface of events, his working life consumed in the service of technics and his leisured life diverted and still kept on the surface of things by the products of technics, a life more and more deprived of the depth, meaning, and relevance that comes from some conscious affirmation of ultimate purposes and ultimate values, a life which estranges the man who lives it from the heart and substance of the tradition of civilization which he inherits. If it is true that our technics is peripheral to our civilization, the danger now is that the actively technical and the passively technified man may in his turn become peripheral to our civilization also.

Another dangerous by-product of the obsession of our age with technical problems and achievements is the purely pragmatic or instrumentalist philosophy to which we have already referred in passing. Now it is perfectly true that there is a realm of thought and inquiry within which purely instrumentalist values are dominant, a realm of thought and inquiry, that is, within which we must be, and ought to be, pragmatists. This realm of thought and inquiry is the realm of technics. When we are seeking to invent and create new expedients to solve our problems and implement our purposes, the pragmatic test of usefulness in operation is the only one which it is necessary to apply. The wise man should certainly be pragmatic about practical things, instrumentalist in his attitude toward his instruments. That is reasonable enough, but the fallacy lies in generalizing this state of mind into a total and dogmatic pragmatism about everything. And so we get pragmatism in politics, pragmatism in education, pragmatism in ethics, and pragmatism in religion. The mistake lies in supposing that in a world in which many things are pragmatic, everything must be pragmatic; that in a world in which many instrumental values are real, all absolute values must necessarily be rejected. This is to substitute a dogmatic, absolute pragmatism about everything for a discerning and appropriate pragmatism about the purely practical issues of life.

In dogmatic pragmatism, the pragmatic and experimental attitude toward life runs riot and every human problem is turned into a technical problem. This is a profound philosophical mistake. As we have already seen, questions about the means we are to employ are essentially pragmatic questions, but questions about the ends we are to pursue are always in the last resort absolute questions. A purely pragmatic philosophy is a philosophy that finds means everywhere and ends nowhere, but the very conception of means is irrational without some recognition of the reality of ends, for a means of doing something implies the recognition and willing of the ends to which it is a means. The question 'What ought we to do?' is different in kind from 'What is the best and most efficient way of doing it?' and it demands to be answered in a quite different way.

In practice, no doubt, what the pragmatist really assumes and implies is that we already know so well what ought to be done that it is a waste of time to give any particular thought to the matter. If this were true the only human problem would be the problem of finding out how best to do it. I do not think that we can realistically say that this is true. Our society is now much more profoundly torn and divided by conflicts about ends than by conflicts about means. There is in fact little general agreement, even within the area of one particular form of civilization, about what ought to be done. Even if there were general agreement about what ought to be done, this fact would not save, or lend rational plausibility to, the pragmatic philosophy, for even in that case it would still be necessary to show within the terms of the pragmatic philosophy how it is that we all know what ought to be done.

The plain fact, however, is that not all human problems are technical problems. Indeed, the profoundest human problems, those that lie most deeply at the roots of our present conflicts and discontents, are not technical problems, and a merely pragmatic attitude can make no contribution toward their solution.

Indeed, it is at precisely this point in our discussion that we may be able to observe and define what I may call the central paradox of the narrowly technical mind. The technical mind glories in the notion of its pragmatic efficiency. It prides itself on being supremely good at getting things done and producing results. Yet at the same time — perhaps because it has so little sense of history and of the subtle impact of so many human factors in human history which if not absolutely imponderable have as yet never in fact been successfully pondered — it is on the whole an inadequate and unsuccessful historical agent. For obvious reasons technical action is by its very nature purposive action. It proceeds by the calculation of consequences, by the adjustment of carefully scrutinized means to desired ends. What it forgets is the narrow limitations to which the human mind is subject when it sets before itself the task of calculating future consequences. It is probably true to say that man as a historical agent is least successful in those activities which most of all demand intelligent foresight and a careful calculation of future consequences; and most successful where he concentrates on bringing present action carefully into line with present vision. Thus man is immeasurably more successful as artist and poet than as politician and economist. Indeed, it would be no exaggeration to say that politics and economics are the spheres of activity in which man throughout the ages has been least successful. Our political techniques cannot avoid recurrent crises and catastrophes. Our economic systems, all of them, whether individualist or collectivist, never succeed in evading the periodic slumps and depressions which are a judgment on the blindness and complacency of our passing prosperities.

The trouble is not so much that the consequences which

the technical mind foresees fail to take place. On the contrary, to an increasing extent in the technical age, the shrewdly foreseen consequences do take place. Man's perennial difficulty is rather to be found in this: that all our purposive acts have many other consequences besides their foreseen and intended consequences. The purely technical or economic action concentrates narrowly on bringing about one particular, desired and possibly desirable, physical or economic result, but any economic or technical action will have many other results besides that which was foreseen and desired. Thus it may have psychological, social, and cultural consequences which not only were unforeseen but, had they been foreseen, would not have been desired. Again and again we find that our manner of solving one problem is the cause of several more new problems, some of them perhaps more bothersome and intractable than the problems that have been solved. Thus if we consider it as a whole the technical age is not a period during which the number of outstanding problems that agitate our minds is steadily reduced. On the contrary, the number of such problems is actually increased, and man finds himself more harassed, more frequently at a loss, than he was before. The great illusion of the technical mind is the notion that through technics, more and more technics, bigger and better technics, man may become the lord of his future. Yet if we compare the impact of the future upon us in this technical age with the sense of the future as we find it in a simpler society possessing far less technical equipment, we shall see at once that in many important respects we are more and not less worried by a sense of foreboding, of unknowable and imponderable hazards and uncertainties waiting for us round the corner in the blinding darkness of the not-yet.

An interesting and, to me, embarrassing example of the philosophical inadequacy of mere pragmatism is to be found in Professor Henry Steele Commager's recent book, *Freedom, Loyalty, Dissent.*[4] I find this book embarrassing because, while I agree entirely with all that it positively seeks to uphold and commend, and entirely also with all its denunciations and repudiations, I find myself in equally complete disagreement with most of the reasons on the basis of which Professor Commager seeks to establish his position. For Professor Commager, pragmatism is the true Americanism, and it is in the very nature of pragmatism to demand freedom, nonconformity, and a critical and experimental attitude in both thought and practice toward the problems of life. Thus for Professor Commager the true American loyalty is a loyal insistence on living up to the pragmatic ideal. For him those who would insist that all Americans should conform to an arbitrarily and authoritatively defined Americanism, or any standardized stereotype of the so-called 'American way of life,' are guilty of participating in what we might call the supremely un-American activity. I repeat that in so far as his applications of this reasoning to contemporary social and political problems in America are concerned, I find myself in complete agreement with Professor Commager. Yet the reasoning itself strikes me as unconvincing and on the philosophical level self-contradictory. For Professor Commager's plea is a plea that we should conform to something, i.e. to the pragmatic ideal. He refers to what he calls 'the first lesson of pragmatism: damn the absolute!' [5] but at the same time he is himself pleading that we should receive the pragmatic ideal as if it were an absolute. The philosophy that damns the absolute is thus strangely revealed as the absolute philosophy.

4. Oxford University Press, New York, 1954. 5. Ibid. p. 51.

The truth is that at some point or other in our philosophizing we can none of us escape the absolute. Nonconformity cannot, in the very nature of the case, be total. In some matters, at least, even the resolute nonconformist believes in conformity. Indeed, it is a man's conformity with that in life which he either recognizes as the absolute, or mistakenly absolutizes in his own thinking, that is the motive and basis of his nonconformity with those other realities and standards in life and society which he does not regard as absolute.

Thus, to speak personally, in one sphere of life and in one sphere only I am a conformist: I am an orthodox Christian. But this does not mean that I am a conformist all along the line. On the contrary, it compels me to be a nonconformist in every other sphere of human existence. No doubt I shall find myself a total conformist in the Kingdom of God, on the basis of the very questionable supposition that I shall ever find myself there, but in a fallen world the very fact that I am a conforming member of the Christian Church forbids me to be an out-and-out, unquestioning conformist in any other sphere of existence. I am not and cannot be a conforming member of any particular political party; I do not and cannot conform to the *mores* or prevailing social ethics of any human group to be found anywhere on earth; I am not and cannot be a cultural conformist, acquiescing passively in the prevailing climate of intellectual opinion; all my secular allegiances I must place under the authority and judgment of God, 'so far as the law of God allows.' It is my conformity that makes me a nonconformist. We are not nonconformists because we believe in nonconforming for its own sake. We are nonconformists because conforming to that to which we do conform makes it quite impossible for us to conform to anything else. That to which we conform is either an absolute whose absoluteness we have recognized, or some non-absolute which we have absolutized through some kind of emotional perversion or intellectual error; it is either the living God or some sort of idol, for in this realm of absolutes and ultimate ends and purposes our real choice is not between religion and irreligion but between faith in the living God, who reveals Himself, and one or another of the innumerable forms of idolatry, the dark shadows of which are the gloom of mankind. Thus an absolute pragmatism is Professor Commager's idolatry, an idolatry rendered plausible by the obsession of a technical age with technics. It is an idolatry which has the advantage of ruling all other idolatries out of court, but it has also the disadvantage of concealing from our eyes the true absolute, the one sphere in which ultimate conformity is permissible and necessary. Again I would emphasize my entire agreement with almost everything Professor Commager explicitly says and lays down. I disagree only with his reasons for saying it, which seem to me quite inadequate. The roots of our democracy are not to be found in the technical age, or in any merely pragmatic attitude toward life, and hence the kind of philosophizing to which a technical age is most prone provides but a poor basis for the interpretation, commendation, and defense of democratic civilization. Democratic convictions must be rooted in absolutes of some kind, not in an idolatrous absolutizing of any particular phase of democratic development, or any particular area of democratic achievement, but in a more deeply rooted insight into the ultimate value of human existence, a conviction that man is made in the last resort for God, and an apprehension of the way in which fallen man inevitably tends to destroy himself if there is committed into his hands too much power over either himself or his neighbor.

THE PSYCHOLOGICAL CONSEQUENCES OF OUR PREOCCUPATION WITH TECHNICS. Large-scale technical devices are essentially forms of power. The extent to which our society employs them has brought about a much wider dispersal of the sense of power, and the delights of feeling powerful, among the great mass of the population than has in all probability ever been experienced before in any previous type of social order. In technically simpler societies the most important form of power was political power, the prerogative of command concentrated into the hands of some relatively small ruling minority. Even in a democracy this is still in some sense the case, for a democracy is in effect ruled from day to day by a minority. This minority, of course, is always in theory and to some extent in practice responsible to the great mass of the people, but it is nevertheless a genuine oligarchy. Democracy is not a proposal to eliminate the oligarchy of rulers; it is simply a new and greatly improved technique for selecting them. There is a fundamental truth in Mosca's once widely discussed and celebrated 'law of oligarchies.' All political power is oligarchic in nature. Even in a country which is in theory an absolute monarchy a great deal of political power is quite inevitably not in the hands of the king himself but in the hands of the 'king's friends.' Similarly even in a democracy what is democratically determined is not the day-to-day detail of government and policy making but the actual personnel of the ruling oligarchy. In one form or another the distinction between the rulers and the ruled turns up in every form of society.

Political power was never, of course, the only form of

power experienced and enjoyed in any society. Normally, the most widely dispersed and familiar form of power is domestic power, the power of a husband over his wife, or of parents over their children. But a technical age makes power not so much power over people as power over things, and makes the wielding of power a familiar ingredient of the life style of the overwhelming majority of the population. For the Christian analyst looking at the social order this is a highly significant development. For the Christian doctrine of man emphasizes the extent to which power and an obsession with the delights of exercising power constitute one of the most corrupting elements in human experience. The great mass of people in a technical age feel themselves to be and really are more powerful than the great mass of common people have ever been in any previous society. How difficult men find it to feel and know that they possess a giant's strength and yet not to use it tyrannically like a giant. The sense of power brings with it a certain ruthlessness; the consciousness of mastery inevitably makes men feel like masters. Hence it is that the sense of power again and again in human history predisposes men to violence — above all when they have succeeded in persuading themselves that they have a clean conscience and a good cause which will justify and redeem their resort to violence.

Thus it comes about that a technical age tends to be a violent age, an age prone to think in terms of imposing its purposes on reluctant and recalcitrant material. No doubt the normal habit of the merely technical mind is to think idealistically in terms of the whole human race harmoniously agreed upon its purposes and imposing them ruthlessly upon impersonal nature. The technician's ideal, at all events in a democratic society, is a social order in which men are sensitive to each other's needs, and forebearing toward each other's foibles, and ruthless and self-assertive only in relation to their physical environment. But this distinction and duality of mood are in practice exceedingly difficult to maintain. Thus human foibles and the attachment of men to their cherished conventions and social institutions may obstruct the technician's program for imposing his will on nature, and in the interests of that program he will find himself compelled to be quite as ruthless and insensitive in his dealings with human habits and prejudices as in his masterful manipulation of his physical environment. He becomes accustomed to being tough and ruthless and he cannot, for all his ideals, cease to be so when he is obstructed not by physical circumstances but by human beings. Again, there is always the possibility that a ruthless and insensitive attitude toward nature may in the long run be as depraving and disastrous as a ruthless and insensitive attitude toward one's fellow men.

In human life character is shaped even more by the means we employ than by the ends we pursue. We usually do not succeed in becoming what we purpose to be; our characters are molded by the pattern of life we adopt in the pursuit of our purposes. Whether a man or a society will achieve its ultimate purposes is always questionable, and in fact most men and societies fail in the end to achieve them. The indubitably concrete historical facts are their patterns of conduct, the modes of action in and through which from day to day they seek to implement their purposes. Thus the communist may seek to justify himself before his own conscience, and before the tribunal of history, in terms of his determination and sincere desire to create the communist society. But to date, on his own confession, he has failed to create the communist society. It is possible, even probable, that he never will create the communist society. In that case when communism is dead and done with, as it will be sooner or later, we shall have to say that the communist contribution to human history was not the communist society, in which, as the communist supposes, all would be justice and order and peace, but the communist propagandas, the communist tactics, the wars that it caused, the persecutions it inspired, the lies to which it gave utterance, the Soviet brutalization of man. This is and will be the distinctive communist achievement, and by this and this alone will history judge the communists. At the Last Judgment such men will seek to defend themselves by crying out, 'Have mercy upon us! We pursued the good as we conceived it.' To which the Judge may perhaps reply, 'But how many of my children did you trample upon in the heat of the chase? You never found your good, and your only monument is the succession of mangled corpses which you left to mark your tracks.'

But the communists are perhaps not the only people who will put in this kind of a defense on Judgment Day, nor will they be the only people to be silenced by this kind of reply. The communists have no monopoly of ruthlessness. Unless our prevalent obsession with technics can be compensated for and balanced by the labors of our preachers and poets, our artists and philosophers, and by a great mass of common people within Western civilization who really love its humane traditions, there is a grave danger that we may find ourselves charged with the same kind of accusation and reduced to the same kind of silence. Men are not justified by the righteousness of their purposes. Men are justified by a divine love which is as swift and efficient in the scrutiny and criticism of means as in the selection of ends. The fact that modern technics has created a situation in which we could conceivably be ruthless to an extent that would utterly transcend all previous ruthlessness only increases the tremendous burden of moral and spiritual responsibility resting upon us to make quite certain that we do nothing of the kind.

Closely connected with the psychological and moral dangers of the intoxicating sense of wielding great power is the way in which an age of fascinating, intricate technical possibilities and accomplishments tends to produce human beings endowed with an overly extroverted mentality. Extroversion and introversion are a useful pair of psychological terms. For our present purpose we may find it convenient to depart very slightly from their conventionally accepted meaning. By extroversion I mean a state of the human mind which is interested in sub-human things rather than in people; by introversion I mean a little more than a man's preoccupation with himself. More generally the term denotes an interest in people rather than in things, although such a state of mind certainly demands a sensitivity and high degree of sympathy, which will be unattainable unless we are very deeply aware of the subtleties and depths of our own self-conscious experience. It is a great mistake to suppose that extroversion is, from a psychological point of view, 'normal' and healthy, whereas introversion is a morbid condition. Presumably the 'normal' and healthy condition of man is to be found in a reasonable balance between the two. Extreme introversion and extreme extroversion are both pathological conditions. The characteristic symptom of extreme and pathological introversion is a morbid depression that immerses a man in a private world of his own gloom and fancy. It may even detach his consciousness from reality altogether. The morbid consequences of extreme extroversion are hysteria and violence. The extreme extrovert lacks the interior resources that would enable him to understand and accept frustration. Hence he tends to react to frustration emotionally, with impatience and violence, which are the product of his inability to comprehend the causes of frustration or to accept the fact of frustration. This is really an infantile condition, the origins of which may be traced in the emotional outbursts of babies when their meals are late or their physical movements are restricted. The same symptoms can often be noticed in immature schoolboys. The unbalanced extrovert is in fact an infantile adult. He is an infantile adult at worst and a grown-up schoolboy at best. Hence it comes about that a civilization too obsessed with technics and the manipulation of sub-human things tends to become an immature civilization, however rich the essential maturity of its traditions.

Maturity is more than a matter of age. The mere lapse of time does not produce maturity automatically. Our Western civilization has in the past been much more mature than it is today. One of the most prevalent European mistakes about America is the notion that America is and must be less mature than the European provinces of our Western civilization simply because it is a much younger country. It is noteworthy that this mistaken excuse is heard as often on the lips of American apologists for America as on those of European critics of America. In fact, however, Americans who love and value and rest upon the great traditions of Western civilization are quite as mature, and for the same reasons, as Europeans who do the same thing. Conversely, the so-called immaturity of America is quite as manifest in contemporary Europe as in America itself. Both areas of Western civilization include large groups who have never been assimilated into the depths and subtleties of the Western civilized tradition. In both areas we find people more influenced by the technical phase of the development of Western civilization than by its deep, underlying values. I am not suggesting that this technical phase is the sole cause of this phenomenon. Another and deeper cause, which we will discuss in a later chapter, is the historic failure of Western civilization to assimilate large elements of its working population into the depths and profundities of its cultural tradition, a failure the consequences of which are visible in America and Europe alike. There can be no denying that those cultural traits and tendencies which European critics of America insist on regarding as characteristically American are quite as popular in Europe as in America itself. On the other hand, all that the most fervent glorifiers of the European tradition regard as essentially European is quite as alive in America as in Europe. There are two Americas, just as there are two Europes, one assimilated to the depths of the Western tradition, the other detached from those depths and consciously aware of Western civilization only in its technical phase. The contrast between Europe and America is not the contrast between the symphony concert and the juke box. There are juke boxes in Europe and symphony concerts in America. The fact is that both these areas of Western civilization, however great and numerous their superficial differences, resemble each other in containing and tolerating the contrast between the symphony concert and the juke box.

Nevertheless, although the advent of the technical phase in the development of Western civilization is far from being the sole cause of the morbid phenomena we are discussing, it is a contributory factor perhaps second to none. It is even closely related to the prevalence of that error, which we have already discussed, which leads many people to suppose that our technics is the essence of our civilization. For large elements of our Western populations, who had never been assimilated into the deeper and earlier traditions of Western culture, have only recently and during the period of this technical phase risen above their proletarian and disinherited status. They can at least say of this technical phase of the development of Western civilization, 'This is where we came in.' Certainly at the point at which they came in the technical aspects of what they came into were its most marked visible features, and their mistaking them for its essence is at least understandable and excusable.

This observation also enables us to understand the deeper psychological causes of the connection between technics and the prevalent cult of the tough mind, with its leanings toward ruthlessness and violence. The cult of toughness is a marked contemporary feature of our popular literature, our popular drama, both in the movies and on the living stage, and not a little of our contemporary philosophical and social thinking. Even in philosophy the positivist tends to be a ruthless and insensitive thinker, and behind pragmatism there lies an evaluation of sheer action which rates it higher than thought. Few characteristics of the present phase of our civilization are darker with a sense of impending fatality than this one, for paradoxically enough the tough mind of the ruthless activist is not really very good at action. Wise action calls for a certain intellectual resilience, a sensitiveness to subtle realities, which the extroverted, activist type of mind can rarely, if ever, attain.

In particular, toughness in politics almost always leads to unwise and miscalculated political policies. The activist is naturally prone to suppose that there is no practical alternative to cutting the cords that bind him with the sword, precisely because he lacks the patience to undo the knots. Oddly enough, the extrovert, who of all men is least able to endure frustration, is of all men the one most easily and most frequently frustrated. His purposes are few, straightforward, and unresilient. He is slow to perceive more subtle alternatives. He rarely dreams of any way of achieving his purposes apart from the way of violence and direct assault. His lack of any capacity for profound self-analysis and self-criticism easily persuades him that his purposes are righteous, worse still, that he himself is righteous because his purposes are righteous. So it is that in his own eyes his impatience and violence are justified. He plays the game of life as a schoolboy plays football. Indeed, even while he is immersed in the perplexities and responsibilities of adult life, he often remains at heart a schoolboy playing football.

These, of course, are not the psychological consequences of an age that merely happens to use technics in the service of its purposes. Ours is not an age that merely uses technics; ours is an age to a very considerable extent obsessed by technics. We may thank God that this obsession is by no means universal, but we cannot ignore the fact that it and its psychological and spiritual consequences are very widespread. Never has Western civilization been so forgetful of its true nature as in this technical phase of its development. Never before has its mind been so hopelessly split between a sense of what, beneath the actual phenomena of its visible history, it truly is, and what it on the surface appears to be. We still possess and cherish in the heart of the Western tradition our Christianity, the magic mirror in which we can see ourselves as we really are. But how easy it has become to look into the glass, and then go out into our world of obsessive technical interests and accomplishments and straightway entirely forget what the glass has revealed. The glass tells us that man is weak, whereas technics reassures him with a sense of his own power; the glass reveals that man is sinful, whereas the illusions of technical accomplishment persuade him that he is righteous; the glass tells him that man can be redeemed, whereas the uncritical self-reliance of the technical age insinuates that he may redeem himself; the glass tells him that man is made for God, whereas the characteristic idolatries of the technical age lure and ensnare him with the enticing notion of making himself for himself. At the end of the process not only is Christianity forgotten but the kindred and derivative values of Western humanism are forgotten also. Technical man is left alone with the dreams that make him feel righteous and the frustrating realities that make him feel aggrieved and impatient.

Is Western man, with this obsession with technics which has reduced him to his present degree of spiritual ineptitude and schizophrenia, as different from Marxist man as he is likely to suppose? Here also we find men left alone with their utopian dreams and their frustrations, sufficiently unimaginative to see no solution to their problems except a violent one, and sufficiently insensitive — or so we fear — to attempt the violent experiment.

Western democratic civilization, even in this technical phase, is still, in my judgment, a vastly preferable alternative to communism, but it is not a complete or total alternative. In its idolatry of technics, in its toughness of mind, in its strange doctrine of justification not by supernatural faith but by humanistic dreams, it resembles communism too closely to argue against it cogently. We in the West cannot decisively reject what we feel alien to our vision, indeed we cannot clearly show that it is alien to our vision, unless we first repossess and experience our vision in all its depths and integrity. It is precisely this kind of recovery which the present obsessive phase of our technics — which is, after all, no more than a mere passing phase in the development of our civilization — has rendered impossible for most of us and almost unbearably difficult for the rest of us.

Thus at no point does contemporary democracy resemble totalitarianism more closely than in this prevailing preoccupation with and unquestioning reliance on technics, far too simple a faith for a great civilization to build upon. We must be reminded again and again, and become more and more continually aware, that technics is concerned with means not ends, and is therefore an inherently servile activity. It is meant to be, and can only be, the servant of civilization. But when a civilization gives more intellectual attention to and derives more emotional satisfaction from the contemplation of the means it employs than the glory of its characteristic ends and values, not merely its integrity but even its very survival as a civilization is in mortal danger.

SIX

The Obsession with Economic Activity

NOWADAYS IT IS almost a platitude to remark that what we may describe as the commercial-industrial phase of Western civilization has been based on a reverence for work, in the sense of gainful economic activity, which cannot be found in the earlier phases of Western civilization. The Middle Ages reverenced contemplation — we shall ask ourselves precisely what contemplation means a little later on — rather than activity, and the most respected groups in society were an aristocracy that gave itself up to military and political leadership, and an ecclesiastical elite which devoted itself to religious and cultural pursuits. Work as such, in the sense of economic effort, was, of course, necessary to sustain the world, but carried with it little or no prestige. The period during which work in this special economic sense has been greatly respected and admired roughly coincides with the period since the Reformation, and this discovery has led some writers, pioneered by the German sociologist, Max Weber, to propagate the view that the Reformation was, at least in one of its most important aspects, a revolution in our attitude toward economic endeavor, and that without it the emergence of capitalism and, of course, socialism and communism at a later stage —

for socialism and communism both agree with capitalism in this high estimate of work in the economic sense of the word — would have been impossible. Sometimes even, although this is an extreme view, the Reformation has been interpreted and represented as primarily an economic rather than a theological revolution.

The central contention of Weber and those who follow him in stressing the important role of the Reformation in economic history seems to be this. The puritan ethic of 'work hard and live simple' perfectly fits the needs of a society in the early phase of capitalist expansion, which requires production for reinvestment rather than production for consumption. An economy that produces primarily for the sake of consumption is bound to be a somewhat static one. To expand an economy necessitates devoting a high proportion of its products to the work of expansion itself. Men who work hard and productively but consume comparatively little are compelled to reinvest their products in further enterprise. In the same way we can see how in contemporary countries a transition from agrarianism to industrialism compels a modern government to impose rationing and shortages in order to check the demands of consumers on current production. In contemporary life this imposed puritanism, so necessary to expansion, is sometimes called 'austerity,' but modern austerity is really a kind of state-imposed puritanism, just as puritanism itself was a kind of voluntary austerity.

At a later stage in the development of industrial capitalism the system begins to require a rather different set of human dispositions. If the system requires thrifty people who will work hard and live simply in order to get it going, its chief need once it has been established is the creation and encouragement of a large and somewhat lavish consuming public. Thus during the New Deal period it was somewhat wittily remarked that President Roosevelt would have liked to rewrite the Church's catechism by incorporating the additional phrase, 'My duty toward my neighbor is to consume his products.' Thus it comes about, from this point of view, that capitalism in its later stages is compelled to repudiate the puritanism that was dominant during the period of its early growth.

No doubt much of this has been greatly exaggerated. It is certainly grotesque and absurd to interpret the Reformation as a whole in these purely economic terms. In any case the tendency in countries that have been through a phase during which puritanism was dominant is too easily to identify puritanism with protestantism. In fact the great sixteenth-century protestant reformers, whatever else may be said for or against them, were not puritans. Puritanism intruded itself upon the scene rather later, and it may plausibly be argued that it has no necessary connection with protestantism at all. The vogue of puritanism in the seventeenth century, though most puritans rationalize it in a theological way, was primarily due to social and economic causes. Its apparent connection with protestantism is an accidental consequence of the fact that protestantism, particularly in its Calvinistic form, made its strongest appeal to precisely those middle classes who were busy laying the foundations of modern industrial capitalism. Thus this primarily economic explanation of the religious changes in the sixteenth and seventeenth centuries is an explanation of puritanism only, and not of protestantism and the Reformation movement as a whole.

Nevertheless, despite these necessary qualifications, Weber and his school of thought made a real contribution to our understanding of religious and ethical developments that have left a lasting impress on the social institutions and the cultural climate of both Britain and America.

The fact is that what we may call capitalistic conduct and a capitalistic way of life was possible, and more or less isolated instances of it occurred, at least three centuries before anything like what we can call modern capitalism established itself as a respected norm in Western civilization. The Italian thinker Amintore Fanfani [1] describes the 'capitalist spirit' — later, of course, to become the ruling spirit of socialism and communism also — as a belief that the production, accumulation, and enjoyment of material wealth is the chief task of man on earth. This is not necessarily an immoral belief, for it may be held that man is still subject to fundamental ethical laws even while conducting his life on the basis of such an assumption. On the other hand, it contrasts sharply with the prevailing outlook of men in the pre-capitalistic phase of Western civilization. At that time, as Fanfani points out, men were not simply concerned, as we are now, with the distinction between producing and acquiring wealth by lawful or by unlawful means. They were also and equally concerned to limit the intensity with which men prosecuted the quest for wealth *even by lawful means.* To devote too much of one's time and energy to acquiring and accumulating wealth, even by the most scrupulously lawful means, was in the medieval view to be guilty of the sin of avarice, and very few men cared to risk being thought guilty of a sin so universally condemned. It was during this period that the Jews in Europe acquired their reputation for commercial astuteness. They were sufficiently outside the social system to be careless of the extent to which they outraged the prevailing

1. Cf. his excellent little book, *Catholicism, Protestantism and Capitalism,* Sheed & Ward, London, 1935.

conventions. The Jew was such an unfashionable person in any case that doing unfashionable things could make very little difference to his reputation. It is a mistake to suppose that there is anything peculiar to the Jewish tradition or to the Jewish racial make-up that causes the Jew's tendency to preoccupy himself with commerce, and to practice the commercial way of life with outstanding success. The historic and fabled commercialism of the Jews is a consequence of the ostracism of the Jew in medieval Christendom. Ostracized people seldom conform to the mores of those who ostracize them. They have nothing whatever to gain by doing so, and perhaps much to lose.

The great change, from this point of view, which the Reformation brought about, was a new concept of the dignity of gainful employment, what we may call a cult of the working layman. In puritan communities in particular the characteristic everyday preoccupations of the working laity became not merely respectable; they were even provided with special theological sanction, for in this tradition a man's secular pursuit was interpreted as his special vocation or calling from God.

THE CHRISTIAN DOCTRINE OF WORK. Here we can do no more than baldly summarize and contrast various approaches to what we may call a doctrine of work which are found in different parts of Christendom, and which are distinctive of different periods in the development of Christian thought.

1. *Work as a punishment for original sin.* This view, historically speaking, is based very largely on the passage in the third chapter of the Book of Genesis in which Adam and Eve are cast out of the Garden of Eden. In this section of the great Eden myth we see man emerging out of the darkness of primitive savagery, a period in which human

beings exist merely by gathering the food so abundantly provided by nature, and becoming a working agriculturalist and pastoralist. Work is thus the price man has to pay for his transition from pure savagery. 'Cursed is the ground for thy sake. In toil shalt thou eat of it all the days of thy life; thorns also and thistles shall it bring forth to thee; in the sweat of thy face shalt thou eat bread till thou return to the ground.' [2]

Work is thus the tragic price man must pay for civilization, with its strange mixture of achievement, anxiety, and sin. From this point of view it is impossible to expect that all the work we do, or even most of the work we do, should be pleasant. It is our punishment for not having tolerated, or been content to rest within, innocent and idyllic savagery. At the moment when man began to use his creative potentialities he was faced with an ineluctible choice of which the contented savage had had no previous experience, the choice between using these potentialities in the service of God or in the service of his own pride and of the demons or perverted forms of spirituality that inhabit this lower world. Work is man's punishment for having chosen the more exacting way in life, and for having rendered himself vulnerable to the more tragic and profoundly perverting forms of temptation.

This view is certainly not adequate if it is put forward as a complete Christian doctrine of work. On the other hand, it does account for some elements in our experience of work. It explains why it is that in all ages a great deal of the work that has to be done if the social order is to be maintained is found unpleasant and uncongenial by those who have to do it. None of us altogether escapes acquaint-

2. Genesis 3, 17–19.

ance with the drudgery of uncongenial toil, and many men have known little else in life. This doctrine gives us at least one reason why even the most uncongenial forms of work must nevertheless be endured and carried on. They must be accepted either as a just punishment for, or as the fair and reasonable price of, civilized existence. No society has yet devised a way of so conducting its affairs as to avoid drudgery, boredom, and frustration.

Our society is no exception to this rule. Occupations that involve drudgery, boredom, and frustration are found throughout our industrial and administrative system. We rightly try to reduce these elements in our working life to the barest minimum, but we are not and cannot conceivably be even within reaching distance of eliminating them altogether. It is impossible to watch men working at a conveyer belt, or to pay tolls at our turnpikes and toll bridges to men who stand for hours a day in little glass boxes passively accepting dimes from passing motorists, without feeling that the price of civilization measured in human terms is still a very heavy one indeed. The romantic view of work, characteristic of some artists and craftsmen, has clearly no validity here. This kind of work is done only because it has to be done. It can be carried on on the basis of purely economic motivations, because those who carry it on know no other way of earning a living, or as a humble service to mankind, but if it is not thought of as in some mysterious way or other part of the penalty of being civilized the boredom and the frustration of it can be endured only in a spirit of resentment and revolt or in one of dumb incomprehension and unimaginative acquiescence.

We cannot entirely set aside a theory, however inadequate in itself, which at least explains facts and experiences so universal as these. On the other hand, the theory entirely fails to explain why so much of the work that has to be done in the world is found so enthralling, satisfying, and creative by those who have the privilege of doing it. People who find satisfaction and fulfillment in their work usually entirely fail to understand why it is that so many millions of less fortunate workers seek by trade-union agitations and sometimes, where possible, by political means to limit the number of hours of the day in which they are called upon to devote themselves to their particular form of toil. The writer, the artist, the minister of the Church, the creative commercial or industrial organizer, and others like them would be anything but grateful for some decree restricting their activities to eight hours a day. But they cannot reasonably expect their own attitudes toward their work to be shared by others whose functions are of a less attractive character, and completely devoid of any possibility of self-fulfillment. I remember hearing a bishop eloquently, and in his case quite sincerely, telling a working-class audience in England that he worked at least sixteen hours a day and asked for nothing better. 'If I were a bishop,' said one workshop foreman in the audience, 'I would work sixteen hours a day, too, but eight hours of my kind of work a day is quite enough for anybody.' It was amusing to hear a bishop being educated, and I hope and believe that this particular exchange was instructive and profitable for the bishop himself.

2. *Work as the exercise of man's creative energy.* From this point of view the capacity for productive and fruitful work constitutes an element in man's make-up which, perhaps above all others, enables us to say that man is a being made in the image of the Creator God. This interpretation of work is most obviously valid in the case of the artistic worker. The writer produces his book, the artist his pic-

ture, the composer his symphony. They create these things not quite out of nothing, as in the Bible and Christian doctrine God creates the world, but at all events they come closer to this Biblical kind of creating than anything else of which we are aware in human experience.

'And God said let there be light; and there was light.' [3] Of course, the writer does not merely say, 'Let there be books.' There is plenty of drudgery involved in the making of books, as this writer is acutely aware at the moment. Nevertheless, there is an important sense in which a book, any book, even a bad one, is an unpredictable novelty, a new creation. Nothing that existed prior to its gradual emergence in the writer's mind and its painstaking transposition to paper logically necessitated or required it. No one could have foreseen it. In the case of the present book, for example, no doubt most of my friends, knowing me, would guess that I should be engaged in writing something or other, but they would have no conceivable means of telling beforehand that I should write precisely this book. I might equally well be engaged upon some other literary task. Even I myself while engaged in writing this chapter cannot precisely foresee all the ideas and phrases that will drift into my mind as I turn to the task of writing the next. The precise value of what eventually emerges out of so many hours of real toil and heart-searching it will be for the reader and the critic rather than for me to say. But at least I shall be able to contemplate the finished volume and say to myself as I do so, 'A poor thing, quite possibly, but indubitably my own.'

We must not confine this interpretation of work to literature and the arts, however. The craftsman, who at his

3. Genesis 1, 3.

highest pinnacle of achievement is very close to the artist, the engineer, and even the administrator, who may perhaps create a whole new social institution in a very real, if relative, sense out of nothing, can contemplate the fruits of their labor with something of the same kind of awed reverence for the creative powers God has placed at their disposal.

On the other hand, it certainly cannot be claimed, as we have seen, that in any conceivable society all work will have this creative character and give this kind of profound interior satisfaction to those who carry it on.

3. *Work as a vocation to service.* This way of interpreting work has the great advantage of pointing clearly to something in the very nature of work which is equally present both in the creative, satisfying forms of work and in the non-creative, frustrating occupations. All valid work renders or contributes to some kind of service to mankind. To bake bread, to paint pictures, to mine coal, to engage even quite humbly in some governmental or administrative enterprise dedicated to maintaining or upholding the state of the world is in each and every case to perform an intelligible service to the social order and the individual people who inhabit it. This is true, as we have said, of even the most unsatisfying and frustrating forms of drudgery.

On the other hand, to interpret work in this way is to put a question mark against the current habit of indentifying work with gainful employment. Not all ways of rendering service to mankind are forms of gainful employment. Indeed, many of the most outstanding ways of serving mankind involve giving something away rather than gaining anything. Thus a millionaire may endow a hospital, or a poorer man may devote some of his spare time and leisure energies to the service of the hospital, without expecting any monetary reward for his activities. Often the reward of such outstanding services, even when there is one, is in no way commensurate with the service rendered or with the time, skill, and energy consumed in rendering it. This is true, for example, in the lives of many dedicated parochial clergy all over the world. It would be monstrous to say of many such men that their work of service is in any way adequately remunerated by their stipends, or carefully proportioned to their earnings. Such men often give their lives, their talents, and energies in return for what from any merely economic standpoint must be reckoned no more than a miserable pittance. A similar kind of generosity can be discerned in many other noble but poorly paid professions — for example, in teaching, nursing, and the social services. Conversely, a good many forms of gainful employment render little or no intelligible service to mankind, and the rewards of labor sometimes far outrun its real value.

The vocational conception of work as necessarily a form of service has thus two important consequences or implications: (1) this conception of work, perhaps unlike the others we have discussed, establishes for us a criterion by means of which we can distinguish between valid work and invalid work: and (2) it enables us to escape from the prevalent habit of identifying work with gainful employment. These two implications are of such importance that we shall discuss each of them separately.

THE DISTINCTION BETWEEN VALID AND INVALID WORK. It is impossible to suppose that all the things which people in any particular civilization think it necessary or desirable to do are things which God wills we should do and calls upon men to do in His service, and in the service of their fellows for His sake. There may in fact be many ways of working for a living which offer no necessary or intelligible service to mankind. The most obvious example of the possibility of working to gain a living without performing any real service to any one in the process is to be seen in that category of activities which we call criminal. But there may also be many quite legal and socially respectable forms of activity which nevertheless fall into the same class.

Thus, to select one example among the many possibilities, a great deal of advertising performs no real and intelligible service to mankind. I should not by any means make this criticism of all forms of advertising. When an advertisement tells me where I can obtain what I require, and the approximate price I shall have to pay for it, it performs a very real and important economic service. The assumption that lies behind this kind of advertising is that I already know what I want, and it says to me in effect, 'If this is what you want, here is where to get it and it will cost you so much money.' But a great deal of advertising is not devoted to helping us to satisfy our needs. According to a theory very prevalent among contemporary practitioners of the art, the purpose of advertising is to persuade us that we need many things which left to ourselves we should never even have thought of requiring. Such advertisements make us afraid of things we should never have thought of fearing, or envious of things we should never have thought of desiring. Their purpose is not to satisfy the human appetite but rather to arouse and intensify it. Their end product is not human satisfaction but human dissatisfaction. For, of course, even the wealthiest of us can hardly afford to satisfy all the desires attractive advertisements arouse in our hearts, and even the hardiest soul cannot quite banish all the irrational fears which they evoke in the depths of his being.

We may illustrate this non-sensical process by imagining an obviously absurd economic activity. I invent and patent, let us say, a new process for making socks out of seaweed. I persuade a considerable number of investors to join with me in equipping a large factory somewhere near the coast where plentiful supplies of seaweed can easily be obtained. I employ a considerable number of people to gather and process the seaweed. Thus a great deal of capital and labor is now bound up with this somewhat speculative and precarious enterprise. Only one difficulty remains. The public is on the whole quite satisfied with the socks it is wearing at present, and sees no particular reason for transferring its patronage to the new socks made out of seaweed. The plain fact is that people left to themselves do not desire seaweed socks. And so I employ advertising experts, probably at fabulous expense, to set about the task of making people desire seaweed socks. There are, of course, many stereotyped and well-worn ways of doing this. There is the sex angle: a beautiful young woman gazing with adoration at a handsome, perfectly tailored man, murmuring as she does so, 'Darling, there is a wild tang of the sea about you which sets my blood on fire.' There is the Hollywood angle: 'All the leading film actors are now wearing the new seaweed socks.' There is the snob angle (for which a British setting may be preferred): the Lord Chancellor in his robes stands on the steps of the House of Lords, talking to the Archbishop of Canterbury, also in his robes; 'Did you observe,' His Lordship remarks to His Grace, 'that all the dukes in the House this afternoon were wearing the new seaweed socks?' There is the fear-of-disease angle: 'Do you realize that the man who wears the new seaweed socks is absorbing iodine into his system throughout the whole day?' There is the science angle: a young man in white overalls peers critically at an unidentified something or other in a test tube; 'Seaweed socks are scientific socks!' And so it goes on. The diligent student of modern advertisements will no doubt imagine many more ways of inducing the public to desire these quite undesirable garments. Of course, all that the advertisements say about seaweed socks will be nonsense, and nine-tenths of it will consist of downright lies. Even the claims that have some vestige of truth in them will be exaggerated to a fantastic degree. The seaweed socks are, of course, an imaginary product; but they are not more fantastic and ridiculous than a great many other products which are in fact now on our markets and are widely advertised.[4] There is obviously nothing criminal about all this activity, yet, judged by our criterion that all valid work performs some valuable and intelligible service, work of this kind must clearly be set aside as invalid work. It need not be done, there is no intelligible reason why it should be done, and our civilization would be the healthier if it were not done.

Nor in a fallen world is the service of desires which men really do feel and cherish necessarily a criterion of valid work. It is possible to earn a living by selling racing tips to amateur gamblers, by advising clients how to evade taxation yet keep within the law, by drawing obscene pictures for the entertainment of secret sex perverts, by composing worthless comic strips for people too lazy to read, and in many other innumerable ways to busy oneself without making any intelligible contribution to the welfare of mankind and yet procure an adequate supply of daily bread. It

4. I emphasize this again because the trouble about fantastic imaginings in the modern world is that they resemble the facts so closely that people often take them seriously. Reality is often nowadays so ridiculous that even the most absurd conceit can look quite real.

would be difficult to frame an inquiry that would enable us to arrive at any precise statistical conclusions, but it is safe to say that an alarmingly high proportion of modern work would have to be condemned as invalid in the light of such a criterion as this.

NOT ALL WORK IS GAINFUL EMPLOYMENT. But this second implication of our doctrine that all valid work renders some intelligible service either directly to God or mediately to man for God's sake is an even more important one, for it points toward a reconciliation of the two concepts of work and leisure. It is no doubt true that the word *leisure* indicates that area of a man's life in which he is not engaged in the economic activities by means of which he earns his living. But once we have distinguished between the concept of work and the concept of gainful employment, we shall no longer make the mistake of supposing that leisure is necessarily the equivalent of not working. For many of us, work is our way of gaining money and leisure our way of spending it; work indicates activity, whereas leisure indicates passive enjoyment. This way of distinguishing between work and leisure is one that lowers the status of both and blinds us to their real nature. Once we have defined leisure not as a cessation from work but as the time left over when our necessary gainful activities are concluded, we shall soon perceive that much of the work which is absolutely essential to the maintenance of civilization has in fact to be carried on during our leisure.

Leisure is not a time for mere inactivity. On the contrary, it is the time for carrying on those activities which are not economically gainful but are nevertheless indispensable if we are to have a civilization worthy of the name. Thus the worship of God, the enjoyment of the arts, the cultivation of the unity and the happiness of the family, the ripening and deepening of friendships, are almost all of them leisure-time occupations. But they are real occupations, and they do involve real work. Yet for many people — and this mistaken idea of the meaning of leisure is based on a false conception of work — leisure is a time for being passively and idly entertained. The Middle Ages had a deeper insight into the nature of leisure, and so it was that medieval men termed the act of religious worship the *opus dei*, or work of God. They saw that contemplating and reverencing the great objective values that confront human existence is not an inactive state of mind. On the contrary, it is a kind of exacting and costly internal work, involving a tremendous concentration of the mind and a profound discipline of the emotions. Thus in music there is all the difference in the world between leaning drowsily back in one's chair and letting some treacly tune, half-heard, spread its sickly substance over our ears, and the intensely alert and active enjoying of a Bach fugue. This latter activity may be one of the peak moments of our leisure, but it is also and in the most proper sense of the word a work, a work which many people, alas, still find beyond their powers. Prayer and worship are also works of a very similar character. One of the worst consequences of the tremendous and in itself quite healthy emphasis laid on the sermon in many of the post-Reformation Christian Churches has been the gradual destruction among large numbers of Christians of any capacity for worship and prayer. For many modern Christians 'going to Church' now means, primarily, listening, or half-listening, or perhaps not listening, to a sermon. The popularity of hymns in modern church life completes the picture. They consist in the overwhelming majority of cases of doggerel rhymes, expressing a sentimentalized, degenerate theology, and wedded to cheap music; they are related to real worship and real prayer very much as the sickly popular tune is related to the Bach fugue.

A return to a truly active conception of leisure and to a deeper appreciation of its function in civilization is an urgent necessity in the present stage of the development of our culture. Nowadays, as a result of new industrial techniques and new methods of commercial and industrial organization, men enjoy more leisure than civilized man has known at any time since he emerged from the savage state. Real savagery, oddly enough, was very leisurely. The women and the children collected food, fruit from trees, berries from bushes, grain from wild cereals, or dug up edible roots, and the men went on occasional hunting or fishing expeditions. They made no clothes; they built no houses. Yet in many parts of the world drawings on the walls of caves and stone carvings and decorated pottery show that such people often knew how to occupy their leisure time creatively. Indeed, the origins and the roots of civilization may be traced even in the behavior of savages. The late Professor J. Huizinga, in one of those little-known books that deserve to be better known, *Homo Ludens*,[5] distinguished between the activities that must be carried on in order to make life possible and the activities that must be carried on in order to make life worth while. The second group of activities he calls *play*, and he argues that all civilization is really a form of play. Civilization is the nonnecessary. This, of course, means that we define necessity in purely biological and economic terms. Civilization begins when we cease to be wholly engrossed in the task of mere organic survival and begin to be human beings in the distinctive sense of the word.

5. Kegan Paul, London, 1950.

Another important book that has recently made substantially the same point, although in rather different language, is Josef Pieper's *Leisure the Basis of Culture*.[6] Here also we find the author insisting that the appreciating and reverencing of objective values is a genuine form of work, involving tremendous inward concentration and activity, a work that is absolutely essential to the being of civilization.

The point seems to be that to recognize, cherish, and concentrate on objective values is essential to the very being of civilization. Civilization, in other words, involves contemplation. The ancient and medieval philosophers were right to distinguish between contemplation and action, and right also, from the point of view of civilization, in estimating contemplation more highly than action, but we altogether misunderstand this distinction if we suppose that contemplation is essentially inactive. Perhaps we shall understand them better if we make the distinction between outward and outgoing activity, devoted to achieving purposes rooted in our finitude, and inward activity centered upon objective values — a religious activity that worships God; a scientific activity that seeks to understand the world; a philosophical activity that reverently probes into the meaning and purpose of human existence; an aesthetic activity in and through which man seeks to make himself sensitive to the beautiful; an ethical activity in and through which a man attempts something much more profound than merely to do good deeds. For the truly ethical activity is not so much an effort to do something as an effort to become a special kind of somebody, or, in religious language — and any really serious effort to be ethical leads into religion — to acknowledge that men are called to *be*

6. Faber and Faber, London, 1952.

saints, rather than just to perform a series of good actions, and under God and with God's help to seek to respond to that call.

Nowadays when we reflect upon the great values of life we are so accustomed to thinking in terms of creating values that our sense of the importance of reverencing and contemplating them is diminished. The result is that too often we regard values as the special business of that small minority of human beings who are endowed with the capacity to create them: art is the special concern of artists, religion the peculiar concern of clergymen, morality the distinguishing characteristic of the ethical genius, science the peculiar business of the scientist, and so on. But in fact the activity that recognizes and appreciates values is the prior and the more important of the two. Many values do not require to be created in any human sense or by any human activity — for example, natural beauty. Even the values that do require to be created by men — in the special sense of the word 'create' which is appropriate to human activity — have first of all to be recognized and appreciated by their human creators. The poet does not necessarily set down in print for the rest of us to read any and every poetical idea that occurs to him. Some of them he judges not worth setting down. It is the idea that sets his mind on fire when it occurs to him which he subsequently gives to mankind, that it may set other minds on fire in their turn. Behind any act of human creation there lies an implicit judgment that what is created is worth creating. The artist appreciates and recognizes the value of his inspiration before he sets about acting in obedience to it. Thus the contemplation of values is even more fundamental to civilization than the creation of them. We may even define a civilization as a state of human being in which certain absolute values and ultimate purposes are contemplated, reverenced, and enjoyed. This is the essential activity of civilization, and it is essentially a leisured activity.

WESTERN CIVILIZATION AND MASS DEMOCRACY. Even the most casual observation of the way in which the great masses of the citizens of our modern democracy divert themselves in, rather than actively employ, their rapidly expanding stock of leisure time will serve to illustrate one of the greatest of the failures and weaknesses of the present phase in the development of Western civilization: its failure to convey and make intelligible to its working masses its own profound and characteristic values. In its earlier phases the task of embodying and securing the survival of the characteristic values of Western civilization was entrusted to small minorities or elites, to the clergy in the Middle Ages, to the aristocracy in the early modern period, and more recently, to the upper bourgeoisie and to that gifted if somewhat uprooted section of the bourgeoisie usually called the *intelligentsia.* The task of these minority groups was to embody the characteristic values of Western civilization while the great mass of their compatriots merely worked for it in a more or less uncomprehending way.

Democracy instinctively and rightly feels this to be an unsatisfactory state of affairs, but merely to perceive the defects of a particular class system does not suffice to remedy them. The problem of democracy is not simply that of giving votes and political status to the submerged proletariat. That can be achieved relatively easily, and has been achieved throughout nine-tenths of the Western world, sometimes by slow evolution but more often by political revolution. But the profounder problem of democracy demands more than the mere enfranchisement of the submerged proletariat. What it really requires is the elimination of the proletariat altogether, by a process that initiates this proletariat into the values and deeper satisfactions embodied in the great traditions of Western civilization. In most parts of the Western world this problem has not only not been solved, its solution has not even been seriously attempted.

In Western history there have been two ways of establishing democracy. The more familiar way is that of political revolution, which overthrows aristocratic privilege and erects the structure of political democracy over its grave. The danger inherent in this method is that men may be misled into supposing that Western civilization itself begins with the revolution, and this anti-historical dogma may deceive them into denying the great contributions which the aristocratic phase made to civilization. A democracy that is consciously anti-aristocratic can hardly escape decrying and repudiating many of the profoundest and most deeply satisfying elements in the Western traditions. The same thing is true, of course, of a democracy that is consciously anti-ecclesiastical or anti-clerical. Not all modern democracy, however, is the product of political revolution. By far the most outstanding example in the Western world of the achievement of democracy without political revolution is Great Britain. Here democracy has been achieved without the abolition of aristocracy. On the contrary, the very essence of the process by which the British have attained their democracy is the gradual extension of aristocratic privilege to other sections of the community. The aristocratic class itself made large and striking contributions to this process. In particular the development of the characteristically English 'public school' — so-called presumably because the public as a whole does not attend it — which educated the sons of the aristocracy and the sons of the upper bourgeoisie side by side, and orientated their education toward ideals of leadership and service, played a very large part in assimilating the traditions of the upper bourgeoisie in Britain to those of the aristocracy. Nevertheless, even in Britain the evolutionary pattern by no means entirely prevailed. For if Britain escaped any kind of political revolution analogous to the French revolution, it experienced another kind of revolution, the Industrial Revolution, in its worst and most violent form. Precisely because Britain was the first nation to experiment with this pitfall-ridden process, it carried it through clumsily and with a maximum number of mistakes. Hence it cannot be said that Britain has been so successful in initiating its working classes into its basic traditions as it was with its bourgeoisie. In consequence the phenomenon of contemporary British leisure provides us with the same visible evidence of failure to solve the basic cultural problems of democracy as we find in other Western countries.

For modern mass leisure, with its tremendous and elaborately organized techniques, designed to save the masses from the boredom and emptiness of mere non-work by a bewildering variety of superficial diversions, is radically out of harmony with the great traditions of Western civilization. It is a measure of the failure of Western civilization in its present phase to solve what we may call the central cultural problem of democracy. For this central cultural problem of democracy is not to be solved by the creation of a new culture. We cannot truly claim that we have integrated Western civilization by admitting the working classes upon whose labor it depends into full membership if in fact we have diluted the values of Western civilization in the process. If we promise men milk to drink the promise is not honestly redeemed by providing them with a mixture containing 25 per cent milk and 75 per cent water. What Western democracy really requires is the transference to the working masses of the richness and value of Western civilization in its depth and integrity, and this is a feat which in general, it is true to say, has most manifestly not been accomplished.

The most searching criticism of democracy is not to be found on the lips of modern totalitarians and antidemocrats. It is to be found in Plato, and in many writers since his time who were perhaps in this matter Platonists without knowing it. It is the charge that democracy inevitably means the reign of the second best, or even of the third or fourth best, that in transmitting our civilization to the masses we are forced to water it down or spread it thin. This is always the aristocratic charge against democracy, and Plato was in fact an aristocratic thinker. The democracy of the Greek city-state was not democracy in our modern sense. The comparatively small minority of fully enfranchised citizens, who indeed behaved toward each other and collaborated with each other in something like our modern democratic way, nevertheless constituted in fact an aristocratic oligarchy. Now we may rightly question the inevitability of this tendency of a democracy to water down its cultural standards. Indeed, we must question it, for we have now no alternative. Another, non-Greek, element in our Western tradition will not permit us to tolerate any longer the conception of a working proletariat which toils in the service of a civilization without belonging to it. It is the Christian element in our heritage — which sees all men as the objects of the divine love and the embodiment of the divine purpose, which reverences as the very king of men one who came that men might have life and that they might have it more abundantly — which clearly forbids us to toy with the aristocratic idea any longer. As Alexis de Tocqueville saw so clearly, and expressly stated more than a century ago in his great book *Democracy in America,* Christianity has never really been at home in Europe. For centuries historical conditions rendered an aristocratic form of society inevitable, but Christianity never really succeeded in making itself at home in that form of society. There is something not so much in what democracy now is but at least in what democracy in its best moments is trying to become that naturally fits and coheres with Christianity, something of which we cannot find even the germ in any other kind of social experiment. The idea that all men are equal can be a very mistaken one if it leads us to suppose that all men have the same talents or the same tastes, and that civilization requires neither leaders nor experts. Yet if we understand it properly it has profoundly Christian roots. Christianity does not tell us that all men are equal in the abstract, or even in the empirical concrete. What it does tell us is that all men are equally, because infinitely, beloved of God. This is the ultimate theological sanction of our often rather crude and confused belief that all men are equal — in some sense which we cannot perhaps define, but yet inarticulately perceive. This is the underlying dogma that makes sense of the equalitarian ideal and motivates us to persevere, despite many depressing failures, in the quest for a 'free and equal' society. Hence it is the Christian element in our Western tradition which compels us, despite the general indebtedness of our civilization to Plato, almost incalculably great, to reject the pessimism of Plato about the democratic experiment.

Nevertheless it is worth while bearing the Platonic criticism of democracy carefully in mind, if only because it will remind us that we have not really achieved democracy so long as our society presents such an abundance of evidences which appear to lend weight and support to Plato's strictures. We shall not in fact have achieved real democracy in depth until we can see the working masses inheriting the whole richness of Western civilization, pouring into the churches and the symphony concerts, consciously aware of the excellence of its rationalism and its mysticism, comprehending its poets, and acquainted with its philosophers. And when I say pouring into the churches, I have very definitely in mind those churches — a comparatively small minority of the bewildering variety of denominations that cater to America's spirituality — which really keep alive the full extent and richness of the Christian tradition, not radical revivalist and fundamentalist sects that preach a special brand of Christianity lately devised to suit the still somewhat crude religious tastes of the newly enfranchised working masses, a caricature of Christianity, related to authentic Christianity at best as Lamb's *Tales from Shakespeare* and at worst as a comic-strip version of *Hamlet* (which I saw the other day) are related to Shakespeare himself.

Democracy cannot be said to have achieved its aim so long as a proletariat still survives. The proletarian is not simply a man without property — that is a Marxist error — nor is he simply a man without a vote — that is a mistake which belongs to the superficial childhood of democracy. More fundamentally he is a man without a civilization, a man not truly rooted and grounded in the values of the culture to the service of which he devotes his labors. He is the slave of a civilization to which he does not belong. He lives and moves and has his being in the midst of cultural treasures which he cannot comprehend, like a color-blind doorkeeper employed in an art gallery.

This failure to initiate great masses of our citizens into the richness and profundity of our civilization is more than merely a failure to carry our democratic principles to the farthest possible point. It is also a source of present weakness. It means that the Western democracies fail to a significant degree to embody their own values, and are constantly betrayed into disloyalty toward their own values. It may even mean that in important crises many of our voting citizens, through no fault of their own, cannot be relied on unhesitatingly and undeviatingly to choose and prefer the characteristically Western democratic way. They fall easily into the hands of demagogues and false prophets who appeal to their fears and their prejudices, and who may even succeed in leading the tremendous popular forces which democracy unleashes in an anti-democratic direction. The characteristic values of Western democratic civilization will remain in a precarious position so long as so many of those to whom democratic privileges are extended do not really understand or appreciate the basic values of our civilization. In the twentieth century democracies have not always or even usually been overthrown from without. More often they have been overthrown from within by popular mass movements which from a superficial point of view may even appear to be essentially democratic. The communist revolutions in Russia and Asia were not, of course, of this character. They merely substituted one form of autocracy for another, and the peoples of these countries cannot properly be said to have repudiated democracy. In fairness it must be acknowledged that they never knew democracy. But the Nazi and Fascist movements in western and central Europe were essentially popular mass movements among peoples who had known the externals of democracy but had never become fully aware of its inner spirit.

Of course, it can truly be said that this is no new thing. As we have seen, in previous phases of western civilization there has always existed what Arnold Toynbee in his *A Study of History* calls the 'internal proletariat,' a great mass of working people who are physically within a civilization to which they do not spiritually belong. But these earlier forms of Western civilization were not and did not pretend to be democratic. They tolerated the presence of the internal proletariat because they could not conceive of any way of getting rid of it or doing without it, so that for them it existed, we might almost say, by natural law. But the democratic program is essentially a program to abolish the internal proletariat and thus create a more cohesive and united civilization. A democracy that has not manifestly abolished the internal proletariat cannot be said to have fulfilled its program.

That we have as yet failed to fulfill this program, that Western civilization still does contain an internal proletariat, seems to me quite manifest, and nowhere more manifest than in those places where the masses gather to divert and disport themselves in their leisure time, in the Piccadilly area of London, or in New York's Times Square. It is in such areas as these that Western civilization most visibly waters itself down in order to accommodate itself to the tastes of its internal proletariat, and improvises a form of leisure almost completely divorced from its characteristic values. Here is the evidence of our weakness and the measure of our failure to fulfill the democratic promise.

SEVEN

The Obsession with Economic Doctrines

BY FAR THE most serious and damaging secular schism in the contemporary Western world is the controversy between capitalism and socialism, or between what is called private enterprise and public control or public enterprise. This is a squabble about niceties of economic doctrine, involving of course many private and group interests, which is pursued in many countries with most unhealthy fanaticism and uncalled-for ferocity. The terms socialism and capitalism are perhaps incapable of any precise definition, but most readers will be familiar, in somewhat hit-or-miss fashion, with the kind of issue with which the controversy between the two is concerned.

The matter is a serious one because the controversy divides Western civilization into two more or less equal camps. The socialists have their strength in Britain and western Europe; the devotees of private enterprise are well-nigh all-powerful in America. The important thing is to see this controversy in a perspective that will diminish its stature and importance, so it will cease to be sufficiently serious to divide and weaken the West in the face of the communist challenge. So long as people continue to believe in either the private-enterprise principle or the socialist principle with too much zeal and conviction, the danger that the West will be weakened by such contentions will remain a real threat to its unity and survival. On the one hand, extreme devotees of the private-enterprise principle profess, perhaps sincerely, to be unable to distinguish clearly between socialism and communism, quite forgetting that Western socialism's devotion to democratic methods is in itself a quite fundamental distinction. On the other hand, many European socialists believe that what they call the contradictions and basic insecurities of capitalism are the chief cause of the vogue of communism among the European working classes. In their view socialism is the great alternative to communism. Nevertheless European socialists are sometimes inclined to take the views of capitalist critics of socialism in America perhaps more seriously than is necessary, and to draw the fatal conclusion that despite their basic opposition to communism they are closer to and more in sympathy with undemocratic communism than with democratic capitalism. This is the chief cause of the tendency of some European socialists toward a neutralism that does indeed impair the unity and the strength of the Western world. Thus the very existence of this controversy within Western civilization is a real menace to its security and survival.

It is our purpose in this chapter to argue that the controversy, if we consider it in the light of facts rather than in the light of alleged ultimate principles, is very largely a spurious one, and that the enthusiasm with which so many people engage in it is quite uncalled for.

THE UNDESIRABILITY OF DOGMA IN ECONOMICS. Economic science is not a proper context for dogma or ultimate principles. Of course, as a Christian I believe in the possibility and validity of dogma in the right place. Dogma is permissible and necessary where we have to do with ultimates and finalities. If there is indeed an ultimate reality that has made itself known to men then such knowledge of this ultimate reality as we possess — in the nature of the case it will be minimal and inadequate, however precious — must properly and necessarily be dogmatic in form. Similarly if there are any absolute values, apart from which human existence makes no sense and life itself is not worth living, then again such knowledge of these absolute values as we possess must properly and necessarily be dogmatic in form. But where there are no such absolute values and finalities there can in the nature of the case be no dogmas.

It is a mistake to suppose that the confession of the great Christian dogmas logically leads to, prompts, or sustains a generally dogmatic attitude toward life all along the line. On the contrary, belief in the great Christian dogmas, by observing dogma in and confining it to its proper sphere, leads to and sustains an undogmatic attitude in all other areas of human thought and concern. It is precisely the people who question or deny the validity of dogma in the place where it properly belongs, in religion and ethics, for example, who are most likely to create pseudo-dogmas, and the ugly fanaticisms which invariably accompany them, in those spheres of life where we have constantly to adjust ourselves and our institutions to changing circumstances, areas of human concern in which dogma is emphatically inappropriate.

The economic sphere is most certainly one of these non-dogmatic areas of human existence. A study of human history and of the varieties of social institutions acquaints us with a large number of different economic systems. In appropriate circumstances none of them is altogether unsatisfactory, but none of them on the other hand is perfect.

Mortal men, so far, at all events, have never devised or experienced a perfect economic system. In all probability they never will. Even if we did succeed in devising an economic system perfectly adapted to one particular set of circumstances and conditions, the slightest change in those circumstances and conditions would to some extent at least outdate the system and start us on our quest for a perfect economy all over again.

Thus there are no perfect economic systems, and no absolute economic principles. The claim to possess, or at least to know how to create, a perfect economic system is part of the communist propaganda, not ours. When one party to a controversy makes an absurd and ridiculous claim, the best way of answering him is to expose this absurdity in principle, not to put forward an equally ridiculous claim on the other side. I recollect that years ago, when I was acting as a hospital chaplain in England, I was called in to talk to a patient who had been making trouble in the mental observation ward. He explained to me quietly and rationally that he very much objected to being put in a ward with a collection of lunatics. 'Why, sir,' he said, 'this man in the bed next to me thinks he's Julius Caesar.' I was completely taken in by his sensible manner of speech and I exhorted him to behave himself quietly so that the doctors would soon perceive their mistake in suspecting his sanity. 'Yes, that's all very well, sir,' he replied, 'but, you see, I happen to be Julius Caesar myself.' The proper reply to a regime that claims to possess the secret of the perfect economic system is not to say, in effect, 'You're a liar, we're the boys with the perfect economic system,' but to explain quite clearly and decisively why it is that the perfect economic system does not and cannot exist.

Since in economics we have to deal with constantly

shifting circumstances, we are inevitably in the realm of the pragmatic and the relative. There has been a long and acute controversy among modern Western philosophers between those who believe in absolute truths and values, on the one hand, and those who believe in various forms of pragmatism and relativism on the other. Like so many of our modern controversies this particular quarrel is very largely spurious and superfluous. It is impossible to make a cogent case for being pragmatic and relative about everything, just as it is ridiculous to suppose that we can be absolute and dogmatic about everything. The proper task of the philosopher is to distinguish clearly between the realm of the absolute and the realm of the relative, for we cannot dispense altogether with either relative mental judgments and processes on the one hand or absolute judgments and affirmations on the other. The wise man knows how and when to combine the two attitudes. The point I am making is that economic judgments fall entirely within the realm of the pragmatic and the relative. An economy is a system of expedients. There are no economic ends, only economic means to social ends. One type of economy will be more expedient in one set of circumstances, and quite another kind of economy in another set of circumstances. It is even possible that one kind of economy may be expedient in one area of Western civilization, say the European, and quite another economy equally expedient in some other province of Western civilization, for example, the American. There is no reason in principle why different economic systems should not co-exist within the area of the same civilization, for an economic system, like our technics, is essentially peripheral to our civilization and does not affect its essential substance. To hold that an economic system is central to a civilization and determines all its social and cultural forms is the central Marxist heresy and forms no part of our Western philosophy of life. Indeed, one of the intellectual difficulties of the West in attempting to combat communism in the realm of ideas is the extent to which many of our most fervent anti-communists really agree with Karl Marx that the economic system is, so to speak, the business end of a civilization, and must determine all its other social and cultural forms. Once more we are reminded of the serious extent to which many of us in the West, even among the most sincere anti-communists, are already half-Marxist under the skin. To suppose that economics is the most important thing in life, and economic activity the primary activity of society, is not any the less Marxist because the type of economic activity preferred and recommended is capitalist rather than communist. The basic Marxist position is not really its preference for the communist system but its belief in the primacy of economics. It is with this philosophy that we must do battle, even when we find it on our own doorsteps and advocated by people who purport to be, and sincerely suppose themselves to be, our most enthusiastic friends.

We have already referred to the late Professor Huizinga's book, *Homo Ludens*. This work has the merit of making it quite clear that a civilization is much more than the cultural aspect of an economy, the icing and decoration, so to speak, on the top of the economic cake. Civilization is what happens when an economy is so successful as to provide men with leisure time in which they are released from preoccupation with the merely economic problem of survival, liberated from the influence of merely economic pressures, and set free to busy themselves about more permanent values and more absolute ends. The true triumph and achievement of any economy is to release men, during at least part of their time, from thralldom to economic forces and preoccupation with economic purposes. An economy, like a system of technics, is the servant of civilization. It cannot of itself constitute or determine a civilization.

How does it come about that so many economists, professional and amateur, both of the socialistic and the private-enterprise persuasion, so often delude themselves into supposing that they are concerned with absolute and ultimate principles? Their error may perhaps be traced to two basic mistakes: the notion that economics is a science, and an even more mistaken interpretation of what science itself is and does. To suppose that economics is a science — and after all in some special sense of the word this claim must doubtless be admitted — would not matter very much provided we really understood what a science is. Unfortunately many people, including a few scientists and especially economic and social scientists, still suppose that in some mysterious way science is concerned with absolute and ultimate truths. In fact science is never concerned with the distinction between absolute truth and absolute falsehood, but rather with the transition from less adequate to more adequate interpretations and descriptions of empirical realities. It is only during the last fifty years or so that we have become increasingly aware that the so-called 'scientific law' or doctrine is rarely and perhaps never an absolute truth. It is simply the best way of interpreting and describing the phenomena in question which happens to be at our disposal in the present state of our knowledge. Even an outworn system of scientific doctrines, such as Ptolemaic astronomy or Newtonian physics, is not set aside as false, any more than the new astronomy or physics is asserted as absolutely true. Both these systems were once the most adequate ways of describing and interpreting empirical realities that men knew. Now, of course, we have more adequate methods in our grasp. The trousers I wore as a little boy were perfectly adequate in their time. I do not set them aside as false or spurious trousers which were not really trousers at all. It is simply that I have outgrown them. No doubt our present scientific doctrines and laws will in their turn give way to more adequate formulas at a later date. Unfortunately many of our economists and our social scientists attribute to their own formulas the absoluteness that was once attributed to the basic laws and doctrines of the physical sciences.

But in fact economics is much more like the merely and obviously descriptive social sciences than many economists would care to admit. Let us take an example of what I mean by the obviously descriptive social sciences. 'The Walla-Wallas of Central Bollaboloo wear rings through their noses, marry only their first cousins, and dance all night whenever there is a full moon.' This is simply a description of the behavior of men in a particular society. Is economics really any more than a highly rationalized description of the economic behavior of men under the conditions prevailing in a particular economic system? No doubt it is true that in an absolutely free market prices will be determined by the interplay of supply and demand. But absolutely free markets are always rare, difficult to contrive and to maintain in their condition of unfettered freedom, and in some societies absolutely unknown. And so the economists have to go on to consider the factors that limit the freedom of markets, and the precise way in which these limiting factors in any particular economy impede the determination of prices by the interplay of supply and demand. There are no absolute laws here, only more or less adequate descriptions of what actually occurs. I recollect that when I was studying economics twenty years ago in London, I attended a series of thirty-two lectures imposingly entitled, 'The Elements of Pure Equilibrium Analysis.' Each of the lectures took precisely the same course. During the opening, and longer, section of his lecture the professor triumphantly demonstrated, with the help of fascinating graphs drawn on the blackboard, precisely what would happen in an absolutely free market impelled by internal forces toward an abstract equilibrium. In the concluding portion of his lecture, he regularly explained, to the accompaniment of ironical cheering on the part of the students, that what according to his analysis was bound to happen never in fact did happen because there never was an absolutely free market. In other words, the facts always compelled him in the end to move away from high abstract dogma to more or less adequate descriptions and explanations of what actually happened. Thus it is that the so-called laws of economics do not determine what men have to do universally and in any conceivable situation; they merely describe what men actually do do in some given situation. There is no harm in calling such descriptions scientific laws if we want to, provided we are careful to remember that scientific laws as we now understand them do not amount to absolute and universal truths. Indeed it would be the very death of science if they did. It is precisely because science does not and cannot attain to absolute and universal truth that science is able to continue from generation to generation, moving always not from falsehood to truth but from less adequate to more adequate descriptions.

The lesson for economists of both the socialist and the free-enterprise variety is thus clear. Let them disabuse their minds of any illusion that their judgments and preferences are matters of absolute truth. On the contrary let them concentrate on observing under what particular conditions their particular recommendations are expedient, and in what circumstances they are rendered inexpedient. When and where are socialistic devices and experiments necessary and justified? Under what conditions is free enterprise feasible and desirable? These are the real questions, and there is no reason why people who are altogether disagreed in the realm of abstract theory should not reach agreement about the proper answers to such questions as these.

GETTING DOWN TO BRASS TACKS. If this analysis is correct, arguing about the alleged merits or demerits of either socialism in the abstract or free enterprise in the abstract makes little sense. The real issue is not the high controversy between socialism in the abstract or free enterprise in the abstract, between universal socialism or universal free enterprise — the fact is that we are unlikely to have either in its pure form — but whether some particular enterprise in the local conditions now prevailing will be better carried on in the one way or the other. Even in any one locality the question may receive different answers when we ask it in relation to different industrial enterprises. Thus in a country in which it has become desirable, perhaps even necessary, to nationalize the railways it may be quite ridiculous even to think of nationalizing the ice-cream industry.

In what circumstances is free enterprise most at home? Surely it fits best the mood of an expanding and adventurous economy. The emphasis of the advocates of free enterprise is almost always and rightly on securing maximum production and maintaining an adventurous experimental spirit throughout the whole economy. That is why free enterprise suits the American scene so well, and as long as present conditions continue the American mind is almost certainly right to prefer it, at all events in general. Socialist advocates, on the other hand, usually put all their emphasis on the problems of just distribution. They assume that the size of the cake is more or less fixed, and they are mainly concerned with securing reasonably fair shares for those who have to consume it. In other words, their basic assumption is a static rather than an expanding economy. Without question there are areas of the world, and in Western civilization, in which this assumption is fairly close to the truth. The case for nationalization is strongest, however, when and where we find industrial enterprises which in the national interest must be carried on somehow, but which are no longer sufficiently profitable to attract private capital in a volume that will re-equip and maintain them. Where the profit motive cannot persuade the private investor to invest in a necessary industry then clearly the community as a whole, through its agent, the government, must step in and shoulder the burden itself. This is often true in the case of railways in relatively small countries. Few railways nowadays profit out of passenger trade. They depend for their sustenance on freight traffic. In spacious countries the volume of this is still sufficient to make the enterprise profitable and attractive, despite the rise of other and competing forms of transport. In many smaller countries, however, the railways, although their maintenance is absolutely essential to the national interest, cannot survive the competition of other forms of transport. Under these conditions there is no alternative to socializing the railways.

But the fact that it may be necessary in some particular area to socialize railways and some other industrial enterprises does not necessarily mean that it is right and desirable to socialize them in another area where quite different conditions obtain. Nor does it mean that even in the area where it is necessary to socialize these particular enterprises it is equally necessary to socialize other enterprises that may still be quite successful in attracting to themselves the necessary capital to maintain and perhaps even expand them. In other words, there are no clashes of eternal principle here, only considerations of relative expediency. White-hot enthusiasm, on either one side or the other, is quite unnecessary and undesirable. It will certainly divide the nation and probably darken counsel.

When we turn from listening to the arguments of the zealots, whose noisy disputing may easily give us the impression that the chasm which divides the European area of Western civilization, where socialism is strong, from the American area of Western civilization, where the ideal of private enterprise is almost completely dominant, is very deep and broad indeed, and turn to the actual facts we find the differences less great than so much disputation would lead us to suppose. What we find on both sides of the Atlantic in actual fact is a mixed system, government enterprise and government control mingled with, sometimes clashing with but often collaborating with, private enterprise and private control. No doubt the blends are compounded in different proportions in different places. But all Western countries agree in fact in avoiding the logical extremes of pure socialism on the one hand and pure private enterprise on the other. There is no Western country in which some things are not socialized by almost universal agreement.

Max Weber, the great German sociologist, dated the beginnings of modern socialism from the abolition of private armies at the close of the Middle Ages or, as he termed this epoch-making event, the 'nationalization of the means of force.' Nowadays nobody proposes that the armed forces should be desocialized. The same is true of the post office in all Western countries. Again, in all Western countries government interests itself in one way or another in such social-security schemes as exist, and normally feels under some kind of moral obligation to see that provision for the social security of at least the wage-earning classes should be made more and more adequate. Broadly speaking, this is as true of governments of a right-wing complexion as of governments of a left-wing complexion. Let there be an economic depression, either on a national scale or in some important area of the national economy — agriculture, for example — and the government, whatever its party color, would either feel responsible or be made to feel responsible for guiding and leading the people out of their misfortunes. Let it fail to assume this responsibility, or discharge its burden of responsibility inefficiently or at least unsuccessfully, and it will almost certainly pay a heavy penalty at the next election. This is true throughout the whole area of Western civilization, whatever the attitude of the people may be toward the doctrinal squabble. On the other hand, there is no Western country in which private enterprise is not an extremely important factor, and no responsible Western socialist party even proposes to abolish it entirely. The mixed system is here among us with general consent, and it is safe to prophesy that it will remain with us for a very long time. The Western reality is thus neither pure socialism on the one hand nor pure private enterprise on the other, but some subtle blend of the two. All this shows how remote from the facts, impractical, and abstract are most of our heated discussions of this too well-worn subject. In any existing area of Western civilization the achievement of either pure private enterprise or pure socialism is about equally unlikely.

Of course, particular arguments and particular differences in local practice still remain and will remain. Thus the great majority of British people — and this is as true of those who vote Conservative as of those who vote Labour — are delighted with their national health service and it will quite certainly be retained. Americans, by and large, do not desire a national health service of this kind. It suits neither their traditions nor, perhaps, their federal constitution. That is as it should be. There is nothing to argue about here; no clash of ultimate principle whatever. The essential and important thing is to avoid any kind of ideological schism within Western civilization over minor issues such as these.

In some ways even more dangerous to Western unity than the zeal of the partisans in this particular controversy, with their abstract and rather artificial principles, is the tendency of each side to indulge in the gloomist suspicions of the other side's purposes and integrity. It must be insisted that the sincerely socialist elements within Western civilization are not in general thinly disguised communists, deliberately blazing the trail that will one day be made up into a great high road to serfdom. In their own belief, and to some extent in fact, they represent in Europe and for the European working classes the great democratic alternative to communism. Certainly if the socialist parties were abolished in countries like Britain and France the communist party in those areas would be immensely stronger than it is. We may compare their position and function in Western civilization with that of the Anglo-Catholic party in the Anglican Church. Low Church Anglicans, and many Protestants in other churches, sometimes charge the Anglo-

Catholics with being Romanists, and treat Anglo-Catholicism as a mere stepping stone to Rome. In a small minority of cases, of course, that is just what it is, but the overwhelming majority of Anglo-Catholics live and die as loyal members of the Anglican Communion. The critics of Anglo-Catholicism rarely pause to ask themselves how many people would have gone to Rome if Anglo-Catholicism had not existed. Roman Catholics are often more critical of Anglo-Catholics than of any other group of non-Roman Catholic Christians. Similarly the communists, in their private minds, and when it suits the party line quite openly, dislike the socialists more than any other of the Western democratic parties. Whether we like it or not the socialist parties in the Western political world are our allies in the struggle against communism, and we should be hard put to it indeed if we had to dispense with their assistance.

Conversely, Western capitalism, as it exists in America and elsewhere, is not necessarily the selfish and socially irresponsible thing which so many of the socialists suppose it to be. It has long ceased to be merely the rapacious, predatory, exploiting economy which perhaps it once was. It has learned how to pay good wages, and to care about the welfare of its wage earners in a socially responsible fashion. The Marxist notion that under capitalism the material living condition of the wage earners would necessarily be pressed lower and lower to the level of mere subsistence, and perhaps below that, has certainly been falsified by the facts. This of course is a fallen world, and capitalist practice and socialist practice are both alike subject to corruption, but each, taken at its best, is superior to what the other supposes it to be.

The corruptions, as we should expect, are in both cases remarkably alike. The kind of man who ruthlessly and unscrupulously forces himself to the front under the one system would almost certainly do the same thing under the other. Only the technique of selfish advancement would vary. There is a socialist ladder of success just as much as there is a capitalist ladder of success, and it will be climbed by very much the same sort of man in either case. Socialist administrators at their worst can be as preoccupied and obsessed by the strict rules of the processes they operate, as insensitive to the subtleties and varieties of human need, as capitalist businessmen at their worst. Conversely, capitalist businessmen at their best can be as sensitive and socially responsible as socialist administrators at their best. Even the bogy of bureaucracy is as characteristic of the one as of the other. Bureaucracy is the inevitable accompaniment of all large-scale economic or administrative undertaking. Large-scale private enterprise is quite as bureaucratic as modern government. The general social outlook and day-to-day activities of a bank manager or a big insurance executive differ very little from those of similarly placed civil servants. If bureaucracy means, as it does at its best, the efficient conduct of large-scale enterprise, with the requisite care in planning and administration, there is no harm in it whether it is the bureaucracy of government or that of private enterprise. If it means, as it so often does, an endless and self-multiplying chain of irresponsibility, then it is equally undesirable whether its sponsorship is private or public.

We may thus sum up the whole course of this discussion by asserting that this particular controversy is fundamentally misconceived, doctrinaire, and abstract, remote from and untaught by the real trend of development in Western civilization, and that the charges recklessly thrown at each other by the partisans in the heat of the discussion are exaggerated and unfair. How unfortunate it is for Western civilization that this particular strife should be carried on with such bitterness and heat by many of the extremists as to impair and threaten the unity of Western civilization in the very hour of this present grave challenge to its values and threat to its survival.

EIGHT

The Balkanization of the West

THE INDEPENDENT, sovereign nation-state, accompanied, as it nearly always is, by its characteristic emotional undertones, loyalties, and prejudices, is now so familiar a part of our mental furniture, so basic and universal an assumption, that it is difficult for us to realize that the nationalistic phase is in most areas of Western civilization little more than four or five centuries old. Nationalism, as distinct from ordinary patriotism, which is a man's feeling of contentment and at-homeness in the locality and among the people he knows and understands, is a phase through which civilizations and culture pass rather than something permanently rooted in human nature. In its period of birth and growth and lusty boyhood, Western civilization was not in any modern sense of the word nationalistic. The civilization of western Europe in the Middle Ages was Latin and predominantly ecclesiastical in its cultural forms, and despite the fact that the people unified by this culture were ethnically distinct, roughly half-Germanic and half-Mediterranean, their unity was something they all recognized in theory, and to some extent experienced and enjoyed in fact. The concept of the 'foreigner' was relatively undeveloped. Thus the medieval King Stephen of Hungary, in his last political testament to his heirs, urged them to encourage settlers from Germany and elsewhere on the grounds that each nation has its own particular skills and capacities and that the kingdom would be stronger if it contained citizens drawn from many different nations. In the same way scholars and high ecclesiastics could hold office in many different parts of Europe without any kind of nationalistic complaint. Few people grumbled in medieval England if the Archbishop of Canterbury was a Greek or a Frenchman. After all, leading and distinguished English ecclesiastics could be found occupying similarly high positions in continental Europe. One of them even became Bishop of Rome. Even the widespread prejudice against the Jew, which arose spontaneously in many different places about the time of the first crusade, in some ways contributed to this general sense of the unity of Western civilization. Anti-Semitism concentrated the thoughts of men on real cultural and religious differences, and made them relatively indifferent to and tolerant of national and linguistic differences. It is only at the close of the Middle Ages, and the beginning of the modern period, that the national idea begins to assert itself as a dominating passion.

Of course, nationalism has greatly enriched our culture. For example, it inspired and fostered the rich vernacular literatures which Western civilization has produced during the modern period, a term which we apply roughly to the last five centuries. (The word 'modern' is often used conversationally as though it meant contemporary, but properly speaking it should be applied to the whole modern period since the close of the Middle Ages.) Of course this distinction must not be pressed too far or drawn too sharply. Thus Dante is medieval and Milton modern, but what about Shakespeare? He falls within the modern period and he has many noticeably modern characteristics — e.g. he writes in the vernacular, not in Latin — yet the influence of medieval ideas and cultural forms is still very strong, in some ways stronger in Shakespeare than in his contemporary Christopher Marlowe, who was much more profoundly influenced by Renaissance ideas. There were, in fact, transitional years, and transitional people who tended to belong to both phases of Western civilization at the same time. The conventional date for the beginning of the modern period is 1453, the year of the capture of Constantinople by the Turks, but that, after all, is just convention and no more. It is noteworthy that the history of the new world, the new Europe overseas, in Australia and the Americas, which Western civilization created by its colonizing activity, falls entirely within the modern period. This does not mean of course that these new nations have no medieval history. Up to the colonial period, for example, the history of America is the history of Europe.

Arnold Toynbee has shown in the brilliant opening chapter of his *A Study of History* how it is that the historian detects the existence of the great areas of civilization, which, rather than nations, are the true units and themes of historical study. We find in charting out the histories of several different nations that we are compelled to employ again and again the same basic concepts and ideas. Thus whether we are considering the history of England, France, Australia, or America we must refer to such concepts as the Industrial Revolution, the colonization of the new world, the Renaissance, the Reformation, the wars of religion, the close of the Middle Ages, the heritage of the high Middle Ages, the Dark Ages, the zenith and decline of the Roman Empire, Roman law, the genius of classical Greece, the tremendous impact of Hebrew religious ideas, and so on. On the other hand it would be possible to write the history of China, India, or even Russia with very little or no reference to most of these basic concepts. The area of Western civilization is precisely the area whose culture it is impossible to understand without some reference to all of these concepts.

The nationalistic phase of Western civilization has no doubt weakened the sense of unity in the minds of the component peoples, but it has not destroyed that unity, still less obliterated the evidences of that unity. Despite linguistic and other important differences it is still possible to travel within the area of Western civilization, from Germany to France, from France to England, from England to America, and feel very strongly that all the time one is still in the same place, moving from one province to another of the same civilization. This is not only a possible experience, it is also a very thrilling and exciting experience, and I for one am grateful that it has been my privilege to enter into and enjoy it on several different occasions. We make much of our differences, and some of them, particularly the linguistic ones, are obviously very important, but beneath the differences there lies the common heritage, exemplified everywhere in subtly different blends. That common heritage is the great fact of Western civilization, and the Western unity that persists despite the very rough handling it has received during these last few centuries.

Thus what I have called the Balkanization of the West, the nationalistic schisms, in some ways very much like the religious schisms that have divided Western Christendom against itself, does not make manifest the whole truth about the West. Just as there is still in some sense one Christendom, despite the existence of many different churches separated by schism, so there is still in a very deep and profound sense one Western civilization, despite the division of the West politically and emotionally into separate nation-states, always separated from each other and sometimes, indeed too often, at war with each other.

So far in this book I have felt impelled to talk more about Western civilization than about its component nations, to speak more often of the German, French, or American provinces of Western civilization than of Germany, France, and America. It is perhaps a pity that we are not in the habit of employing such language more often. It is not a language that corresponds closely to contemporary political fact, or to the prevalent emotions of most of the peoples concerned, but it is a manner of speaking that conforms very closely to the underlying cultural facts and emphasizes and brings back into our consciousness a reality that is too often ignored. The Russo-Marxist challenge is a challenge to Western civilization as a whole rather than merely to the independent existence and prevailing political and economic policies of the separate Western nations. Thus it may at least have the merit of reminding us of our underlying unity and teaching us the danger of overindulging our feelings of national separation and independence.

There are indeed signs, in many parts of Western civilization, that the nationalistic phase of our cultural development is drawing to a close. In most areas of Western civilization popular nationalistic feeling is still very strong, but it is less and less appropriate to contemporary circumstances and increasingly irrelevant to prevailing needs. In its heyday nationalistic feeling, this glorying in the fact of being a separate and independent community, was at least in harmony with prevailing conditions. The nations really were separate in the physical sense and they could for the most part, and for most of the time, get along without each other economically and politically. Their cultural interdependence, of course, was always strong and inescapable. Throughout the modern period to be culturally isolated has meant for any Western community becoming a kind of backwater. Still, throughout most of this period the sense of isolation and independence at least fitted the facts. This real state of independence and isolation was perhaps particularly true of America during the nineteenth century, and it is still more of a possibility, however undesirable, in America than in any other part of Western civilization. But it was also true to some extent of Britain and of European Western nations such as France and Germany. Now, however, it is almost everywhere breaking down. The nation in Western civilization is ceasing to be a feasible military and strategic concept. There is now no Western nation that could possibly feel happy about the prospect of having to face the enemies of Western civilization alone. At the same time, and to some extent for the same reasons, the Western nations are ceasing to be independent and isolated economically. More and more the economy of one Western nation is finding that the economic health of the others is vital to its own economic well-being. In other words the unity of Western civilization is ceasing to be a profound cultural unity surviving with difficulty and almost unnoticed in the midst of political and economic disunity. The cultural unity of the West is being slowly, and under the impact of harsh and inescapable realities, reinforced by a newer and higher degree of military, political, and economic unity. In the long run these great and irreversible changes cannot but begin to make their impact on the popular consciousness and emotions. The time may well come when the great majority of us will be more profoundly and deeply aware of being Western than of being

German, French, English, or American as the case may be.

Indeed one of the strange paradoxes of the contemporary world is that just as we in the West are slowly beginning to recover from our violent attack of nationalistic fever, non-Western peoples in Asia and Africa are beginning to succumb to it as never before. A recollection of our own characteristic behavior when the disease was at its height among us should help us to understand and be patient with what now seem to us its irritating manifestations elsewhere. We should try to understand why it is that contemporary India wishes above all things to be isolated and neutral, for that is what we ourselves once desired. The very fact that we find the political attitudes of contemporary India so irritating is itself evidence of the extent to which we ourselves have now left these attitudes and emotions behind. The desire to remain neutral and to be disentangled from the wars of the bellicose Western peoples is after all very like the once prevalent illusion that America could isolate itself from Europe and refrain from participation in the warlike behavior so characteristic of that stormy but creative and gifted continent.

Nevertheless it is not possible to dismiss the nationalistic phase of the development of Western civilization as a mere unfortunate interlude, a sickness from which we are now in a process of gradual recovery. It will not even be sufficient to set it on one side as a dream and illusion which, although it had many unfortunate consequences which divided and enfeebled Western civilization, had at the same time many compensating virtues, the great vernacular literatures and such like. For the fact is that when Western man turned to nationalism he found elements already present within the Western tradition on which he could draw for nationalistic purposes. For the origins of Western nationalism, like the origins of almost everything else deeply embedded within the characteristic traditions of Western civilization, are both Greek and Hebrew. The Greeks, over and above the conflicting loyalties to the different city-states, which divided them, were imbued with a deep loyalty to the Greek idea itself, which united them. Thus it was that they came to divide mankind very simply into the Hellenes on the one hand and the barbarians on the other. They felt themselves to be the superior people, the one truly civilized people in an otherwise rude, ungifted, and uncreative world. This was never in fact quite true, as some of the greatest Greeks such as Herodotus were well aware. Nevertheless it was one of the basic and ineradicable assumptions of the Greek mind.

The Hebrews worked with a somewhat similar distinction. For them mankind was divided by the great dichotomy between Jew and Gentile. The Jew was not, even in his own eyes, a superior kind of man, endowed with a higher civilization and greater intellectual and spiritual gifts than others. The Hebrews thought of themselves not as a greater people but as the *chosen people,* the messianic people whom God had raised up above other people and through whom He purposed to institute His kingdom. At its best this idea caused the Hebrews to think of themselves as the great missionary people, the servants, often the suffering servants, of mankind, 'a light to lighten the Gentiles.'

Modern nationalism has taken and to some extent fused these two ideas of the greater and more gifted people, and of the chosen, messianic people, and applied them to the nation. Almost all Western nations during the nationalistic phase have indulged in an extravagant mythology which assures them first of all of their own superiority to other nations, and secondly makes them dream of some great historical purpose of which they will be the instruments and which will find in and through them its fulfillment. We find both these themes manifestly present, for example, in the German nationalism of the last two centuries, which achieved its most violent expression under the Nazi regime. This nationalistic philosophy included the notion that the Germans are a separate and superior people, a notion developed sometimes on a racial, biological level, which delighted to dwell on the idea of a special German heredity; or on a psychological level, which demonstrated the superiority of the German intelligence; or on a historical level, which pointed to the unique greatness and glory of the German cultural achievement. Side by side with this went a messianic conception of the historical mission of the German people. It was their office to lead and civilize the world, to give to mankind the blessings of disciplined German government and the glories and privileges of the great and creative German culture.

The idea that the great achievement of some particular nation will inaugurate a new era of happiness and peace for mankind is present even in the emotions of contemporary communism. For whole decades before Russia became communist we find Russian writers — Dostoevski, for example — dwelling on the innate spiritual superiority of the Russian peasant to the rest of mankind, and the messianic office of the Russian people in world history. At a later stage this fused with a new sense of the Russian leadership of world communism. Now Marxist communism has become, for the Russian mind, the fulfillment of the true Russian idea, and the role of Russia in world history is to confer the blessings of communism on the whole of mankind.

But we can find the same motifs and mythologies nearer

home if we look for them. Thus for many British people the British Empire, later transformed into the British Commonwealth of Nations, represents a newer and higher way of common life for mankind, and it is the destiny of the British people, and the purpose of the British achievement, to reveal and teach it to all their neighbors. The late Mr. Lionel Curtis even ventured to use the phrase 'Civitas Dei' (the community or polity of God) as the title of a book in which he expounded the ideas and ideals underlying the development of the British Commonwealth. There are messianic elements of this kind present also in the American tradition. The first settlers came to these shores filled with the idea of building up a new and purer community, a kind of kingdom of God on earth. Nor have these notions altogether departed even yet.

I do not wish to argue that these notions have no validity whatever. They are part of our Western tradition, and in one form or another we cannot entirely avoid them. My point is that they are misapplied when we employ them to interpret the nature and historical functions of the distinct Western nations. The Greek idea of the superior people has perhaps less validity, and less reality, than the Hebrew notion of the messianic or missionary people. In so far, however, as we do retain the Greek idea of the superior people, always, of course, in some form compatible with our Christian inheritance, we must apply it not to some one of the several Western nations, such as France, Britain, Germany, or America, but to Western civilization as a whole. Western civilization is quite distinctive and — at all events in those areas of human activity in which it has chosen to excel — it has surpassed and still surpasses the rest of mankind. Of course for Christians it is our faith that 'God has made of one blood all nations of men to dwell upon the face of the earth,' that in Jesus Christ 'there is neither Jew nor Gentile, neither Greek nor barbarian.' In the last analysis, therefore, there are for Christians no superior peoples and all peoples are chosen peoples. Nevertheless in the economy of history, in the strategy of divine providence, there may indeed be phases of human development during which it is for particular peoples to assume a real ministry of cultural leadership. Manifestly the peoples who inherit the traditions of Western civilization have been such a people for several centuries, are such a people now, and must continue to be such a people in the foreseeable future. For them to cease to be such a people at this present juncture of world history would be a disaster for mankind, but, I repeat, this is true of Western civilization as a whole rather than of any one of the great Western nations in particular.

Again, the Hebrew idea of the messianic, missionary people is misapplied in a fashion quite false to the Biblical message, taken as a whole, if we use it to interpret the historical role and mission of some one modern people such as the Germans, the French, the British, or the Americans. This particular error is due in part to the tendency of so much post-Reformation piety to concentrate on the Old Testament rather than on the New, and to ignore the central place of the Church in the Christian Gospel. If we examine carefully the wonderful transmutation of the great Old Testament themes which we find in the New Testament we shall see that the Hebrew idea of the chosen nation is not superseded in the New Testament, or even replaced by something else, but continued in the new idea of the Christian Church open to men of all peoples and tongues. From the New Testament standpoint it is this Christian Church which is now the chosen people of God. The Christian Church is the second Israel upon whose shoulders falls the mantle of the first Israel. It is this great theme — rather than, as so many have supposed since the Reformation, the inward spiritual process of justification by faith, divine election, and predestination — which is the central preoccupation of the epistles of St. Paul. That the Church is now the Israel of God, that its failures and backslidings are fundamentally similar to and continuous with the failures of the Hebrew people, lashed and exposed so unmercifully again and again by the Hebrew prophets, that this Christian Church is now the 'light to lighten the Gentiles,' that in it and through it God wills and purposes to establish His Kingdom — these are among St. Paul's central and dominating convictions. Hence in the New Testament to preach the Gospel is inescapably to proclaim the Church, to bring men to Christ is to baptize them into the Church, to inherit the Kingdom of God and eternal life is to enter into the fullness and the fulfillment of the Church in that ultimate dimension of its being in which the notion of the Church and the notion of the Kingdom of God melt into each other and are seen to be one.

Thus properly understood the messianic idea of the chosen people must be applied not to the modern Western nations but to the Christian Church. Now we are in a position to see the connection between the Reformation and modern nationalism. For the Reformation, by putting the Church, so to speak, in lower case, by shifting its emphasis from the universal Church, visibly greater than any of the nations, to the local churches so apparently smaller than the nations that contain them, prepared the way for a new application of Hebrew messianic ideas to the nations themselves. It is precisely when men cease to feel that deep sense of belonging to a great universal Church that they experience the need to identify themselves with some messianic nation. The Biblical idea of the chosen people must surely be applied to something that falls within the orbit of the experience of modern Christians, and since the great universal Church has ceased to shine so brightly within that sphere as once it did, it is very easy to apply the Hebrew nationalism of the Old Testament to our modern national consciousness, and to ignore the fact that we are short-circuiting the witness of the New Testament in the process. And so we find texts from the Old Testament employed again and again by nationalistic preachers, quite literally but with one significant change: the alleged chosen peoples are no longer the Hebrews but some modern nation or community to which the preacher belongs. It is no longer the Canaanites who must be destroyed that God may establish His people in the land He has chosen, but the Slavs or the Indians. It is no longer the ungodly who must be hewers of wood and drawers of water for the chosen people, but Negro serfs or slaves, either discovered and subjugated in their own lands or transported across the oceans for the same purpose. The old ideas are taken at their face value, as proper Biblical and Christian notions — the way in which the New Testament transmuted them being entirely ignored — and simply applied quite literally as they stand to new peoples and new places. We may even say that there is something radically heretical in the semi-religious way in which so much modern nationalism has professed and proclaimed itself. At no point in our analysis is it quite so easy to see how desperately Western civilization needs the Church, for the doctrine of the universal Church is still the doctrine that enables us not only to glimpse the reality of Western unity but also provides us with a foundation upon which to build it. Unless the piety of the Western peoples constantly interprets the Old Testament idea of the chosen people as something fulfilled under divine providence in the reality of the universal Church, then the tendency to relapse into an idolatrous nationalism — already and for so long chronic among us — will continually recur.

The word 'idolatrous' is carefully chosen and intended in its literal sense. Behind the emergence of nationalism lies that dark confusion of categories which is characteristic of all forms of idolatry at all times and in all places: the decking of the natural in the garments of the supernatural. Nationalism transfers to the nation the attributes of the Church, it reverences as a goddess what should be loved as a woman, it worships what should be merely loved and accepted, it is awed where it should most of all feel comfortable and at home. Nevertheless the mistake was, as we have seen, one natural and native to the Western tradition, for at the very roots of that tradition lies the strange unique phenomenon of the Hebrew people and their dealings with God, the strange and fateful ambiguity of Israel, too like a church to be quite a nation, too much of a nation to be precisely what we mean by a church, in fact neither a church nor a nation, and yet the prototype and the original of them both. And yet this unique phenomenon of the chosen people lies at the very roots of our whole tradition of civilization. Spiritually we Westerners are all Semites. We cannot escape or evade the Hebrew categories. We aspire and enthuse and interpret our existence in Hebrew terms as inevitably as we think in our mother tongue. If we will not or cannot discover and recognize the fulfillment of the Hebrew idea in the Church then we shall mistakenly suppose that it is fulfilled in the nation — unless, of course, we happen to be communists, in which case we shall even more mistakenly identify the fulfillment of the essential Hebrew idea with the communist party. It is thus at least understandable that it was within the traditions of Western civilization that conscious nationalism was first invented.

The reader will fail to follow this analysis and misinterpret the purpose of this chapter unless he is very clearly aware of the very important distinction between nationalism and patriotism. Patriotism is a quite universal and natural phenomenon. It is not really an 'ism' at all in the sense of a developed ideology. It requires neither rational defense nor rational interpretation, and hence it is not usually rationalized. A mother does not feel called upon to provide a philosophical defense and justification for her strange habit of loving her children. For a mother to love her children is a natural and spontaneous state of affairs, and it is through loving her own children that a mother understands why other mothers love theirs. She not only understands, she strongly approves. She need not claim that her children are superior to other children, or more significant in some historical or theological sense. She loves them simply because they are hers. It is so with patriotism. True patriotism does not conceptualize or vindicate the nation. The patriot does not love his country and his people *because* . . . He simply loves his country. It is the place where he feels at home, where he finds and knows the people he understands, a place that belongs to him precisely because he belongs to it. The patriot sympathetically comprehends precisely why other people love their countries just as much as he loves his own. He does not need to romanticize or invent some pseudo-philosophy about the race to which he belongs. His people need not be superior to other peoples, or somehow more significant from either a theological or a historical point of view. His people have only to be his, and he is satisfied with a sense of identity, warm kinship, and comfortable at-homeness.

True love, certainly love as we understand it from within the Christian religion, is not called upon to justify itself by vindicating and white-washing the beloved. It does not feel guilty of having thrown its love away unless it can delude itself that what it loves is supremely great or morally perfect. If it were impossible to love anything that is small or imperfect we human beings here on earth would do very little loving. Where the lover feels constrained to justify his love, by making false and inflated claims for what he loves, there is something very defective indeed about the reality and mode of his loving. Thus nationalism is not simply an extreme and exaggerated form of patriotism. It is something profoundly perverted and quite different. It is a guilty patriotism that is unpatriotic enough to feel the need of defending itself, as though a man could be justified in loving the place and people in which he was born and nurtured only if he could show that it was great and good enough to deserve his love. Real love is never deserved; it does not even ask or expect to be deserved. Real love is always ungrudgingly given. There is only one place in which we can profitably study the nature of love, only one context in which to discover the meaning of this terse but tremendous word, and that is the New Testament.

It is useless to reply to this comment that what I have said may indeed be true so far as 'sacred love' is concerned but that there remains a profane love whose meaning must be sought elsewhere and in other ways. The distinction between sacred and profane love is an invalid and misleading one. All love is sacred in so far as it is love. All love is profane in so far as it wears the mask of love and employs the language of love but knows not love's essential spirit. Profane love is not a special kind of love, it is just love profaned, profaned by a false glorifying of the beloved which in fact glorifies and inflates the egoism of the lover. The final effect of a nationalism that is not satisfied with a merely natural patriotism, but seeks to justify itself by making all sorts of pseudo-metaphysical, pseudo-theological, and pseudo-historical claims on behalf of the nation, is that it ends by intensifying the pride and heightening the group egoism of the false patriots. To glorify the nation in this false ideological manner is really a kind of secondhand and unconfessed way of glorifying ourselves. The true patriot is content to love his country in a natural, spontaneous, unsophisticated manner, but the nationalist inflates this natural love of his country into a metaphysical necessity, a moral obligation, and a work of personal merit. Nationalism is patriotism sicklied o'er with a rather pale and ominous cast of thought. The distinction between the two is in fact an ultimate and absolute one. Patriotism never menaces the world; nationalism has again and again set the Western nations over against each other in a manner that both obscures the essential character of Western civilization and seriously imperils the West's capacity to defend itself by concerted action.

Hard circumstances, as we have said, are making all this more and more clear. The pressure of events is driving the Western nations together, making us increasingly conscious of our common heritage. Nevertheless in Britain, Europe, and America alike the old nationalist emotions and jealousies, the outworn isolationist sentiments still survive. The last five hundred years or so of Western history have been of such a character that all the Western nations can find good reasons for being suspicious of each other, and cherishing grudges against each other, if that is what they really desire to do. The trouble is that these outworn emotions are out of harmony with contemporary circumstances. Necessity has thrust the Western nations together, but it cannot yet be claimed that we are glad to be together. There is an absence of rejoicing in our reluctant acceptance of our new-found unity. We have not learned to interpret it as part of a pattern of tragic withdrawal and happy return. 'For perhaps he therefore departed for a season, that thou shouldest receive him forever.' [1] Many people still cherish in their hearts a false conception of what is sometimes called 'normalcy.' They acknowledge that we are driven together by the present unfortunate circumstances, but they cherish the idea that once the dangers have been successfully confronted and survived, once 'normalcy' has been restored, we shall be able to retreat once more into irresponsible and introverted isolation. The historical perspective of these people is too short. It is in fact this slow rediscovery of the unity of the Western nations, and of the one Western civilization, now so gravely challenged and menaced from the East, that constitutes the true 'normalcy.' The more the Western nations draw together in unity, and rediscover their true spiritual kinship with each other, the more normal their situation in fact becomes. It is the long period of the Balkanization of the West that is abnormal. We must learn to be reassured by the manifest symptoms of its decline, and to rejoice in the prospect of its forthcoming demise.

1. Philemon, 15.

NINE

The Divorcing Society

'WE HOLD THESE truths to be self-evident: that man is endowed by his Creator with certain unalienable rights, and among these are life, liberty, and the pursuit of happiness.'

The precise phrase 'the pursuit of happiness' has for modern ears a somewhat archaic, eighteenth-century ring, which is, after all, not surprising since the Declaration of Independence is an eighteenth-century document, and bears all the marks of its time. As it stands the phrase 'the pursuit of happiness' smacks of an outmoded utilitarian philosophy. Happiness is something that comes almost unbidden into the life of a man who is busy pursuing other things that are intrinsically worth pursuing. The pursuit of happiness for its own sake is an artificial and superficial proceeding which will almost certainly be frustrated.

Perhaps the nature of human happiness has never been more profoundly misunderstood than by the utilitarian and hedonist philosophers. They reduced the concept of happiness to that of a mere succession of pleasant experiences uninterrupted, or interrupted to only a minimum extent, by unpleasant ones. According to their view of the matter, to maximize pleasure and to minimize pain is the essence of human wisdom and the sole aim of philanthropy. The happy life, for them, is simply what a large variety and long succession of pleasures add up to. But there is a fundamental difference between happiness and pleasure. Pleasure is the satisfying and soothing tone that accompanies a congenial occasion. Pleasure is essentially transitory. Even an unhappy man may enjoy a pleasure while it lasts. Indeed it is above all unhappy people who are characterized by an inordinate appetite for pleasure. Pleasures are desired by such people precisely because, as they sometimes say, they 'take them out of themselves,' or 'make them forget themselves.' Happiness, on the other hand, is essentially a permanent state of well-being and satisfaction. Of course, the happy man will enjoy his pleasures, but he will not allow his happiness to be dependent on them. The essential constituents of happiness are the things in life we can count on and depend on, certainly in good times but above all in bad times, rather than the passing things that surprise, please, and delight us so long as they last. Of these utterly dependable things no doubt religious faith, where a man has it, is the first and chief, but certainly the stability and reliability of the home and the family and the whole domestic background come second.

But although the phrase 'the pursuit of happiness' raises some doubts in the minds of those who have seen through the fallacies and inaptitudes of the utilitarian philosophers, its place in the Declaration of Independence was nevertheless a proper one, fully justified by any adequate political and social philosophy. In the long run no form of social order, however great its other advantages and however profound its essential values and purposes, can hope to endure and prosper unless it is among other things an area of corporate human existence in which it is possible for people to find, enjoy, and preserve genuine personal happiness.

The good society must be concerned about the happiness of its citizens. The accusation against a society that it is not in fact an area of human existence in which people enjoy a profound personal happiness is a charge which menaces its right to existence. Not a few of the critics of our Western society make precisely this charge against it. They point out that contemporary Western society, particularly in the form in which it exists in America and the British countries, is by its own account a society haunted by desperate fears and anxieties, chronically neurotic and dependent upon the ministrations of psychiatrists and psychoanalysts and similar practitioners to an extent probably unexampled in the history of civilized man. Thus we are told by some pro-communist propagandists that there is a remarkable absence of neurotic conditions in Soviet society, that even where the desperate need to build up a new social order imposes drastic restrictions and limitations on the well-being of the people, the sense of participating in a social enterprise that is purposive and creative more than compensates men for their frustrations and enables them to find a real contentment and happiness in the midst of their relatively impoverished lives. No doubt there is considerable exaggeration here, and the difference between communist society and our own in this particular matter is not so great as such writers claim. Nevertheless, the charge that Western society is not, in an embarrassingly large number of cases, a good place to be happy in is a serious one which cannot be contemptuously set aside as a mere illusion of anti-Western propaganda. Whatever may be the case in Soviet society it is undeniable that our own Western society, particularly in its present phase of development, does house and cause an enormous amount of unhappiness, psychological deprivation, and spiritual frustration. The most evident example of this is to be found in the widespread instability of our family life and the enormous and increasing number of broken marriages.

There is perhaps no one of the social factors composing the texture of daily life in human civilization which is so closely and vitally bound up with human happiness as the harmony and stability of our domestic relationships. Ordinary experience as well as innumerable sociological studies reinforce this conclusion at almost every point. The family, the network of mutual intercourse and relationship between children and their parents, is indeed the most vital spot in any particular social system. In this context all the first and most basic lessons in life have to be learned. Here we acquire our initial mastery of the mother tongue, in terms of which subsequently every other lesson which we need to learn in life has to be communicated to us. And here, too, we get our first training in the art of social existence and the self-discipline it requires. How many of the disharmonies and maladjustments of later life are rooted in unstable and unsatisfactory family relationships is a truth which the psychological study of neurotics and the sociological study of delinquents and misfits only serve to illustrate more and more emphatically as these sciences develop. The family is indeed, as has so often been said, the true unit of human society, the basic stuff or raw material out of which all society is composed.

If this is true, and few will endeavor or even desire to gainsay it, a society in which matrimonial and domestic relationships are notably unstable and unreliable, a civilization in which the family functions inefficiently, will almost certainly constitute an area of human existence which contains and tolerates, perhaps almost ignores, an enormous amount of anxiety, frustration, and unhappiness. Unfortunately, it must be sadly admitted that at no point is the record of Western civilization in its present phase of development more disconcerting than at this one. As we said in an earlier chapter, it is in precisely those provinces of Western civilization that have made the most marked strides toward expressing and understanding democratic ideals and values — America, the various British countries, and Scandinavia — that the family is most unstable and inefficient.

We can illustrate the growth of this domestic instability by glancing at the divorce rates in some of these countries. Thus if we consider the divorce rates in every tenth year in the United States from 1889 to 1949 we find the following figures (expressed in terms of the number of divorces per thousand of population): 1889 — 0.5; 1899 — 0.7; 1909 — 0.9; 1919 — 1.3; 1929 — 1.7; 1939 — 1.9; 1949 — 2.7. The figure for 1952 was 2.5. This means that five people out of every thousand living in the United States were involved in successful divorce actions during 1952. Of course, these people were husband or wives. A certain number of children would also be vitally and gravely involved. This rate (2.5) really means that in 1952 there was a gross total of 388,000 divorces. If we estimate that on the average there were two children to each of these broken marriages, then the number of people actually involved in these unhappy proceedings amounted to 1,152,000. This is a staggering figure. *It means that if divorce were continued at this rate for ten years almost 10 per cent of the present total population of the United States would be involved in divorce proceedings during that period.* Things are slightly, but not very much, better in Britain and Scandinavia. Thus in Great Britain there were 0.15 per thousand divorces in 1939 and 0.98 in 1949. In Sweden there were 0.56 in 1939 and 1.09 in 1949. With this we may usefully compare the figures for a less highly developed Western country such as Portugal. Here there were 0.10 divorces per thousand in 1939 and 0.12 per thousand in 1949. In Mexico there were 0.23 in 1939 and 0.28 in 1949. Even in such cases as Portugal and Mexico there is a slow but steady drift in the direction of increasing domestic instability, although nowhere is this tendency so chronic and nowhere has it reached such horrifying proportions as in the United States.

In considering and assessing this course of development it is important to emphasize that it was entirely unforeseen by the first founders and architects of our divorce institutions a century or more ago. Hence we may justly claim that the time has come to reconsider the projects and proposals of the enthusiastic advocates of divorce in the light of our experience of the social consequences of divorce and of the impact of divorce institutions and divorcing habits and conventions — for that is what they have become — on our social system.

I had occasion some years ago to make a careful study of the report of the Royal Commission and the subsequent parliamentary debates that preceded the passage of the first Matrimonial Causes Act in Great Britain in 1857. I was struck by the almost total lack of sociological insight and foresight that characterized almost the entire discussion. For these people divorce was to be a kind of optional legal expedient. Their reasoning was somewhat as follows: 'There are inevitably a certain small number' — all were agreed, and perhaps rightly then, that the number was very small — 'of unsuccessful and unhappy marriages. We shall therefore provide a legal and merciful means by which the victims of these unsatisfactory marriages can escape from their miserable condition. So far as the great mass of mankind is concerned, however, all will be as before. Happily married people do not need to avail themselves of divorce facilities, and so the existence of these facilities will make no difference to their mode of life.'

Only one speaker, a bishop in the House of Lords, displayed any realization of what was really happening. He hazarded the opinion that once divorce was established and divorcing habits became visibly widespread, the existence of divorce facilities would not merely remedy the unhappy marriages already existing but also cause unhappy marriages that might otherwise have been more harmonious and satisfactory. He foresaw that divorce, once established as a recognized social institution, would transform the social context in which marriages are entered into, and alter the assumptions on which they are based. Divorce would become a part of the climate of marriage. At the time this wise counsel was neither heeded nor understood, for most men in those days had little sociological insight. They did not understand how it is that an accepted legal enactment slowly creates a living social institution, and how a living social institution in its turn slowly creates conforming social habits and attitudes. Thus a monogamous society tolerating divorce in exceptional circumstances slowly transforms itself into a divorcing society in which monogamy is no longer a ruling social institution but a worthy and desirable religious and ethical ideal. There is a profound difference between an institution and an ideal. The institution can summon to its aid both the idealism of the idealists and also the strong tendencies toward social conformity at work in any and every society, even among non-idealists. But the ideal has nothing to rely upon except the idealism of the idealists alone.

It is obvious that monogamy is gravely weakened in a divorcing society, but we have to ask the further question whether marriage in a divorcing society is really monogamous in the proper sense of the word at all. No doubt according to the strict letter of the law each marriage in a divorcing society is a monogamous one so long as it lasts, but, since all marriages in such a society are permanent by accident rather than permanent in principle, what a divorcing society tends to produce is a kind of serialized polygyny and polyandry. We are familiar with societies that are either polygynous or polyandrous, rarely, perhaps never, both at once, across the dimension of space. Our society is becoming both polygynous and polyandrous concurrently through the dimension of time. The difference between the man who has several wives at the same time and the man who has several wives one after the other is not so great that we can justifiably claim that the latter is a monogamous creature whereas the former is not. On the contrary, in many of the definitely polygynous societies the natural human tendency is to concentrate on the latest wife at any particular moment of time, and simply to retain the earlier wives as, so to speak, retired pensioners. The difference is very real but not so great as at first sight appears. At least we can claim that the basic assumptions of a divorcing society are no longer unambiguously monogamous. I use the phrase 'divorcing society' because a divorcing society, from any realistic sociological standpoint, is a very different thing from that legalistic fiction, a monogamous society, which tolerates and permits divorce in exceptional and appropriate circumstances.

The main point of my argument at this juncture is that those who conceived and founded our divorce institutions really believed in this legalistic fiction. They sincerely supposed that it would be possible to create a society which tolerated and provided for divorce, but which would not for that reason become a divorcing society. In the light of our experience during the last half century it is quite impossible any longer to entertain this illusion. The consequence of divorce is the divorcing society, exposing marriage to the rigors of an unhealthy and uncongenial climate, and indeed transforming the very nature of marriage by altering the assumptions predominating in the minds of those who enter into it.

This contention requires and demands to be reinforced by some consideration of the way in which the existence of divorce institutions, and the prevalence of the divorcing habit, influences and modifies the matrimonial and family life even of those who do not seek a divorce, and never experience any particular desire to seek one. Once the question is asked the answer is fairly obvious. The divorcing context imposes upon even the non-divorcing married couple a persistent burden of insecurity and anxiety. Nowadays even the marriage in which divorce does not happen is one in which it could happen at any moment. It is the specter at the family table, the skeleton in the family closet. Of course we may know, or think we know, that in our case it will not happen, but we never quite lose the feeling that it might. Even those who are about to enter into the marriage relationship, however sincerely and responsibly, do so with the secret, perhaps almost unconscious, knowledge that they could get out of it if ever they really wanted to. Even after a marriage has been contracted, the very awareness that the divorcing expedient exists makes it possible to magnify and dwell upon differences and frictions which in a healthier state of society would be laughed at and forgotten.

It is perhaps not altogether surprising to observe how many of our magazine and newspaper advertisements select this particular kind of anxiety for their underlying theme.

These advertisements explain to the young wife again and again and in many different ways how it is possible for her to fulfill her wifely and maternal functions, keep the house clean, care for the children, and prepare attractive meals which will infallibly find the way to a man's heart through his stomach, yet still remain as attractive and desirable as she was when he first fell in love with her. What such an advertisement is really saying, and refrains from saying only because most people would be revolted by the crudity of such direct language, is this: 'How can you contrive to double the role of wife and mistress? Feed your husband nightly on our canned peas!'

There is inevitably something nightmarish, neurotic, and tormenting about a marriage accompanied by such insidious and secret fears as these. The divorcing society provides an uncongenial climate for the happy and stable marriage. Hence it comes about that the tendency of a divorcing society is to accumulate and multiply the divorces, and thus to accumulate and multiply the evil consequences of divorce — the neuroses, the juvenile delinquencies, the frustrations and disappointments of the wasted years, the disillusioning of love, the psychological privation of children robbed of one of their parents, the cynical conviction of the ultimate emptiness of romance which drives so many men and women into more and more sordid experiments with quite unromantic forms of sexual behavior.

In addition to this consideration of the influence of the habits and the assumptions of a divorcing society on our matrimonial institutions and practices, we may also distinguish and discuss three distinct elements in the current climate of opinion which do much to determine current attitudes toward and current assumptions about marriage. It is a great mistake to suppose that because the great majority of people are not philosophers there can be no philosophical elements in their general outlook on life. On the contrary, people who are not philosophically minded in any formal or technical sense probably entertain as many philosophical beliefs, if not more, than most professional philosophers do. The philosophy of the non-philosopher differs from the philosophy of the philosopher in being a matter of uncriticized assumptions and presuppositions rather than of conclusions arrived at by some process of critical reasoning.

INDIVIDUALISM. The essence of individualism is its strong belief in analysis as the proper way of arriving at the truth, and its inability to treat union, unity, and synthesis really seriously. No doubt in real life we are always confronted with complexes and compounds but, according to this view, we arrive at the truth by resolving these complexes and compounds into their primary constituent elements. Reality according to this doctrine consists of simple primary elements in isolation from each other, joined together by relationships that remain somehow external and accidental to the true being of the elements they relate. We may call this the *analytic fallacy,* and we can trace its influence again and again in modern and contemporary thinking.

In social philosophy this analytic fallacy results in the doctrine that is usually known as individualism. A society, whether it be a nation, the citizens of a city, a functional group, a church, or a family, is simply, from this point of view, a certain number of separated and separable human units living in relationships to each other which are, so to speak, external and accidental to the true being of each of them. Thus marriage is conceived as a relationship between two separate human beings, each of whom has entered into the marriage for the sake of securing or furthering his or her own happiness. The inevitable implication is that each party to a marriage uses and treats the other party instrumentally to his or her own happiness. There is an inescapable element of exploitation involved in the individualistic conception of marriage. It is obvious that, from the standpoint of this logic, either party will desire to escape from the obligations of marriage, and should be permitted to escape, if at any time the marriage ceases to be an arrangement that contributes to his or her private security and happiness. The marriage that is entered into on the basis of hedonistic and individualistic motives and purposes has clearly failed to do what it was intended to do if it has not achieved and intensified the private individual happiness of both parties.

The logic is impeccable. Once we accept these particular philosophical premises, and so long as we are looking at marriage in the abstract, as an isolated relationship between a man and a woman, the theory is at least a plausible one. But marriage does not in fact exist in the abstract, and in the normal case it is not an isolated relationship between a husband and a wife. Marriage as we know it in reality, as it normally exists and functions in society, is only for a very short time a relationship between a husband and a wife. Normally and for most of the time it is a relationship between a mother and a father. Most married people, throughout most of their married lives, are the joint parents of the same children. So that the norm of marriage is not the husband-wife relationship but the father-mother-child relationship. Now if it is true that the husband-wife relationship can at least plausibly be analyzed and dissipated in the individualistic way, the parent-child relationship makes nonsense of individualism. For here we are confronted not with separate and separable units of being but with a kind of being that actually produces another kind of being and is responsible for its existence and maintenance. Thus it is that the family is both a sociological and a metaphysical unity. We may say that if the individual is the abstract atom of society, the family is the concrete molecule of society, the smallest unit of human existence which can conceivably exist and flourish in concrete actuality. The parent-child relationship is manifestly rooted in actuality. It cannot plausibly be pretended that it is the creation of law or social convention. The proof of this is that whereas it is possible for a judge in a divorce court to say to a woman, 'This man is no longer your husband,' and to a man, 'This woman is no longer your wife,' at all events without obviously talking nonsense, what he cannot possibly say to either the man or the woman is, 'This child is no longer your child.' Here is a relationship which lies beyond law and which defies individualistic analysis. Here are profound ties and mutualities, the very stuff out of which society is everywhere composed, which cannot be dissolved into nothingness by any conceivable technique of philosophical analysis or any possible code of law.

Perhaps this is why the family has always appeared to be something of a problem and a scandal from the point of view of democratic thinkers of the highly individualistic persuasion, from John Locke to the present day. For them basic ties and mutualities, responsibilities and obligations rooted in reality, and lying far beyond the realms of human choice, have seemed to trespass on their highly individualistic conception of human rights. In their thought they are forever seeking to dissolve the unity of the family, to turn it into a crowd of isolated individuals. Now the family in the very nature of the case can never really be what the individualistic philosophers say it is. But in so far as the prevailing climate of opinion has been formed and influenced by the individualistic philosophers, men will be inclined to feel that they ought to make the family resemble the individualistic account of it as closely as possible, and although this presupposition will not, because it cannot, destroy the unity of the family altogether, yet it will subject it to great strains and do much to mar its efficiency. We have already remarked that the so-called 'democratic family' of some of the individualistic social thinkers and sociologists is really no more than the inefficient family, or the 'unstable' family, as the French sociologist Leplay used to call it. This is simply a form of the family whose unity, authority, and spontaneous cohesion has been so whittled away, almost to a vanishing point, that it can no longer fulfill its basic functions and obligations with any degree of efficiency.

The idea of the democratic family is an example of the fallacious notion, already discussed, that in a democracy everything ought to be somehow democratized. This error has already been analyzed. It is not the purpose or function of democracy to weaken or to destroy the basic and universal human institutions, which emerge spontaneously, in some form or other, wherever men are men, and which we must regard as in some sense natural. Rather it is the purpose and function of democracy to give them new strength, depth, and stability. We have already noticed that where the natural and spontaneous human institutions are weak, the state inevitably becomes correspondingly more powerful, so that a highly individualistic doctrine of man and the family, far from being the philosophical alternative to and antithesis of the collectivist doctrine of the state, is, on the contrary, part of the normal stock in trade of the totalitarian state. Totalitarian states almost always seek to weaken the strength and unity of the family, because they can tolerate no alternative form of social unity to the comprehensive and collective one which they themselves seek to impose. It is an odd and unhappy paradox that where a totalitarian regime succeeds a democratic one it sometimes finds that in this matter half its work has been done for it already. The radically individualist way of life which slowly erodes away all the spontaneous human unities and cohesions and finally leaves the isolated individual to confront the state alone is not in fact the fulfillment of democracy but the preparation for totalitarianism. Tocqueville, the French social philosopher and prophet, observed this more than a hundred years ago, and in the twentieth century his diagnosis has been verified again and again.

THE OBSESSION WITH ROMANTIC LOVE. We have not here the space at our disposal to embark upon an inquiry into the history of the notion of romantic love. So far as our civilization is concerned the cult of romantic love originated during the Middle Ages in those parts of Europe which had been profoundly influenced by the anti-sexual Manichean heresy, a doctrine characterized by a deep-rooted horror of marriage and childbirth. In its original form the cult of romantic love had nothing to do with either marriage or childbirth, and perhaps at first very little to do with sexuality in the ordinary sense of the word. Thus Dante's devotion to Beatrice — to take an example of romantic love in its most ethereal form — neither achieved nor desired for itself any normal physical expression whatever. They met no more than two or three times, and even then in the most passing and casual fashion; she married another man, he another woman; and yet it is she who in Paradise conducts the poet to the very threshold of the beatific vision.

Thus the notion of romantic love in its pure form is concerned with an emotional relationship between a man and a woman which has nothing to do with marriage. At a later date, however, our civilization began to attempt a kind of synthesis of the idea of romantic love and the idea of marriage. This attempt at a synthesis was particularly characteristic of the English-speaking, Anglo-Saxon areas of Western civilization, and of those that have been influenced by puritan movements. For puritanism the problem of somehow justifying and spiritualizing sexual behavior is almost always an acute one, and this need fosters the growth of the idea that sexuality is justified by the motivations and attitudes characteristic of romantic love. This attempt at a difficult synthesis finally produced the characteristically modern view that marriage ought to be based on romantic love, and that its morality is questionable whenever it possesses no such romantic foundation.

At a later stage the advocates of free love and easy divorce — for example, Ibsen in his famous play *Ghosts* — deduced from these premises, logically enough, the conclusion that marriage in itself does not add anything of any substantial importance to romantic love, and should certainly be abandoned the moment a husband and wife are disenchanted and the spell of romantic love no longer presides over their relationship in its magic fashion. No doubt it is an important enrichment of human experience, and of the marriage relationship itself, if and when a phase of romantic love precedes marriage and transfigures the early years of married life. The trouble about this prevalent obsession with romantic love, however, is that it leads to a depreciation or even a complete ignoring of the characteristic form, values, and beauties of married love. For married love is different from romantic love. It is something that grows up within and out of marriage, a comradeship and solidarity based on common interests, shared responsibilities — above all the joint responsibility of a father and a mother for their children — and mutual gratitude for the loyalties and unselfishnesses experienced and recognized within the intimate association of married life. Romantic cultures like our own assume that love must come first, and that love is the proper cause of marriage. Unromantic cultures, on the other hand, suppose that marriage must come first and that marriage is the proper cause of love. The difference is a very profound one, but we have no reason to believe that all the concrete advantages are on our side. On the contrary, all the available evidence suggests that marriage tends to be more stable and successful in unromantic societies than in romantic societies, perhaps because in unromantic societies marriage is more securely based on married love. Nevertheless it may be possible to claim that at its best modern and contemporary Western civilization is attempting a kind of synthesis of the two views, a new ideal sequence in which first romantic love causes marriage, and then marriage in its turn brings about married love, so that the warm, steady glow of married love begins to come into operation just as the fitful fires of romantic love are dying down. If this synthesis represents the contemporary Western ideal we cannot deny that it is a noble and ambitious one, but it must be said that our society is not at present conspicuously successful in its efforts to rise to the heights of this ideal. The notion of romantic love still contains recalcitrant elements which have not yet been successfully reconciled to marriage and child-bearing, imposing and necessitating as they do faithful collaboration and association, steady mutual obligations, and inescapable joint responsibilities. Where marriage is popularly envisaged as no more than simply a lifelong continuation of romance, the danger is that it will prove disappointing and unrewarding, for marriage is anything but permanent romance. It has its own beauties and its own values, and its own characteristic kind of love, but it is too realistic a condition to be endlessly romantic.

Another dangerous mistake to which the contemporary obsession with romantic love has rendered our civilization prone is the notion that all men and women are so to speak ripe for the experience of romantic love. The plain fact is that some people never experience romantic love at all. There is no reason why they should not make excellent and happy husbands and wives on that account, but their cool and deliberate marriages fail to conform to the current romantic conventions, so that they themselves may feel guilty, or if not guilty at least deprived. The spectacle of so many unromantic people expecting romance because current social conventions have taught them to expect it, looking everywhere for romance, and not finding it, is an unhappy one.

Worse than that, many people may be led by such social conventions into supposing that they are experiencing romantic love when in fact they are experiencing nothing of the kind. Very prevalent in our society is the tendency to mistake for authentic romantic love the emotional glow and haze that accompany mere sexual passion and desire. It cannot be stressed too strongly that genuine romantic love is much more than mere stupefying and intoxicating sex haze. It is a profound personal relationship which, of course, includes passion and desire, but which nevertheless transcends them. True romantic love *is* real love. The characteristic mark of the experience, as in the case of all loving, is the blinding revelation that some other being can be more important to the lover than he is to himself. Love is always a blessed release from our self-centeredness. This is as true when we are speaking of a romantic relationship between a man and a woman as it is when we have in mind some self-forgetful saint's passion for the living God. Without love we should necessarily carry the intolerable burden of self-centeredness, with the isolations and false perspectives it imposes, and the unrewarding idolatry it renders inevitable, from the cradle to the grave. It is not possible to escape from this self-centeredness merely through the way of sexual passion and desire, for they in themselves are as self-centered as any other form of passion and desire. The prevalent identification of romance with mere sexuality is the corruption rather than the essence of the obsession with romantic love. Nevertheless it is a corruption to which an unbalanced and one-sided emphasis on the importance of romantic love is peculiarly inclined.

THE OBSESSION WITH SEXUALITY. This confusion of the romantic with the merely sexual is perhaps one of the most characteristic and familiar of the basic errors presupposed in and by the contemporary climate of opinion. It has led to the widespread notion that sexual fulfillment, far from being a high and spiritual vocation, and one of the great glories and attainments of human existence, is in fact a quite essential ingredient in human existence itself. So it is that for many thinkers love is merely a highly spiritualized, and marriage an overmuch regimented and socialized, form of sexuality, and it is the sexuality itself that constitutes the essential substance and stuff of such relationships. The indispensable thing, from this point of view, is that man should recognize and fulfill his sexuality in sexual experience. It may be better that he should fulfill it in genuine love, and preferable that he should stabilize this fulfillment in fruitful marriage, but it is the fulfillment itself which is absolutely indispensable to physical and mental health and the achievement of human maturity.

Now it is true that man is by nature a sexual animal, and always at least potentially a sexual agent, but in human life it must be recognized that men in general have too many potentialities for each man to realize them all in practice. In the life style of human personality some potentialities must be neglected that others may be encouraged, and it cannot be denied that sometimes the sexual potentialities may rightly and usefully be numbered among those selected by some men for non-realization. The plain fact is that deliberately chosen celibacy has made important contributions to the development of our civilization. Of course, like all other human things it is liable to corruption. The self-glorification of celibacy by complacent celibates is an unlovely and sinful thing. But we cannot, because of the prevalence of this perverted attitude among celibates, deny the essential goodness and creativity of celibacy itself.

In the Christian tradition as a whole the idea of holy virginity runs side by side with the idea of holy matrimony. Indeed, the idea of holy virginity is indispensable to the idea of holy matrimony. Marriage can be accepted and embraced as a high vocation, a great calling from God, only in a world in which there exists some feasible and proper alternative. In many societies marriage and sexuality are not optional and vocational things to be accepted or rejected but — such is the pressure of economic conditions and social convention — sheer necessities to be accepted and acquiesced in without question. In such a society the Christian conception of holy matrimony can have no meaning. Marriage, from this point of view, is a necessity, an economic necessity, a social necessity, a physiological necessity, or even a psychological necessity. Under such conditions the vocational element in marriage, the deliberate choice of such a way of life under God and as a means of fulfilling one's duty to God, is necessarily unrecognized and superfluous. In such a society not to be married is either slightly scandalous or quite ridiculous, and there are, unfortunately, many such societies. It was from this situation that we were rescued by the insistence of the early Church on the possibility and goodness of holy virginity. Where holy virginity is possible and praiseworthy, and only there, is holy matrimony, marriage embraced and accepted as a high calling from God, a feasible conception. It is undeniable, of course, that the fathers of the early Church used exaggerated and misleading language in celebrating the glories of virginity. Theirs was the language of reaction, and reaction tends almost always to overstate its case. Nevertheless by making virginity possible and respected in Western civilization, they were enlarging the bounds of human freedom and rendering a tremendous service to marriage itself.

For there is a real threat to marriage, and to the stability of sexual relationships, at work in any society that cannot and does not respect virginity. Where the customary outlook and the traditional mores of the people conspire together to render sexuality and marriage necessary rather than vocational, we shall inevitably find a great many people contracting marriages and entering into sexual relationships who are not really well fitted for such a way of life. We must face the fact that not all human beings, if we take them as they are, are suited to marriage or capable of participating successfully and creatively in the profound intimacies of sexual relationship. Just as the most confirmed anti-prohibitionist must agree that, although it is permissible for human beings to enjoy alcoholic liquors without shame or blame, yet there are some human beings so constituted that they ought never to touch alcohol in any shape or form — because they seem incapable of doing so except to an immoderate degree — so there are some human beings who ought to refrain altogether from sexual behavior. If they marry, they will almost certainly ruin their marriage; if they participate in even casual sexual intercourse, they will do it like animals rather than like human beings. Such people will be happier and healthier without sex, and such people exist in most human societies in not inconsiderable numbers.

We may also add in passing that a society which contains a sizable proportion of celibates, and respects celibacy, is in a much better position to deal with the problem of homosexuality than a marrying society like our own which interprets 'single blessedness' as an unparalleled misfortune and has no respect for celibacy at all. In effect our current moral code tells the homosexual that he must sublimate his homosexuality and embrace the celibate life. From the point of view of the widespread modern attitude which interprets sexuality as a psychological and physiological necessity such an attitude may seem unduly harsh. On the other hand, it is difficult to see what else any responsible moral code could say to the homosexual, for any less rigorous and exacting rule would in effect open the floodgates to a large-scale exploitation and perversion of youth. The moral code is compelled to be stern with the homosexual for the sake of society as a whole. But it is difficult for a socicty that does not honor celibacy in heterosexuals to insist on celibacy in the case of homosexuals with any real conviction and justice. The homosexual may very well reply, as he often does, 'Why pick on me?' to bear a burden which in the case of heterosexuals is regarded as abnormal and undesirable. A society that respects responsible celibacy as resolutely and emphatically as it reverences responsible marriage is thus a society that can offer the homosexual an honored and valued place in the social order, one in which he need not feel an outcast and underprivileged oddity.

We must not assume, of course, that the Christian doctrine of holy virginity means that the celibate state is good only for such people as these. On the contrary, what makes virginity holy is not the renunciation of marriage and sexuality because these things are evil but the renunciation of marriage and sexuality for the sake of rendering a peculiar kind of service to God and man which only the celibate can render. Nevertheless the existence of a recognized and respected way of virginity in human society does provide a richly creative alternative to marriage and sexuality into which men may enter for many different reasons. Certainly the existence of such an alternative tends to protect and enrich marriage, by eliminating the contracting of marriage by people spiritually unsuited to the married state, and by making marriage itself a free act of deliberate human choice.

Thus the re-emergence in Western civilization of any psychological dogma or social convention that tends to put marriage and sexuality back into the realm of the humanly necessary and indispensable is an inherently retrogressive development. It is thrusting us back into the prison house from which Christianity once released us. The great central tradition of Western civilization is one that reverences holy virginity and holy matrimony alike. It is desirable and essential that we should refrain from exalting either over the other. They should possess and enjoy parity of social esteem, for only where the possibility of holy virginity is recognized is the true glory of holy matrimony even imaginable, and only where the goodness of holy matrimony is frankly acknowledged can holy virginity be seen and respected as the noble renunciation it really is. Robert Bridges once described a great and characteristically medieval Christian saint, St. Francis of Assisi, as the man who 'abjured what even good men will call good.' There is no particular glory in the renunciation of evil, but the renunciation of one manifest good for the sake of some other good which beckons perhaps from farther away is indeed a glorious thing. Thus the Christian respect for holy virginity is based not on a low view but on a high view of marriage, the highest perhaps that the world has ever known. Marriage, from this point of view, is so utterly good and glorious a thing that to renounce it for the sake of some high and noble purpose must be numbered among the supremely great sacrifices, and the renunciation honored accordingly.

The Christian ascetics of the early Church and the Middle Ages are strongly criticized and even despised by some modern Christian historians, but to some extent at least this is because the ascetics are so often misunderstood. Often they are confused with the later puritans, but this is a profound error. There is a world of difference between the ascetic and the puritan. The emphasis of puritanism is on the avoidance of evil, whereas the ascetic concentrates on the pursuit of good. The puritan abjures many of the good things of this life because of his secret suspicion that what seems to be good is in fact evil, a concession to man's baser nature which the Christian conscience ought not to tolerate. The ascetic, on the other hand, abjures the good things of this life because, although he knows them to be good, he seeks some other and further good which lies beyond and above him. Thus it is that the puritan corrupts and poisons the well-springs of human existence by calling good evil, whereas the ascetic enriches human existence by adding good to good.

THE CHRISTIAN DOCTRINE OF SEX AND MARRIAGE. But although we must distinguish between the asceticism of the early and medieval Church and the puritanism of some of the post-Reformation sects — strongly, as it seems to me, in favor of the former — yet it must nevertheless be admitted that both asceticism and puritanism have conspired together to obscure the Christian doctrine of sex and marriage. At no point has the essential Christian tradition been made less clearly explicit; at no point is the responsibility of the theologian greater or more relevant to the needs of today. His task is to grope, so to speak, within the dark recesses of the Christian tradition, and bring up into the light of day rich elements of that tradition which up to now have for the most part been only latent and implicit within it. The ascetic doctrine of marriage sees clearly that marriage is good, but nevertheless tends to relegate it to the realm of the second best. Of course, even during the long reign of the ascetic mentality over the Christian mind, the great majority of Christians married and were given in marriage, but always with a sense, not indeed of having done anything evil, but of having missed and forfeited something even more supremely good. The general tendency of puritanism is to regard sexuality as somehow unclean *per se* and to treat marriage, the one permissible form of sexuality, as a kind of concession to the fallen flesh. Under a puritanical regime almost everyone gets married, but always with a latent sense of guilt and shame lingering in the background, because of the puritanical feeling that sexuality and its characteristic joys are tainted and unclean.

Thus the explicit Christian tradition has for different reasons consistently fallen short of a wholesome and whole-hearted affirmation of the inherent goodness and splendor of marriage, and in particular of the sexual elements within marriage. Yet the Biblical tradition taken as a whole is singularly free from any morbid and unclean horror of sexuality. Sexuality, like every other aspect of fallen man's nature, presents him with a problem that is both ethical and religious at the same time, but sexuality as such — the Bible makes this very clear — is part of the God-given natural endowment of man and cannot conceivably be regarded as unclean *per se*. If much of our human sexuality and sexual behavior is sinful and unclean, it is because we ourselves have made it so, perverted it with elements of selfishness, desire, and mastery, welded it into the pattern of our sinful self-centeredness, indulged in it inordinately, so that man's indulgence in his sexuality often produces the unwholesome suppression of other equally important and equally basic elements of his nature. But sexuality itself remains a God-given and beautiful thing, however much we may abuse and spoil it in our human practice.

What is the problem of sexuality? Fundamentally it is the problem of integrating this element with the rest of human nature, with the whole realm of man's aspiration and experience. Considered simply in itself sexuality is something which man has in common with all mammalian creatures. Some writers conclude from this — Dr. Kinsey, for example, tends in this direction — that human sexuality is simply an example of mammalian behavior, and that it makes no particular difference to its nature if the creature who is indulging in sexual behavior at the moment happens to be a man rather than some other mammalian creature. This seems to me a gross error. Sexual behavior never happens in the abstract. Human sexuality has a context from which it can never escape, and that context is human nature itself. Man's sexuality must fit the rest of his being, be adapted and reconciled to his nature, if it is not to cause morbid internal conflicts within the human personality. The danger is that our sexuality may become a kind of isolated function, having no deep relationship to or consonance with the rest of human behavior and aspiration. The important thing, in other words, is simply that human sexuality should always be *human* sexuality, not just sexuality in the abstract.

If the fundamental problem is the problem of the integration of our sexuality with the rest of our nature, then three things must be true of our human sexuality which need not be true, either not at all or to anything like the same extent, of the sexuality of other mammals. (1) Since man is a personal being, his sexuality must be personalized. In other words, all sexual relationships must be personal relationships, the sexual intimacies instrumental to and expressive of personal intimacies. Mere physical sexuality without real love is less than human. (2) Since man is a social being living consciously and responsively in association with his fellows, human sexuality must be accommodated to social needs and requirements. A mode of sexuality that estranges a man from society and from social responsibility will frustrate his gregariousness however efficiently it may satisfy his sexual cravings. (3) Since man is a spiritual and religious being, a being made for God and with an eternal destiny, his sexuality must be unified and harmonized with his conscious spiritual life. To put it briefly, the personal nature of human beings demands the element of love in our sexuality; the inherently social nature of man demands the social recognition of a responsible sexuality in marriage; the spiritual nature of man and of human destiny demands the spiritualization of our sexuality in the sacrament of holy matrimony. Only so can our sexuality be truly human, completely integrated with all the other elements that compose man's nature and fit him for his destiny.

The formula in terms of which I am proposing to state the Christian doctrine of sex and marriage is one that owes a great deal to Sören Kierkegaard's doctrine of the three 'stages on life's way,' an analysis of human moral and spiritual development which sees it as moving from an aesthetic stage, in which human behavior and impulses are refined and become more perceptive, through a moral stage, in which man's life becomes a consciously responsible one, to a religious stage, in which man's life becomes a consecrated existence based on a sense of eternal realities and purposes and of that inescapable dimension of our being in which we are related to God. Kierkegaard himself does not apply his analysis in particular to the problem of the Christian doctrine of sexuality and marriage, yet I feel that my attempt to do so here is in deep accord with the spirit of his teaching.

1. *The personalization of sex.* When sexual relationships are not also and at the same time profound personal relationships, human sexuality degenerates into a sordid traffic in and exploitation of human bodies. This would hardly matter, no doubt, if men and women were no more than animated bodies, but, since this is not the case, it cannot but do violence to their non-physical potentialities. Such a sub-personal sexuality would become what it must be and can only be, and therefore ought to be, in the case of a large number of sub-human mammals. Man has an animal nature, but it is a mistake to suppose that he is therefore *an* animal. Animalism in man in fact thwarts and frustrates other elements in his nature. Human sexuality must be based on love and warm personal regard; it must be so employed and indulged in as to express and foster profound and lasting personal relationships, or it will be somehow unworthy of and out of harmony with other, non-sexual elements in human nature. This is perhaps the great truth grasped in the tradition of romantic love. Sexuality without love is literally beastly, and therefore sub-human. The failure of the romantic tradition, on the other hand, as we have

seen, is its inability to perceive that there are other kinds of profound human loving, which may properly express themselves through sexuality and integrate it with our personal nature. Normally — indeed throughout most of the years of companionship between a man and a woman — it is married love rather than romantic love which performs this function.

This insistence that our sexuality must function within the context of our personality, that it must be adjusted to and worthy of the kind of being which we call personal, is the basis of the Christian objection to sheer promiscuity, and all other forms of frivolous and irresponsible sexuality. Human sexuality is too noble and beautiful a thing, too profound a form of experience, to turn it into a mere technique of physical relief, or a foolish and irrelevant pastime.

On the other hand, the Christian judgment upon all forms of illicit sexuality outside marriage cannot properly be, and ought not to be, an indiscriminate one. On this level of analysis it must be recognized that some sexual relationships outside marriage may be, and often are, profoundly personal and enduring ones. There is a great deal of difference between a lasting liaison based on deep love and comradeship and loyalty and a merely promiscuous wandering from bed to bed. The Christian mind must object even to the lasting liaison, but on different grounds (which we shall discover on the next level of analysis), but the Christian mind must nevertheless prefer an illicit sexuality which includes important elements of loyalty and love to merely frivolous promiscuity. The serious moral theologian is in my view bound to say that these two very different, although in each case defective, ways of life are far from being equally sinful.

2. *The socialization of sexuality.* It is when sexuality is

publicly declared and publicly recognized in marriage that it assumes a new and higher stature. The sexual relationship is not, in the normal course of nature, a private relationship between two people with which the rest of society is unconcerned. It brings new lives into existence, and it is responsible to them and for them to society as a whole. The trouble about unmarried sexuality, even at its best, is that it contains an element of social irresponsibility which it can never quite escape. There is something inherently juvenile about unmarried sexuality, a failure of the two people concerned to grow up together in the ways of social responsibility. Often it is sly and furtive, but even when it is openly declared it fails to assimilate sexuality with the whole social nature of responsible men. This does not mean, of course, that all marriages are necessarily responsible, and to be regarded with moral approval. Some marriages — for example, deliberately childless ones, or marriages entered into for sub-personal motives such as financial gain — may actually be worse from the standpoint of Christian moral judgment than the nobler kinds of illicit union. The socialization of sex and marriage cannot compensate for the complete absence of any personalization of sex and love. All that we saw to be true on our first level of analysis remains true on this second and deeper one. We are not saying that marriage is higher and nobler and more responsible than love, but simply that married love is higher and nobler and more responsible than illicit love. The cult of mere respectability, which is quite satisfied if marriage is present even though love is absent, and which may even be foolhardy enough to use marriage to whitewash the consequences of the most frivolous promiscuity, is responsible for a great deal of social misfortune and a great many foolish and ill-assorted marriages.

I remember when I was a parish priest interviewing in my study two distraught and anxious parents. 'I'll make him marry her, the dirty young scoundrel,' cried the angry father as he strode up and down the room. The young man in question indeed deserved the description of 'dirty young scoundrel.' I knew him well and I could not contradict a single epithet, but I did suggest to the parents that this attempt to give an undesirable permanence to a most unfortunate relationship was not in the best interests of their daughter. My advice, however, was quite in vain, perhaps not even understood. The unhappy parents were obsessed by the idea of respectability, and for them marriage was a form of necessary whitewash. Fortunately for the young lady concerned, the 'dirty young scoundrel' was an even greater rascal than we thought, and, perhaps not surprisingly, refused to do the 'honorable thing.' She was luckier than a great many other girls in the same situation.

The reduction of marriage to the status of a mere means to respectability is not only the cause of a great many undesirable marriages but is also the cause of a great many equally undesirable divorces. I mentioned earlier in this chapter the study I undertook a few years ago of the debates and discussions that preceded the enactment of the first divorce law in Great Britain. A second prevailing characteristic of these discussions was their marked puritanical flavor. Many of the speakers seemed above all concerned to maximize the extent of respectability in social life and sexual behavior. They were shocked by the spectacle of so many people living together, as men say, 'without benefit of clergy,' of so many illegitimate children being born. A divorce law, they felt, would enable many of these unions to be rendered respectable. This motive has often been uppermost in many subsequent demands that divorce should be made easier to obtain. Thus about ten years ago an English member of Parliament secured a great deal of publicity by advocating divorce at the will of either party after three years of separation. She declared that there were 100,000 couples living together in Great Britain outside the bonds of marriage, and argued that her proposal would enable them to rehabilitate and conventionalize their irregular unions.

There is something puritanical, almost 'Mother Grundyish,' about such arguments and proposals. Marriage is interpreted as merely a means by which society renders sexuality respectable, and it is supposed that society will somehow become more moral if some means can be devised for the mass production and mass distribution of marriage licenses to as many sexual delinquents as possible. Marriage, from this point of view, is a mere remedy for sin, and the people who put forward or are convinced by such arguments as these are in effect proposing to unsettle the basis of matrimonial institutions for the sake of whitewashing fornication and adultery. It is safe to say that if marriage comes to be regarded as no more than a mere means to respectability, then true marriage, real adult, responsible sexuality, based on the mutual and permanent self-giving of a man and woman to each other, will cease to exist in our society.

3. *The spiritualization of sexuality.* But Christianity cannot remain content with the social institution of marriage alone, even in its best and highest forms. It distinguishes, and must distinguish, between the social institution of marriage and the sacrament of holy matrimony. The sacrament of holy matrimony is more than a social institution. We have already seen that it is possible for marriage to be as defective in its own way as illicit sexuality, and even to fall below the level of illicit sexuality at its best, when

considered from the point of view of a deep and personally satisfying relationship. On the whole it is true to say that one of the gravest and most consequence-laden errors of the puritans and the Reformed theologians was their rejection of the conception of the sacrament of holy matrimony, and their tendency to content themselves with the assertion that marriage is a divine ordinance. As we have seen, this easily degenerates into the conventional, vulgar prejudice that marriage is simply that which makes sexuality respectable, and this in turn leads to the notion that divorce is quite as important and necessary, in the interests of respectability, as marriage itself. In order to preserve respectability at all costs we must destroy marriages as well as make them. But the Christian ought not to be concerned with preserving respectability at all costs. For him there are higher values than respectability, and the prejudices and prudishnesses of modern middle-class society have no ultimate theological sanction.

What do we mean when we say that marriage is a sacrament? The concept is indeed a little ambiguous. We may mean no more than something like this: marriage is a state of life that has its own characteristic difficulties, tensions, and perplexities; through the sacrament of matrimony, consciously embarked upon in the context of the Christian spiritual life, there comes to married men and women a special divine aid or grace that enables them to solve and survive the testing experiences which the mutual solidarity of husband and wife has to endure. If we mean no more than that, we shall undoubtedly have in mind a great truth, but I doubt whether we shall have sounded the concept of the sacrament of holy matrimony to its depths.

For Christian marriage is a sacrament in a much deeper sense than this. The union of a man and a woman in holy matrimony, a union in which each gives himself or herself utterly and entirely to the other for the duration of their lives, is an experience that positively enriches and deepens the spiritual life of both parties. It deepens their perception of God, and enriches their experience of their relationship to God. Holy matrimony is one of the great means in and through which we abdicate our self-centered claim to individual autonomy. The married man is not his own, but his wife's. The married woman is not her own, but her husband's. In marriage they learn to surrender themselves, not merely for the moment, in a gust of self-forgetful emotion, but coolly and deliberately for life. It teaches them that they must lay down their lives in order to have them, that the supreme moment of possession is precisely the moment in which we give, utterly and entirely and without reservation. To be consciously married in this sense is to possess within the narrow orbit of one's own existence a vivid and pregnant analogy to our relationship to God. Marriage as we experience it in the sacrament of holy matrimony is of all earthly, temporal experiences the one that most closely resembles the spiritual life, the one that best trains us in that inward and spiritual technique of self-giving which the spiritual life, as the Christian understands it, persistently demands. Thus as marriage is reinterpreted and more profoundly understood in the sacrament of holy matrimony, permanence, fidelity, self-giving without reservation of any conceivable kind are its essential characteristics. We are not merely concerned here with making human relationships look respectable, we are concerned with the very salvation of man's immortal soul; we are concerned not merely with the relationship between a man and a woman but with their common relationship, working in and through their relationship to each other, to God. So our sexuality, which rises to the heights of moral responsibility in marriage, rises to still further heights of spiritual being in the sacrament of holy matrimony. Once marriage is seen and interpreted as the raw material, the essential stuff, in and through which the sacrament of holy matrimony affirms itself, then at the same time divorce is seen to be impossible, a mere social device that contradicts the essential nature of marriage, represses its most fundamental characteristics, and frustrates its ultimate purposes. Hence the Christian insistence on the vanity and unreality of that essentially puritanical, respectability-seeking social device and expedient which we call divorce.

It is important to insist that there is nothing penal or retributive about the Christian prohibition of divorce. The Christian prohibition of divorce is not a punishment for adultery, nor does it suggest that in the mind of the Church and the Bible adultery and fornication are, for some obscure reason, graver and more serious than other kinds of sin. The contrary is the case. In the New Testament, the smug, self-satisfied Pharisees, who, in their own view, have saved their souls by a painstaking obedience to the moral law, are assured that in many cases the corrupt and venal publicans and the sensuous harlots will go into the kingdom of heaven before them. When adultery is repented of and confessed by a member of the Church, the Church dares to proclaim the divine forgiveness, and it must urge the wronged spouse to rise to the same heights.

This truth has sometimes been obscured by reckless and theologically quite unwarranted talk by theologians and Churchmen about the so-called 'guilty party' in a matrimonial dispute. There have even been Christians who have urged that the so-called 'innocent party' should be allowed to remarry after divorce, whereas the so-called 'guilty party' should be prohibited from seeking and finding the same relief. This is from every conceivable point of view a non-sensical notion. How can one party conceivably be released from the obligations of the marriage bond and not the other? In any case, the distinction between the guilty and the innocent party is of a most dubious character. Almost always in matrimonial disputes grave faults, of which adultery is not necessarily the gravest, can be observed on both sides. From the point of view of Christian theology this is a fallen world, and although the offenses of some people may indeed be graver than the offenses of others, an absolutely innocent party never exists. In a fallen world innocence is unknown; there are only different degrees of guilt. It is precisely because we are all fellow-sinners that it behoves us to forgive each other, even 'until seventy times seven,' and to look upon each other's failings and infidelities with pity and love. Human beings have no right to be overstern with each other, either in the married relationship or anywhere else. The Gospel exhorts us to forgive in any area of life in which forgiveness is called for, precisely because there must certainly be some other area of life in which we ourselves need to be forgiven.

No, there is nothing penal about the Christian prohibition of divorce. It is the measure neither of the Church's wrath nor of the divine wrath. It is simply the practical conclusion that logically follows from the Christian insight into the true nature of marriage, and the Christian desire at all costs to preserve the fullness and richness of holy matrimony; at all costs, even at the cost of mundane respectability itself.

Just as the prohibition of divorce is not penal in its intention, so it is in no sense puritanical in its conception. Puritanism, on the contrary, tolerated divorce from the first, and it is indeed precisely those parts of Western civilization most influenced by the puritan outlook which have carried the social habit of divorcing to its farthest extreme. The tendency of puritanism to encourage divorce, almost to assist at the birth of the divorcing society, may be traced to two elements in the puritan outlook on life. The first of these is its extreme horror of sexual offenses. In many puritan societies the word 'sin' is almost synonymous with sexual irregularity, and the word 'morality' connotes in the first place the accepted code of sexual ethics. From such a point of view sexual offenses are so serious as to be humanly speaking almost unforgivable. The wronged partner of an unfaithful wife or husband, or so it seems to the puritan, cannot reasonably be expected to overlook so terrible an affront. Certainly such an offense can easily be supposed, from a puritan point of view, to disrupt and destroy the entire foundation of marriage.

Behind this error there perhaps lies a perfectionist doctrine of marriage, as of many other things in personal and social life, which is frankly disruptive. Only the perfect marriage, from this perfectionist point of view, is a real marriage, truly 'made in heaven,' as we say. When some manifest imperfection exposes itself the proper conclusion to draw is that such a union never was a real marriage at all. The trouble about perfectionist doctrines of this kind is that they are totally unsuited to the needs of a fallen world. If only perfect marriages are real marriages, then in this life we have no marriages. The same thing is true of the doctrine of the Church which underlies the teaching and existence of so many of the puritan sects. For them the only real Church is a 'pure Church' of the elect. The empirical Church of history which contains so many obvious sinners and so many flagrant corruptions cannot, from this point of view, be regarded as a real Church at all. It subsequently turns out, of course, that the new Church of the elect is no more exempt from sin and corruption than the great empirical Church of Christian history, and this leads to the ultimate conclusion that we cannot have any real Church Militant here on earth at all. Perfectionism is a disruptive doctrine, for it would void all our social institutions of any claim to validity and reality.

Again, the puritanical form of society, as we have seen, is characterized by an overwhelming desire to procure the respectable marriage of as many couples as possible who are living together in some illicit kind of sexual relationship. Puritan society, especially once the fires of living faith have departed, and where only the habitual puritan way of life survives — once, that is, puritanism has become no more than a drab morality without religion — easily degenerates into this depressing cult of respectability. Indeed the fundamental error of many Christians during the last few centuries has been this kind of confusion between the conventional ethics of the Western middle classes and the Christian ethic itself.

Puritanism is predominantly a lay religion, and lay religion is particularly inclined to identify its spiritual ideals with its everyday social habits and objectives. After the Reformation the lay life was robbed of that vivid and visible contrast with the monastic life which might have helped it to attain a degree of humility about its achievements, and to question sometimes its everyday assumptions. The monastery might at least have served to remind a puritanical society that there is a real distinction between middle-class morality and respectability and Christian sanctity. The lack of such a stimulating contrast made it easy for puritan society to identify the two.

It is perhaps worth pointing out that this hazardous project of securing and spreading at least the appearance of respectability by injecting into the social body more and more, and heavier and heavier, doses of divorce has in fact proved extremely unsuccessful. There is at least no evidence to suggest that in a divorcing society such as our own there is any decrease in the incidence of adultery and fornication. In fact we are quite as familiar with these evils as any non-divorcing society. We have undermined the foundations of marriage, and weakened the strength of the matrimonial bond, in order to reduce the evidence and frequency of visible sin, and we find ourselves at last with the foundations of marriage indeed undermined and the strength of the marriage bond gravely debilitated, but with at least as much sexual irregularity and delinquency as before. We have taken a great risk to achieve a questionable purpose, and we have incurred the losses inherent in the risk without achieving the purpose. Surely we have the weightiest reasons for reconsidering and criticizing anew the basic assumptions of our society about this matter.

THE DILEMMA OF THE CHURCH IN A DIVORCING SOCIETY. It is only comparatively recently, and in a comparatively few areas of the Western world, that the Church has been brought face to face with the problem of the divorcing society. Too many discussions of the Christian view of divorce confine themselves to the abstract theological question of whether or not, and in what possible circumstances, divorce is permissible. This is an interesting speculative problem, but it is not the problem with which the Church is now faced. The Church is now confronted with the concrete fact of a divorcing society, not just a Christian society in which divorce is legally permissible and occasionally happens, but a society in which the divorcing habit has become chronic, in which an increasing proportion of those to whom the Church much speak and minister are, whether we like it or not, divorcees, or perhaps the emotionally impoverished and spiritually deprived children of divorcees.

This is not merely a problem but also a dilemma for the Church, because it is at the same time a prophetic and a pastoral problem. The Church has a prophetic duty toward our civilization. It must declare, in season and out of season, whether men will hear or whether they will forebear, that the word of the Lord is against our civilization in such enormities as these, that in the long run the civilization that abandons itself to such courses must weaken and confound itself from within and ultimately perish. If the Church does not remind the people of the true nature of marriage, there will soon be no true marriages, only a perpetual succession of vainly whitewashed fornications, bearing fruit in one unhappy, neurotic, and frustrated generation after another. The fathers and mothers have eaten sour grapes and the children's nerves are set on edge, as indeed they are to an almost visible extent.

But if the divorcing habit and its prevalence in our society confront the Church with a prophetic problem, it is equally true that the divorcees themselves and their unfortunate children confront the Church with a pastoral problem. 'My song shall be of mercy and judgment.' The mind of the Church must be set as much upon mercy as upon judgment, and at the same time. Hence it comes about in the Church that the prophetically minded tend to concentrate on constantly reasserting and reiterating the Church's judgment on divorce, whereas the pastorally minded are chiefly concerned with the problem of ministering to the spiritual needs of the divorcees. Hence also there tends to be a certain amount of discord and tension between these two equally Christian types of mind, and that perhaps, in the circumstances, is as it should be, for both the prophetically minded and the pastorally minded are preoccupied with valid and important concerns. The compromise that seems to be working itself out, however, in both the Roman and the Anglican Churches is not an entirely satisfactory one. It consists in publicly and officially maintaining what is sometimes called a 'rigorous' view of the matter, while at the same time, through private and discreet channels, finding ways of relaxing the full rigor of the Christian principle in favor of rather arbitrarily selected individuals. Rome is perhaps the Church most notoriously guilty of this practice, and most strongly criticized on that account, but it must be confessed that something very like the Roman practice is to be found in other Churches.

Indeed, we may well ask, in a society so given to divorce as ours, and in which the Church has both prophetic and pastoral duties at the same time, what alternative, if any, exists? The Lord's word must be spoken, and yet at the same time the Lord's mercy must be made plain. There are no perfect pattern solutions of this problem. As so often in a fallen world, the perfect solution to its characteristic dilemmas does not exist. We feel ourselves bound to and obligated by contrasting and to some extent mutually exclusive duties, and we are compelled, through our own implicatedness in the sinful situation, to work out an uneasy compromise which will enable us to do rough justice to both of these obligations at the same time. It is not an enviable situation for the Church Militant here on earth, but the plain fact is that the situation of the Church Militant is not, and in the nature of the case never can be, an enviable one.

CHRISTIAN MARRIAGE AND THE WESTERN TRADITION. We have already noticed that such an integrally Christian analysis of the nature of marriage as I have summarized in this chapter has never been a part of the explicit Western tradition, except perhaps here and there. The ascetics in one age and the puritans in another have seen to it that a completely Christian account of the nature of marriage should continually evade the conscious mind of Western civilization. Hence in this particular instance the plea of this book is not for some kind of return to the fullness of the Christian tradition but rather for an advance toward an apprehension of the Christian reality such as our civilization has never yet experienced.

But if a completely Christian view of marriage cannot be said to form any part of the great tradition of Western civilization, it is equally true that the divorcing habit is not deeply rooted in that tradition either, although it does arise out of and express perversions very deep-seated within the Western tradition. Indeed it is far from fanciful to trace its origins to the hatred of marriage so characteristic of the medieval Manichean heretics.

It is sometimes claimed that a more recent factor contributing to the rise and prevalence of the divorcing habit is the feminism of the late nineteenth and early twentieth centuries. It is certainly not more than a contributory factor, but no doubt its influence ought to be taken into account. It is true also that a considerable number of social thinkers and propagandists have supposed that easier divorce is a mark of our signal progress in the so-called 'emancipation' of women. Feminism is not the characteristic creed only of aggressive, masculine women. It is also the fashionable creed of sentimental men with a guilt complex about the relations of men with women. In the sentimentalized picture of a divorce situation, divorce is constantly presented as a merciful device by means of which a pathetically wronged woman attains release from the perverse cruelties and tyrannies of a detestable husband. It is the persistence of this somewhat sentimental stereotype of divorce that so often gives the impression that divorce institutions favor the feminine rather than the masculine ideals and objectives in life. In fact, however, if we consider the impact of divorce upon our society as a whole, we can see clearly enough that it is primarily a masculine and man-made expedient. Normally the primary objective of the woman who has become a wife and a mother is to secure and possess in security a stable foundation for the family life at the center of which she functions. The fact is that in a fallen world men desire to change their wives far more frequently than women desire to change their husbands.

Feminism — and I hasten to acknowledge that our civilization has profited in many ways from the feminist movement — has never really represented the interests of the married woman. It has been the creed, almost the ideology, of the spinster making her way through the rough and tumble of industrial, commercial, and professional life side by side with men and on a footing of increasing equality with them. But the interests of such a woman are by no means identical with those of her married sister, and it is a mistake to suppose that those interests can be comprehended in terms of the same philosophy or furthered by the same propagandas. The wife with her yearning for domestic stability, the mother striving to nourish and nurture her children in security and peace, these are in fact the chief victims of divorce, and no right-minded feminist can pretend otherwise.

Our main concern in this chapter, however, is with the effects of the characteristic institutions of this particular phase of Western civilization on the long-term prospects for its survival. A civilization that does not know how to create stability and security in the domestic relationships which lie at the very roots of human happiness is bound to be a civilization in which great numbers of frustrated and neurotic people are tortured by demons of discontent and deprivation. To pretend to ourselves that these conditions are signs of progress is to delude ourselves almost to the point of madness. On the contrary, at no point is the contemporary weakness of the West more obvious. To nurse and foster the social institutions that produce in increasing quantities such tensions, dissatisfactions, and frustrations as these in the very heart of the social body is to nourish a cancer.

I am continually surprised, perplexed, and distressed by the extraordinary strength, throughout the English-speaking world, of reforming movements and propagandas devoted to such aims as the suppression of all indulgence in alcoholic refreshment, cleaning up of alleged immoralities on the stage, or the abolition of gambling, when the greatest social evil of all in our Western civilization is to a very large extent ignored, allowed to continue unabated, or sometimes even celebrated as a priceless achievement of progress. I am not suggesting that the Christian citizen could or should demand and propagate the total, immediate, and outright abolition of divorce. That would be but to repeat the errors of the prohibitionists and similar fanatics. Nevertheless, much could be done by a widespread reforming movement seeking to reduce the incidence of divorce, by judicious legal and social means, and by continually bearing witness to the social evils of which divorce is the underlying cause. This is not the place to discuss the form such a propagandist movement might or could take, but if ever there should arise some kind of anti-divorce-law league in the future it would be striving not merely to remedy and remove a great and prevalent social evil; it would be working also, and at the same time, for the defense and strengthening of Western civilization itself.

TEN

The Secularity of the West

To the reader who has persevered thus far the main thesis of this book must by now be quite clear: the present secular mood or phase in the development of Western civilization is sapping its vitality and menacing its future. This prevailing secularity as we know it in Western civilization is a somewhat untidy phenomenon. It consists very largely of a number of conflicting but converging doctrines and presuppositions loosely associated with a set of social habits and attitudes which have emerged out of our common life by accident rather than by design. Marxism, on the contrary, is an intellectually ordered secularity, secularism turned into a coherent doctrine. It fits too many of our present habits, shares too many of the prevailing assumptions, for us in our secular mood to resist it wholeheartedly. Our secularity impairs our unity, enervates our will to resist, and weakens our capacity to wage the war of ideas with any real cogency and success.

We have examined in turn our tendency to transform our belief in our characteristic political institutions into something more like an idolatrous cult than a reasoned political faith; our almost superstitious reverence for and trust in our technical efficiency; our preoccupation with economic activity and doctrine; the way in which our nationalism bedevils and dissipates the unity of our civilization; and lastly our failure to root and ground the happiness of the people in its proper and appropriate soil, a secure and stable mode of family life which can fulfill and discipline our sexuality at the same time within a pattern of coherent and ordered social institutions. But the task of Christian social thought and analysis is not fulfilled, as is the task of the 'private eye' in the 'whodunit,' merely by unmasking the villain and handing him over to the police. We have to ask ourselves: what are the causes of the present secular mood, and what, if any, are the prospects of its death or removal in the foreseeable future?

In my view there are tenable grounds for a cautious hope that the secular mood is now entering into its period of decline. It is such a belief that enables me to conclude this book with a relatively, if somewhat tentatively, optimistic chapter. In our fallen world history moves not along pathways of smooth and unimpeded progress, each generation an epoch which carries the attitudes and presuppositions of its predecessor to a logical conclusion; history moves dialectically, through a process of action and reaction. (This was a part of the truth which Marx saw clearly, however gravely he narrowed and misinterpreted it in practice. It is this misalliance with a great truth that gives the falsities and errors of Marxism their strength and vitality. Marxism would not have become the menacing historical force it now is if it consisted of pure error and sophistry. It is its grasp of something that is true and its correspondence to a deep-seated human, and indeed spiritual, need which explains its immense appeal to the contemporary mind.) Thus it is in the nature of the case that each of the characteristic phases through which a civilization passes should meet with its deserved end in the appropriate reaction. The present secular phase of Western culture has its roots in the eighteenth century and its flourishing in the nineteenth century. The latter half of the twentieth or the first half of the twenty-first century may well witness its decline and fall. This at least is the kind of pattern we should expect if we have a sense of history, and in my view there are important reasons leading us to suppose that our expectations will not be disappointed in this particular case.

Before we can embark on a discussion of what seem to me reasonable grounds for a cautious and by no means undiscriminating optimism about the passing of this primarily secular phase in our culture, however, we must try to understand the secular phase itself as a historical phenomenon, to take notice of the historical movements with which it is closely affiliated.

The secular phase of our culture, which has endured and grown in strength during the last two and a half centuries, has coincided with the epoch of social and political revolution. But it is important to notice that this epoch is misinterpreted if we think of it as the age of *the* revolution. It is, on the contrary, essentially the age of two distinct revolutions, which have tended from the beginning to clash with each other, and are now locked together in a conflict of ideas and purposes that threatens to engulf the world. This concept of the two revolutions is so essential to the analysis put forward in this chapter that it will be necessary to discuss it at some length.

THE TWO REVOLUTIONS. The middle-class revolution against the surviving power and prestige of the aristocracy and the regionalism and local self-government of the so-called *ancien régime* — of which the French revolutions of 1789 and 1848 are classic examples — and the working-class or proletarian revolutions — of which the Russian revolution of 1917 is the supreme instance — are not merely distinct but successive aspects of the same revolutionary process. If we make the mistake of supposing that the working-class revolution merely conveyed the blessings won by the middle-class revolution even farther, and to a new section of society, we shall fail to understand why it is that these two revolutions come so persistently into conflict with each other. In fact their social aims are as distinct as the sources of their support and strength. The conflict between the democratic institutions that have emerged out of the middle-class revolution and the authoritarian institutions that have emerged out of the working-class revolution is not a recent twentieth-century development. We can trace the beginnings of the conflict even in the course of the first French revolution itself, and in 1848 the necessity and fatefulness of such a struggle were clearly perceived by a brilliantly intelligent observer who was at the same time a participant in the course of events — Alexis de Tocqueville.

In June 1848, the middle-class supporters of the republic which had been established in the previous February came into open armed strife with the working classes of Paris. Tocqueville commented on this singular and ominous event with a full consciousness of its epoch-making significance.

> What distinguished it [the insurrection of June] among all the events of this kind which have succeeded each other in France for sixty years, is that it did not aim at changing the form of government, but at altering the order of society. It was not, strictly speaking, a political struggle, in the sense which until then we had given the word, but a struggle of class against class . . . It must also be observed that this formidable insurrection was not the enterprise of a certain number of con-

spirators, but the rising of one whole section of the population against another. Women took part in it as well as men. While the latter fought, the former prepared and carried ammunition; and when at last the time had come to surrender, the women were the last to yield.[1]

Elsewhere Tocqueville has the following comment on the sequence of events in France during the dramatic months between February and June 1848. 'Socialism,' he says, 'will always remain the essential characteristic and the most redoubtable remembrance of the revolution of February. The Republic will only appear to the onlooker to have come upon the scene as a means, not as an end.[2] In 1870, some years after Tocqueville's death, the same pattern of events was to repeat itself, in the streets of the same city, in the risings of the Commune, and with the same tragic result. The representatives of the middle-class revolution were openly at war with the representatives of the working-class revolution.

Tocqueville himself, in the years that were left to him after 1848, spurred on by what he had observed in those stormy months, because the classic analyst and expositor of the meaning and aims of the middle-class revolution. In his great book *L'Ancien Régime*,[3] he asks and answers the question: what was it that the first French revolution really accomplished? In his reply to this question he sees the first French revolution as the culmination rather than the initiation of a great historical process. The destruction of the aristocratic regime in France was in fact begun, a century before the first French revolution, by the so-called 'grand monarch,' Louis XIV. It was this king above all

1. *Recollections of Alexis de Tocqueville,* Columbia University Press, New York, 1949, pages 160f.
2. Ibid. p. 82.
3. 1856.

who transformed the aristocracy into a generation of courtiers, with their younger sons serving perhaps as officers in the army. Under his rule they ceased for the most part to be a working aristocracy. When it came to the serious task of government and administration he put his trust in able officials recruited from the middle classes. By the time of the first French revolution the substance of power had already been shifted to the middle classes. To the aristocracy as a whole there remained nothing but privilege. Thus the aristocracy which the first French revolution destroyed was not a real, working, responsibility-bearing aristocracy, whose visible services to the commonwealth might to some extent at least seem to justify their privileges, but a painted corpse. There are probably few spectacles in the world more revolting than that of a painted corpse.

Thus the mere destruction of the *ancien régime* was not, as might at first sight appear, the characteristic accomplishment of the first French revolution. The great accomplishment and legacy of that revolution was the completion of the great project of Louis XIV and his ministers for the complete centralization of the administration of France. The French revolution destroyed the independence of the great French regions. It left a mere façade of local self-government and substituted for it everywhere the rule of local careerist administrators appointed from Paris — prefects, sub-prefects, and the like. It made the administrator rather than the businessman the true and authentic representative of the French middle class. In the twentieth century this tendency has become more and more obvious almost everywhere. It has been truly said that the France that emerged out of the revolution is not so much governed as administered. That is why the bewildering succession of cabinets and ministerial cabals so characteristic of French politics does not really imply such a degree of discontinuity in the national life as might at first sight appear. It is this vast army of bureaucrats and administrators who are to this day the true heirs and beneficiaries of the first French revolution; but of course, although these men, rather than the men of business and property, are the most characteristic representatives of the middle-class tradition as it emerged out of the revolution, the two remained akin to each other. They mingled socially and were recruited to a very considerable extent from the same families. Hence the members of this administrative class were from the beginning heavily biased in favor of the maintenance of existing middle-class property rights.

The working-class revolution, however, as becomes clear in the pattern of events in France in 1848 and 1870 and in the Russian revolution of 1917, is based on a new conception of corporate property rights which reflects the much stronger proletarian sense of community, the product of the working-class experience of individual weakness and corporate strength. It is important to emphasize that this marked tendency of the European working classes was the outcome of their experience; they discovered the strength which even weak men may attain in mutual solidarity and in corporate action when they join together in co-operative societies, trade unions, friendly societies, and the like. Regarded as individuals, the members of this class are the weakest and poorest members of the community, but the class itself is often better and more easily organized than other sections of the community. In most places its members constitute a majority of the voters and, particularly where trade unionism is widespread, it is usually a well-disciplined, cohesive group. Thus the class of the least powerful people tends in highly industrialized countries to be the most powerful class. In many large urban and industrial areas it is the politically dominant class, and yet — a paradox which this analysis enables us to understand — its prevailing mentality is nevertheless dominated by the resentments and inferiority complexes characteristic of those who know themselves to be weak. This is why labor movements in so many parts of the world find it so difficult to accept responsibility in mature, adult fashion. It is hard for them to leave behind their sense of being a dissident, opposition group. Bitterness and resentment, which are at least understandable in the weak, ill become the strong. Power shows itself at its worst when it is the hardly gained, perhaps precariously held, power of weak and resentful men.

The conflicts we are now witnessing on a world scale are in essence a continuation of the Parisian conflicts of 1848 and 1870, when the two revolutions came to blows with each other in the streets. I have chosen to interpret the central dilemma of the modern world in terms of French history because, it seems to me, it is in French history above all that the basic dilemmas of modern man have been most clearly diagnosed and defined. This is perhaps the characteristic French service to our civilization, a great ministry of clarification. The French mind has often been praised for its lucidity, but its great virtue is its capacity to ask the right questions clearly and observe and define the real problems. It cannot be said, as a generalization, that the French element in the tradition of Western civilization has shown any parallel capacity to answer the questions or solve the problems. Lucidity perhaps is not enough. But even to this day — for example, in contemporary French existentialism — the French intellect and French literature still display their extraordinary genius for perceiving precisely what the dilemma is. Elsewhere in Western civilization — for example, in America, Britain, and Germany — a certain sentimental and romantic disposition, a distaste for clear-cut dichotomies, tends to blur the edges of such hard and fast distinctions. This second type of mind also has its virtues, for it finds it easier perhaps to avoid otherwise inevitable head-on collisions, and is less inclined to split the community with irreconcilable divisions. It is perhaps true that France — and this is the defect of her great intellectual virtues — is more hopelessly divided than any other modern Western nation. Nevertheless we can see in her divisions the basic and underlying motivations which explain the great world schism of our time.

America and the British countries have, as we have seen, a different tradition of revolution, one far more deeply rooted in Western history. This was first made clear by Edmund Burke at the time he was accused of inconsistency in opposing the French revolution when he had previously sympathized with and supported the American revolution. His answer was in effect that the American revolution had been essentially a claim made by a large group of English colonists to the inherited rights and social privileges — stretching back through a long history at least to the Magna Carta — which the English tradition wholeheartedly conceded to those Englishmen who had remained at home. In his view the great mistake of George III's government was its failure to recognize that Englishmen across the sea were still Englishmen. The French revolution, however, was not based on any such solid historical tradition. On the contrary, its foundation was supplied by the speculative and dubious social philosophies and metaphysics fashionable among the French middle classes during the eighteenth century. No doubt this criticism was not entirely fair. Those who through no fault of their own lack a great evolving tradition of liberty have perforce to make shift without one. The English revolution, however, occurred in the seventeenth century, and had its roots in the Middle Ages. The American revolution occurred in the eighteenth century, and was influenced by eighteenth-century thought forms, particularly in its literary expression, but nevertheless it is essentially closer in spirit to the English seventeenth-century revolution.

As a result the English-speaking democracies have on the whole escaped the intensity of class feeling that has embittered modern history in so many other Western countries. In particular the openness of the upper and middle classes in these countries, their willingness to accept new recruits from below, has created a sense of opportunity, indeed a tradition of opportunity, which enables the working class to interpret itself as at least potentially, and often indeed actually, middle class. There is none of the intense pride in being proletarian, and the contemptuous abuse of the middle class, which is so characteristic, for example, of French working-class life. Just as one of Napoleon's privates might dream — and the dream, although an illusion in the majority of cases, came to pass sufficiently often to sustain it — that he had a field marshal's baton in his knapsack, so the working man in these countries could imagine that he might have a middle-class checkbook in his trouser pocket. As for the English bourgeois of good stock and position, he could even entertain a colorful and enticing dream of a coronet and a seat in the House of Lords. It is not the absence of class distinction — no modern society has ever achieved that — that soothes down exasperated class feeling, but rather the occurrence of visible movements from class to class. The classless society remains an illusory dream. So long as it does so a high degree of class mobility provides an effective working substitute.

Nevertheless in the English-speaking democracies the realities on which class consciousness fastens are undeniably present, the visible contrast between the standards of living of the propertied and professional classes and those of the wage-earning classes. If the social situation in these countries should at any time become more set and rigid than it now is, the stage would be set for an exasperated outburst of class feeling of the familiar west-European kind.

But despite the important differences between them we now find side by side the kind of democracy that stems from the French revolution — weakened by its narrowly middle-class basis but still a strong and flourishing tradition — and the kind of democracy, more deeply rooted in history, which we find in America and the British countries. They are drawn together in a work of mutual defense against the world-wide expansion (in some ways recalling the rapid Moslem expansion which so menaced Christendom at the close of the seventh century) of a new type of social order which stems from the great working-class movements that began to agitate the Western world a century or so ago. It is against the background of the conflict between these two revolutions that we are at present existing somewhat precariously in a critical phase of our history.

From our present point of view, however, the essential thing to notice is that these two revolutions had at least one thing in common. They were both essentially secular in spirit and characterized by a marked hostility toward Christianity. In 1789 the first architects of the French revolution received considerable assistance from the elected representatives of the parochial clergy in winning their early battles, but this did not dissuade them from immediately embarking upon a vigorous attack on the French Church and from a tremendous secularization of French life. The estrangement, both tragic and fateful, between the Church and the revolutionary forces in European life dates from that time. The forces of middle-class revolution were in fact as violently anti-Christian in those early years as the forces of working-class revolution are now.

Nor, especially in continental Europe, have they altogether ceased to be so even yet. In the liberal and republican parties of countries such as France and Italy the association of doctrinaire democrats with the anti-clerical European variety of Free-Masonry still survives. The spirit of the eighteenth-century philosophers and encyclopedists is far from being entirely vanquished. Time has mellowed this hostility to some extent, and some sort of uneasy *modus vivendi* has been established, but the anti-clerical and anti-Christian intelligentsia still exists in its original homelands, as its colonists and sympathizers still exist also in America and the British countries.

On the other hand, it is undeniably true that the bitterness and fury of the strife has died down in the modern world. The old-school anti-clerical in France no longer expects that the Christian Church will in fact be destroyed in any foreseeable future. Perhaps he has even ceased to hope for such a thing with any marked enthusiasm. On the contrary, what we are now witnessing in most Western countries is the beginning of a reconciliation between the

Church and the intelligentsia. If there are any signs among us of what is sometimes hailed and heralded as a return to the faith, they are most manifest among the cultured classes whose former estrangement from the faith precipitated the marked decline of the influence of Christianity on our civilization, and is so characteristic of the eighteenth and nineteenth centuries. Thus in countries such as France and Britain, and possibly America also, the proportion of convinced, worshiping Christians to be found among writers, artists, university professors, schoolteachers, scientists, and similar professions far exceeds the proportion of worshiping, practicing Christians in the general working population. The proportion is lowest among the working classes, who in many vitally important areas of Western civilization include in their ranks almost no believing Christians at all. This state of affairs is much more marked in France perhaps than elsewhere, and more clearly visible in Europe and Britain generally than in America, yet I suspect that in all these countries the general trend is in the same direction, toward an increasing reconciliation of the elite, who think civilization's thoughts and provide it with its ideas, and an increasing estrangement of the working masses, who uphold its foundations. Indeed it is little exaggeration to say that one of the gravest dangers now confronting the contemporary Church is the possibility that it may be gradually transformed by the pressure of events into a kind of high-brow intellectual coterie. Thus in most of the Churches represented in the World Council of Churches, as in the deliberations of the World Council itself, the Christian elite and intellectuals are perhaps bearing a heavier burden of responsibility, and exercising a more commanding influence, than is altogether good for them. But although not unfraught with possible danger, the present situation seems to me a healthy and hopeful one, and this for two reasons.

First, the prevalent trend toward a reconciliation of the intelligentsia and the Christian Church, the way in which so many members of our intellectual and cultural elite are rediscovering for themselves the spiritual excitement of the Gospel and the intellectual fascination of the faith, a breaking of the bars and a bursting of the chains with which the secularistic phase of our culture has imprisoned and shackled the modern mind, at least means that those who are now drawn toward Christianity and the Christian Church are above all others precisely the people who in the natural course of events will exercise a major influence on the ideas and thinking of the generations to come. There is every sign that we are at last at an intellectual turning point, that the inhibitions and denials that seemed so new and exciting in the eighteenth and nineteenth centuries are becoming outworn and conventional, with little in them to attract the alert, seeking, and probing mind. If these present trends continue they cannot but exercise a major and perhaps decisive influence on the course of the history of our civilization during the next century or so.

Secondly, the realization that the secularistic, anti-Christian violence of the first revolution is slowly but visibly losing its grip, that the fires of the anti-religious passion among the heirs of the first revolution have died down, and are now merely smoldering here and there, encourages at least the hope that the same pattern of events will ultimately repeat itself in the second revolution also, that here, too, the fires of anti-religious passion, now burning so furiously, will gradually die down, that first an uneasy *modus vivendi* will be established and that later a process of reconciliation and reclamation will become possible. The bitterness of the Marxists, even at its most venomous, is not greater than the bitterness of the unexciting eighteenth-century deists and the colorful nineteenth-century atheists was in their heyday. *Ecrasez l'infame,* 'destroy the infamous thing,' was once their slogan even as it has become the slogan of the Marxists in our own day. They, too, once labored, even as the Marxists now labor, with passionate enthusiasm to fulfill such a program, and encouraged by an invincible conviction that they were indeed capable of fulfilling it. Nowadays the conviction and the passion are for the most part gone, even where the prejudice and the habitual antagonism remain. It is at least not unreasonable to anticipate that in the same way the vigor of the Marxist anti-Christianity will relax as it grows older and transforms itself more and more into a merely conventional prejudice.

Indeed, all the trustworthy evidence that reaches us from those who are able to give us first-hand reports about the religious situation in the Soviet Union suggests that this dying down of the fires of anti-religious zeal is already taking place. Marxism itself remains, of course, dogmatically atheistic in theory, and the communist party is still, at least in theory, a fraternity of atheists. But the overwhelming majority of the citizens of a Marxist nation are themselves neither Marxists nor members of the communist party, and we have every reason to believe that inside this majority a large number of people remain obstinately Christian in conviction and in practice. Anything like the early officially sponsored and violent persecution of the Church has long ceased. Anti-Christian propaganda still continues, but it is a propaganda conducted by private groups of enthusiasts, as in our Western democracy. No doubt the state looks upon such activities with a favorable eye, provided they are kept within reasonable bounds and do not threaten public order, but it no longer lends them the weight of its official sanction and support. To a communist government the Christian Church remains 'the infamous thing,' but there is no longer the same confidence that it can or will be destroyed, or the same enthusiasm for hastening the process of its destruction. The official view seems to be that Christianity will gradually disappear of itself as the education of the masses progresses and deepens, but even this sanguine expectation will probably die out in the course of a generation or so. There seems no doubt, on the other hand, that atheism is still taught and encouraged by many of the teachers in the schools, though with comparatively little effect so far as the mass of the people is concerned. This is an important difference from the practice of almost all Western democracies. There is a real hostility to religion in some of our schools, particularly in the so-called 'lay' schools of France, but it stops well short of the actual inculcation of atheism.

What we do find in the school systems of many of the Western democracies is the religiously 'neutral' school, a school in which the religious issue is entirely ignored. This type of school exists in the United States and in many other places. It is only fair to say that the Christians themselves have very largely caused the particular educational problem to which the religiously neutral school is supposed to be a solution. It is the scandalous division of the Christian Churches from and against each other that has created the situation in which the religiously neutral schools seem to present the best and only opportunity for bringing about educational peace. There are, of course, other factors and motives that have led people to support this type of school, and no doubt the secularists have used the divided state of Christendom as an argument for an educational settlement which they themselves favor on quite other grounds. Nevertheless the blame and the responsibility must fall primarily on a sinfully and tragically divided Christendom itself. The religiously neutral school does not, of course, if it is true to its own neutralist ideals, as normally it is, in any way teach atheism or seek to influence the pupils in the direction of atheism. Nevertheless the critics of the neutral school have argued, with at least some measure of justice, that the total effect of an educational system that is neutral about matters of religion, and preserves its neutrality by ignoring them, is one that is at least implicitly atheistic. Such an educational system cannot but suggest to those who fall under its influence that the fundamental religious issues of life are somehow second-class issues which an educational institution may ignore without neglecting its duty and forfeiting its right to be regarded as an adequate preparation for human existence. But if the living God of the Bible truly exists, then surely no educational system that ignores the fact of His existence can be regarded as an adequate educational system. How can we prepare the young for life with an educational system that ignores the chief end of man, that ultimate reality which gave him his finite existence and is at once his chief glory and his ultimate destiny? It is a poor preparation for life indeed which excludes the whole question of the ultimate purpose and meaning of life. If the religious issue has any real meaning as an issue at all it cannot conceivably be regarded as a second-class issue and ignored. It is either meaningless, or it is the primary issue in life which must predominate over all the others. To ignore it, or try to ignore it, for reasons however politic and excellent, inevitably suggests that it is possible to ignore it and desirable to do so, and this policy does seem to carry within it the inescapable implication that the religious issue is not in fact the supreme issue of life, but a second-class issue which can be safely set on one side without any danger to the educational project as a whole.

In some ways, the atheist school may even be preferable, from a Christian point of view, to the neutral school. Schools that teach a dogmatic atheism at least have the virtue of raising the religious issue in a direct, inescapable way. I was myself surrounded in my home in the earliest years by influences which, if not quite atheistic in the formal sense, were so bleakly and negatively agnostic as to amount to very much the same thing. I now look back on this upbringing with some gratitude, for at least it can be said in its favor that it confronted me with the religious issue at every stage in my growth. For us it was vitally important not to be religious, and to know the reason why we were not religious. From the moment I ceased to be satisfied with the reasons alleged for not being Christian my feet were set fairly and squarely on the path that leads to the Church. The trouble with the neutral school, particularly when it is allied with a religiously neutral or indifferent home, is that it enables young people to live through their most sensitive and impressionable years without having the religious issue ever vividly brought before them at all. The neutral school and the neutral home have thus made, and are still making, a massive contribution, second perhaps to no other in our society, to the maintenance and spread of the secular mood.

The fact is, however, that educational agnosticism and religious neutrality do not differ so sharply from downright atheism as Western secularists and skeptical humanists often suppose. The atheist thinks and says that there is no

God; the agnostic, more cautiously, will not commit himself on the subject, but he lives in practice as though there were no God, without prayer, without worship, buried and imprisoned in his secularity, not recognizing, that is, the eternal dimension in human life and therefore not recognizing, if he is really logical — which, perhaps fortunately, he rarely is — the eternal and unique significance of human personality. At best the agnostic is inspired by a kind of vestigial Christianity, the implications of Christianity detached from any sure grounding in the assertions about reality which imply them. The atheist is at least aware that if there is a God he will certainly manifest His presence, so that we can know Him and know about Him, and at least asserts the right of the human mind to infer His non-existence from His apparent absence, and to draw the appropriate conclusions.

Like most Christians, or so my experience suggests, I have a kind of intuitive, almost spontaneous, preference for the atheist. When a man proclaims himself an atheist at least we both know where we stand. Nevertheless, as I have said, the actual differences between the atheist and the agnostic are not so great as is often supposed, and an educational system that seems to presuppose agnosticism, or at least the absence of any definite commitment to the divine existence, as a necessary part of the foundations of its methodological procedure is not perhaps an adequate educational alternative to the atheistic school. This is, of course, a delicate matter of policy, particularly while the Christian Churches remain divided, but it would certainly seem to me that those Western democracies which tolerate the neutral school, and even pretend to believe in it with a somewhat uncalled-for enthusiasm, are failing lamentably to bear witness to the traditions on which democracy stands, and to the foundations of their own way of life, at a peculiarly sensitive and crucial stage in the mental and spiritual growth of new recruits to democratic society. In many areas of Western civilization people are growing more sensitive to the acuteness and momentousness of this educational problem — the British Education Act of 1944 is a clear example of this growing consciousness — but in many other areas the tradition of neutral education still persists and still hampers the school in its essential task of initiating its students deeply and profoundly into the perennial well-springs of Western civilization.

THE PROPHETIC OFFICE. But although it is possible to look far forward into the future in a mood of cautious and rational hope, the immediate prospect is dark indeed, for the hostility of the two revolutions toward each other remains unabated. The conflict so unhappily begun in the streets of Paris in 1848 has now become a world conflict, the protagonists armed with more terrible weapons and burning after a century of bitter history with an even more violent mutual hatred. In such a situation, what is the prophetic duty of the Christian Church? 'Is there any word from the Lord?' — in the first place any Word of the Lord to the Christian himself, and in the second place, any Word of the Lord the Christian can proclaim to the world.

The Word of the Lord to the Christian in this fateful historical situation, or in any other comparable one, must first of all be a Word about the Word. What are the general characteristics of the Word of the Lord, when it is given, that enable us to recognize it for what it is? By means of what criteria are we able to distinguish between the true prophet and that dark figure of mingled futility and false guidance whom the Old Testament describes as the false prophet? The Word of the Lord as we see it in the great

Hebrew prophets in the Bible is always a Word of judgment and of mercy, a reconciliation of the theme of doom and the theme of hope, of a judgment that must be accepted in a mood of understanding precisely in order that the mercy may come. Thus when Jerusalem and its monarchy were at the last gasp, when, as the prophet Jeremiah had foretold, the hosts of Babylon were encamped around the city and it was obvious that nothing could save it, Jeremiah chose that precise moment to buy a piece of land and seal up the title deeds in an earthen vessel. He foresaw that at last the judgment would be understood and accepted by the people and that consequently the mercy would flow. 'Thus saith the Lord of Hosts, the God of Israel; Houses and fields and vineyards shall be possessed again in this land.'

The true prophet thus interprets the events of history in terms of the purpose, the judgment, and the mercy of God. He enables the people of God to understand what is happening to them, to endure the calamities of history without faltering in their faith in the righteous and triumphant purposes of God, the Lord of history. Thus the true prophet meets the real spiritual needs of the people. The false prophet, on the other hand, tells the people what they want to hear and frustrates their profounder spiritual needs. He declares that God approves of their present condition and conduct, thus ministering to their complacency, and that God is wholeheartedly on their side in the existing conflict, thus giving a false theological sanction to their presumption. The result is that when at last the calamity comes the disciples of the false prophet are left with nothing to fall back upon and their faith in God is confounded. I know of a particularly clear instance of false prophecy of this kind in England during the early months of 1939. A certain parish priest drew large congregations to hear him preach Sunday after Sunday on the general theme that since God is a God of righteousness and peace He would not permit the coming of the threatened world war, and that those who were apprehensive that war was not far away were in fact men of little faith. It became cruelly obvious in September 1939 that this misguided preacher had most singularly failed to prepare his people for the ordeals that were to come upon them. The more completely he had convinced them, the more their faith must have been confounded and overthrown in the event. True prophecy rouses men to face the realities of a fallen world; it does not facilitate their persistent tendency toward wishful thinking, and exile them to an unreal land of pleasant dreams. Again, true prophecy does not merely take sides in human conflicts. It is an error to suppose that in any human conflict all the right is on one side and all the wrong on the other. 'The scripture hath concluded all under sin.' [4] It is true that at certain moments in human history God has entrusted the care and stewardship of righteous causes to sinful men and sinful nations. But we must never commit the error of supposing that because our cause is righteous it therefore follows that we are a righteous people. On the contrary, it is always our own unrighteousness that threatens and menaces the righteous cause that is entrusted to our unworthy hands.

This is something that the Christian Church must say persistently in season and out of season, for if the Word of the Lord through the lips of the Church's prophets is not always and everywhere to this effect then it is no Word of the Lord at all but a blasphemous deceit. The Word of the Lord never tells us that we are righteous; it never reassures us with the illusion that God is on our side. Indeed

4. Galatians 3, 22.

there is never any question of God's being on our side. The issue for us to consider is always to what extent, and with what degree of depth and conviction, we have placed ourselves on the Lord's side.

This message is to a peculiar degree indispensable once actual armed conflict has broken out. War is in its very nature a raging and almost hysterical period, a period in which it is well-nigh impossible for men to do justice to their own opponents, and escape from soul-destroying illusions about their own righteousness. The prophetic message of the Church to a nation at war is clear: men must learn to wage war without hating their enemies and to long and pray, even while waging war, for a peace founded upon a real will to justice rather than upon mere victory. In the calm that follows the war wise men usually realize this quickly enough, but it is difficult to remember it during the actual heat of the battle, and thus much is said then that the less wise among us find it hard to forget once the battle is over. The trouble about emotion, particularly mass emotion, is its habit of persistence long after the events that originally evoked it are past.

On a summer evening in 1870 a young Victorian clergyman named Kilvert — who achieved no fame in his lifetime, but whose delightful diary fortunately lived after him [5] — sat preparing a sermon for the next Sunday, in the peaceful English village of Bredwadine in Herefordshire, deep in the heart of rural England. He was disturbed by the sound of a commotion in the village street, and shortly afterward the sexton burst into his study to explain its cause. 'Sir,' the sexton cried, 'the Germans have licked the Frenchies at Sedan and the Emperor has surrendered with all his army!' Parson Kilvert immediately hurried out to join a crowd of

5. *Diary, 1870–1879,* Macmillan, New York, 1947.

his rejoicing parishioners, and a service of thanksgiving was straightway improvised in the open air. It had been fifty-five years since Waterloo had brought to a close the long series of wars between Britain and France. Yet to these simple English villagers the French were still the natural enemy, and to hear of their defeat was an occasion for spontaneous rejoicing. If they had known that 1870 was not in fact the last act in the drama of the French wars, but the first act in the drama of the German wars, how different their reactions might have been. The emotions that had been the appropriate accompaniment of the wars against France had absurdly survived into a new period of history in which they were an irrational archaism. Even today one of the reasons France has found it so hard to enter into an alliance with a rearmed Germany, in order to counter the threat of Russian aggression, is largely the survival of anti-German emotions in a period of history in which they are perhaps no longer appropriate — or so we all devoutly hope. But in fact wartime emotions are always archaic survivals the moment the war is over — which is one good reason for trying to damp them down as far as possible even while the war is going on. To proclaim the possibility as well as the necessity of waging war without hate is the primary prophetic task of the Church in a war-torn world.

Thus there is a Word of God that can and must be spoken even to a nation at war, a Word of mingled warning and hope, with a warning that must be heeded if the hopes are to be fulfilled: 'Wage your war,' it tells us in effect, 'without hate, without lust for revenge, and above all without self-righteousness. Never forget that your conflict is a conflict between sinners.' It is perhaps one of the basic errors of the pacifists that they have obscured the possibility of any real Word of the Lord to a nation at war. In their prophesying there is a Word of the Lord to a nation on the eve of war which is the same in any conceivable set of circumstances: Don't. But once war has broken out there can, in their view, be no conceivable Word of the Lord at all. War in their estimate is an irresistible force which imposes its own mental patterns upon and destroys all the moral scruples of those who commit the cardinal sin of embarking on it. I do not wish to criticize the pacifists here, but in this they seem to me plainly mistaken, and they have the whole weight of the Christian tradition heavily against them. With memories of events in Europe in 1938 and 1939 still vivid in my mind, I am convinced that there are worse things than war, black and horrible though war itself must always be.

Another criticism of what, as it seems to me, must be the instant and unflinching witness of the Church throughout a period of war is that of those soldiers and psychologists who tell us in effect it is impossible to fight a war without hate, that deliberate hate propaganda is an essential element in the training of a soldier. This is a point of view which no Christian can possibly accept. Every Christian must rise up and say plainly that if Christianity is true this statement is a lie. And indeed the example of many a Christian soldier through the ages demonstrates how totally false it is. Perhaps what has lent color to this particular lie is the rise of the modern citizen army in mass warfare. Nowadays the great bulk of the people who participate in war are not professional soldiers, and they do not share the motivations and attitudes characteristic of professional soldiers at their best. The psychology of the citizen soldier, who remains at heart a civilian in arms, requires no doubt a propaganda that supplies him with a motive and incentive for activities so remote from his normal way of life and psychology. Emotional hate may perhaps seem the most practical solution of the problem. But it is not really practicable, for in fact the survival of this hate after the war is over often proves a chronic embarrassment to the politicians who have the responsibility of making peace. As so often in life an unsatisfactory way of solving one problem makes it much more difficult to solve the next problem. There are in fact other possible motivations and incentives besides hate to which an appeal is constantly made during the time of war. There is, for example, the defense motive, and the necessity of creating a situation in which a restored balance of power will make it possible for us to rebuild peace on just and tolerable foundations. There is no reason why the forthright and successful waging of war should not be compatible with a certain manly respect for the virtues of the enemy, which can always be found illuminating his vices.

Often the soldier himself finds this easier to do than the civilian at home. Thus there was a storm of criticism among civilians in Britain when General Montgomery invited the captured General Ritter von Epp to dinner in his mobile headquarters immediately after the Alamein campaign. But for the Christian in a matter like this there can be no conceivable evading of what is for him a fundamental moral and spiritual issue. Hatred is the most utterly evil of all the vices, just as charity is supreme sovereign among the virtues. The Christian cannot admit the validity of hatred in any conceivable circumstances whatsoever. He can have a sympathetic understanding of how hatred too often wells up in the hearts of fallen men in a fallen world, but reliance on a policy of hate, a propaganda deliberately aimed at fanning the fires of hatred, is for him the most utterly and absolutely evil of all human sins.

But if there is a Word of the Lord that is searching and relevant and constructive even in a time of war, there is also a Word of the Lord to a nation during a period of uneasy and nervous peace, a time of 'cold war' as we now call it. There is every possibility that this present time of cold war may prove to be a very long time indeed. Even a nation sincerely convinced that it may rationally count on ultimate victory is awed by the thought of what even victory may cost the victorious nation in a war fought with such weapons as are now at our disposal. In these days fear has become rational as well as emotional, and our calculated apprehensions may well cool our martial ardor.

Another factor that may counsel both sides in the cold war to hold their hands and refrain from precipitating a hot war is the fact that rightly or wrongly each side entertains the optimistic belief that time is working in its favor. The communists are convinced by their Marxist analysis of history that the type of economic order they describe as capitalist will, because of what they call its 'internal contradictions,' gradually rot away and destroy itself from within. On the Western side of the great divide, on the other hand, there is a parallel and similar belief that the internal contradictions of a totalitarian political system based on dictatorship and imperialism will, given time, manifest themselves, so that such a system will prove incapable of prolonging its life indefinitely. These two convictions, which, for all we know, may both be right or both be wrong, at least hold out some hope of a lengthy prolongation of the cold war.

From the point of view of Christian theological analysis the confidence of both sides seems somewhat misplaced and excessive. The Christian theologian would say that in one sense both sides are right. In a fallen world all nations and societies contain and are inwardly divided by internal contradictions. Internal contradictions are peculiar neither to economic capitalism nor to political totalitarianism. History does not know of a society that contains no internal contradictions. But if internal contradictions always and necessarily brought regimes and societies to a speedy end, no society known to history would have succeeded in prolonging its existence for more than half a dozen generations or so. Human societies have a way of enduring with and bearing their internal tensions, and we have no reason to suppose that any particular regime or society must necessarily be hastening to its doom merely because it contains observable internal contradictions. As we look at Western democratic and Eastern totalitarian societies in their present condition we can observe deep-rooted internal tensions and contradictions in the structure of both.

Indeed we can even observe in some cases the same internal contradictions in each structure. Thus every society that moves beyond a purely agrarian stage creates a large class of urban workers who are not food producers. Always an urban civilization rests on the foundation of a surplus agriculture, on the use by food producers of agricultural techniques that enable them to produce more food than they themselves require for their own subsistence. This means that in every society there is a deep-seated conflict over food prices between the rural workers who produce the food and the urban workers who consume it. Here in the West this same conflict arises in one form or another in country after country, or, where a highly urbanized country such as Britain depends on imported foodstuffs, it emerges as a factor causing disharmony between different and perhaps allied nations. In Soviet society the same problem is dealt with largely through the institution of collective farming, which turns the rural food producers into something very like the helots and slaves of the urban group which controls the destiny of the nation as a whole. But the problem itself is the same on both sides of the line. We know of no urban society that has entirely escaped the tensions generated by this deep-seated conflict, but nevertheless we know of many urban societies that have succeeded in enduring for a long period of historical time despite the presence of such internal contradictions.

It is true, of course, that history knows of no society that has succeeded in maintaining itself forever, nor do we know now of any existing society that gives us any reason to suppose that it will succeed in maintaining itself forever, but this observation gives us no grounds for supposing that any particular existing society is moving rapidly toward speedy extinction. Of course we cannot say for certain, but it would seem to me rash indeed to prophesy the decadence and collapse of any existing society merely because we happen to observe that it contains deep-seated internal contradictions. No doubt it will collapse sometime or other, but for all we know that time may be a very remote one, too remote for us to take it seriously into account in any of our present calculations.

Nevertheless in the present ideological conflict the conviction of each side that its opponent's time is running short may well prove beneficial if it indefinitely prolongs the cold war and postpones the hot one. At least such a postponement will provide the Church with that necessary breathing space in which to speak prophetically to the nations of their sin and their peace. In the cold war, as in the hot war, it is useless, as well as a betrayal of the prophetic office, merely to take sides. Since the two sides are already clearly defined and know where they stand and why, merely to reinforce either one side or the other is a waste of words. If we have no message for our society except to say in effect, 'You are right and your opponents are wrong,' we may just as well keep silent. There are already too many people in the modern world who have a most unhealthy and un-Christian conviction that they are right, sometimes in the sense of being righteous altogether. Why should we seek to add to their number?

During the past few years I have been invited again and again to lecture to groups of people, sometimes in universities and colleges, sometimes to professional and vocational groups, sometimes in various church parishes, on what is now the well-worn theme of Marxism. I have two different kinds of lecture ready in my mind for use on such occasions. If I have any reason to suppose that my audience contains a proportion of convinced Marxists, I attack the Marxist gospel and philosophy with all the vigor and theological and intellectual acumen of which I am capable, endeavoring to expose the shallowness of its philosophical foundations and its pitiful inadequacy as a gospel for modern man. But if, as more often happens, I have a well-grounded suspicion that my audience contains not a single Marxist, I refrain altogether from delivering a message so ill suited to the condition of those I am addressing. I try to point out that we who are bearing our witness against communism, and preparing ourselves if necessary to withstand any possible communist aggression against our way of life and civilization, must take note of the fact that many of our social institutions in this present phase of our civilization bear an uncomfortable resemblance to much that we denounce and reject. Both are profoundly secular in spirit; both are willing to rely, in almost idolatrous fashion, on technical progress rather than spiritual insight; both are in one way or another inimical to the basic social institution of the family; neither is entirely lacking in virtue on the one hand, or free from sin on the other. I plead, as I have pleaded in this book, that the best way of giving to our Western civilization strength and cohesion, and a real belief in the greatness of its mission and the splendor of its tradition, lies through a return to and a new and deeper understanding of our own Christianity, which is neither a heart-warming emotion, nor a noble, if somewhat impracticable, ethical aspiration, but a dogma and a gospel. If the West were more true to itself and its whole way of life, inwardly and spiritually true to itself before the eyes of God, and visibly and sociologically true to itself before the eyes of men, the false dogmas and pseudo-gospel of Marxism might perhaps find fewer appreciative audiences in the world at large.

Judgment, like charity, begins at home. When the hordes of secularists and materialists menace us from without, we cannot but be reminded of the secularists and materialists in our midst. The sins that we have graven small on our own hearts God has written large on the pages of history, to show us what we ourselves would look like if ever our own sins and failings came to dominate us completely. He says to us in effect: 'Here is real materialism; cast out your own. Here is real secularism; criticize and extinguish your own secularist illusions. Here is real unbelief; fall on your knees.' Even so in the Old Testament, when the armies of the idolatrous empires encompassed the promised land and laid siege to the walls of the sacred city, the prophets of God pointed to the existence of idolatry within the ranks of the chosen people themselves, interpreting the menace of idolatry without as God's just judgment on the presence of idolatry within. One is reminded of the legend of the man who awoke with a shock from a horrible reverie, in which it seemed to him he was confronted with a would-be murderer, and found that in fact he was standing before a mirror. When a secularized and to a considerable extent apostate West looks East it sees among other things the dark reflection of itself; the very horror of the vision is part of its judgment.

But, of course, we cannot entirely account for the tremendous successes of this new kind of civilization in the modern world entirely in terms of our own backslidings and failings. It must surely contain some core of the validity that lurks beneath the tyranny and the sadism and the blood-lust and the persecutions. Just as our Western tradition has excelled and been at its best in reminding men of the preciousness of personality and personal life, and of the individual freedom without which personal life cannot flourish and be true to itself, so this new Eastern civilization has developed a kindred and compensatory stress on the equal importance of the sense of community and the values that can be found only in common life, however greatly it has misinterpreted that stress in the process. Both of these stresses are to be found side by side in the New Testament. Christ is the Saviour of each man, of each unique person with his own unique eternal destiny, and yet at the same time each person who finds the Christ remains side by side with the Christ only in the common life of the Church, which is the Body of Christ, which is the predestined agent of the reunion of all mankind in a single common life, in which the living God who has shown Himself to us in the face of the Christ must for all eternity be all in all to and for each one of us.

In the tremendous chapters that lie at the heart of the Epistle to the Romans, St. Paul has made himself the great apostle of Christian personal religion, a process in which each man one by one learns of his own personal need for redemption and finds that Christ is his own personal redeemer. But it is also St. Paul — and this must not be forgotten — who with burning eloquence lays before us the central doctrine of the Church as the new Israel, the new chosen people of God, the heir to the promises once made to the old Israel, the Body of Christ in which the personal life of each man is essentially part and parcel of the common life of the whole. Protestant writers sometimes call St. Paul the founder of Protestantism. Others point to him as the great architect of Catholicism. In one sense both are wrong, for these things go back to Christ himself, and even back to Moses and Abraham; but in another sense both are right, for our sin in modern Christendom, a sin that estranges us from the Bible, has been the supposition that these two contrasted but mutually complementary points of view are incompatible.

This revived stress on the importance and essential value of the collective life is, in my view, the almost unseen core of validity which is the secret of the East's tragic and frightening success during the last few decades. The Christian mind cannot rest content with the idea of two ultimate and incompatible validities, of the ultimate necessity of conflict between the principle of the primacy of personal life and the principle of the primacy of the collective life. The Bible makes it clear to us that life in the Church, and life in the Kingdom of God, is happily and harmoniously personal and collective at the same time. Indeed, in the doctrine of the Trinity the Christian even dares to assert that this ultimate reconciliation of the essential values of personal life and collective life is to be found even in the final reality, God Himself. It is at this high peak of Christian insight that we begin to see how even in the present context of a tragically divided world the Word of the Lord given through the prophets in the Church, and through the Church to the world, may yet be a word of reconciliation. If we consider our enemies as they show themselves at their worst, then their worst at least has something in common with our worst; we see in them our own sins writ large. But if we see them at their best, then their best complements rather than contradicts our best.

Given time and peace and patience, not merely a willingness to understand but even a desire to understand, some kind of reconciliation may not be ultimately out of the question. But when men are at bitter enmity with each other, though their reconciliation may be *possible* it is unlikely to become actual except through the agency of a reconciler. Surely this must be the role of the Christian mind, and the theme of a Christian speech to which the Christian mind will respond with native enthusiasm. The Christian task is to show in patient theological analysis and in burning prophetic utterance, in mingled tones of warning and hope, that reconciliation is still possible, and that men will neglect such possibilities only to their own ultimate undoing. Thus indeed saith the Lord God; and a prophetic Church has no choice except to repeat His words, in season and out of season, whether men will hear or whether they will forebear.

It is important to emphasize that this is in no sense another, and only very slightly less obvious, way of taking sides. This is not to endorse the point of view of the so-called 'neutralist' forces in contemporary world politics. I find it quite impossible to accept the vigorous and legalistic pacifist position, attractive to the Christian mind though it may seem at first sight. If the East should attack the West, the West has a right to resist, and must do so. This means that the West has the right and the duty to prepare itself for so terrible an ordeal, always with the prayer on its lips that such preparations may ultimately prove to have been superfluous. But if war comes, *it must come because the East attacks the West.* A conflict with the East which even seems to have been prepared and precipitated by some Western nation or nations would be the worst of all possible calamities. It would divide the West itself by horrifying other Western nations into a reluctant neutralism, and fling the existing 'neutralist' nations of Asia into the arms of Russia. There is a small handful of irresponsibles among us who sometimes advocate that we should seize the initiative, as they call it, and launch a so-called 'preventive war.' If we were to listen to their wicked, perhaps lunatic, advice we should not only meet our doom, we should deserve it.

This is what the Church must say, and yet how rarely anything like this does get said in the day-to-day life of our familiar Christian institutions. It seems to me undeniable that in a Church organized primarily on the basis of the parochial system the prophetic office does somehow get neglected. This is due partly to a right and absolutely justified stress on the supreme importance of the pastoral function of the Church in the parochial situation. The good pastor may, not altogether foolishly, entertain in his heart the fear that resolute prophetic preaching may in some cases impede his efficiency as a pastor. When we speak what from a prophetic point of view must be spoken, whether men will hear or whether they will forebear, the fear that haunts and agonizes the genuinely devoted pastor is that in a fallen world some men will choose to forebear rather than to hear. A certain young curate deeply read in the writings of Sören Kierkegaard was once told about a neighboring clergyman who had, or so a former member of his congregation complained, 'emptied his church.' 'Emptied his church!' cried the young curate, 'what a holy work!' We can perhaps understand the young curate's point of view, but we can hardly call it the point of view of a devoted pastor. It is not even the point of view of a genuine prophet, who always nourishes in his bosom at least the hope that men will choose to hear rather than to forebear. But this apparent conflict between the aims of the prophet and the aims of the pastor is always in the last analysis an illusory one. In the long run a pastoral failure always and necessarily follows upon a prophetic failure. A prophetic failure to warn the people, to help them to understand the events of history in terms of the divine purpose and the divine mercy, to equip them spiritually to withstand the shocks and misfortunes of the time, means a parochial life permanently menaced by the danger that the ultimate event may confound the people's faith. It is only on a superficial, short-term view of the problem that the prophetic and the pastoral offices of the Church seem to come into conflict. Ultimately we are driven to the conclusion that the prophetic ministry is a pastoral ministry, and that the pastoral ministry, however devoted, that is not a prophetic ministry at the same time fails to minister to the deepest needs of the flock.

THE FUNCTION OF THE THEOLOGIAN. Any resurrection of the central tradition of Western civilization, as a controlling vital force which will unify its energies and interpret and control its novelties and discoveries so that they may serve and expand our civilization rather than internally divide it, necessarily calls for a revival of theology. For the influence of theology on the most formative, crucial years in the development of the tradition of Western civilization has been so profound and so decisive that Western civilization apart from Christian theology is quite inconceivable. Certainly it could not be the Western civilization we now know and recognize. It is no exaggeration to say that the theologian in the mid-twentieth century bears a burden of responsibility, to the world as well as to the Church, heavier perhaps than his predecessors ever experienced. The task that confronts him is essentially a new one. To understand it merely in terms of the restatement of the original tradition in a new language, with reference to new thought forms and new climates of opinion — although the theologian's responsibility does include all that — is to fail to come to grips with the heart of the matter.

'Restatement' may mean no more than merely repeating the original statement all over again. Certainly one possible meaning of the verb 'to restate' is simply to repeat what was said before. Restatement in this merely repetitive sense would appear to be the aim of those Christian preachers and teachers who are usually referred to as fundamentalists. There is of course a catholic fundamentalism that is as purely repetitive in its aims as the more clearly defined Biblical fundamentalism, but normally, at least in the English-speaking countries, we regard this kind of fundamentalism as the peculiar intellectual vice of a decadent and devitalized Protestant Christianity. This kind of fundamentalism is not really the mere restatement it aims at being, because the ancient orthodoxy which it proposes to restate was not in fact militantly fundamentalist in its original form. Fundamentalism is essentially the refusal to heed the verdict of modern criticism, or to employ the tools of modern criticism, in carrying out the theological task. Fundamentalism is not older than modern criticism; on the contrary, it is younger, for it is essentially a response to modern criticism. There is all the difference in the world between willfully refusing to take any notice of modern criticism, and merely being innocent of it. The great classical theologians, both Catholic and Protestant, often seem to take a view of the scriptures, and of the theological tradition in general, which resembles that of the fundamentalists. But this resemblance is merely accidental and superficial. The great classical theologians adopted an attitude toward their subject matter which resembles that of the modern fundamentalist primarily because they knew of no good reason for doing anything else. To adopt an attitude in defiance of modern criticism is quite different from adopting the same or a similar attitude in ignorance of the very possibility of such a criticism. In the same way a man who believes that the earth is flat in the twentieth century must be sharply distinguished from the man who held the same belief in, say, the fourth century B.C. In classical times there were several good reasons for supposing that the earth is flat, whereas now there are none. Once such a belief was in accordance with all the known evidence; now it can be held only in defiance of all the known evidence. The distinction is quite fundamental.

But the word 'restatement' may also mean — and this is what it usually does mean nowadays — a fresh statement of an old message in new language and thought forms. This is the more legitimate and important meaning of the term, but here also there are dangers to which many who were sincerely dedicated to the theological task have succumbed. At the opposite extreme from the fundamentalist fallacy in contemporary theology is what we may call the 'modernist' fallacy, a theology so liberal and so subservient to the thought forms and the intellectual fashions of the present moment that it fails to be a genuine restatement of the original tradition and, being so much a thing of the day, is devoid of any capacity to survive into the future. It attempts to abstract some alleged core or kernel or essence of the original tradition which can be put forward as though it were an integral part of the contemporary and transitory phase in the development of culture.

The failure of the so-called modernist[6] or liberal theology is a failure to be truly critical. A genuinely critical theology can assimilate and learn to use the new thought forms in the service of its self-expression only by means of a ruthlessly critical process in which it sifts through the new thought forms in order to discover how much in the passing transitional phase of our culture represents a lasting and permanent contribution to the enrichment of the tradition, and how much consists merely of the fashionable illusions of the time.

What the theological task in this age really calls for is neither fundamentalism on the one hand nor modernism on the other, but a ruthlessly critical orthodoxy, a self-critical orthodoxy on the one hand, and an orthodoxy critical of current intellectual fashions and developments on the other. Only a theology with such aims and convictions as these can hope so to restate the tradition that it will be a genuine and honest restatement and at the same time contribute to the unification and development of Western civilization. Fundamentalist theology is irrelevant to the times and the times are irrelevant to fundamentalist theology. Modernist theology is mastered by the times, and for the modernist the so-called spirit of the age dictates his estimate of what is living and what is dead in the tradition.

6. Properly speaking, the word 'modernist' refers to certain tendencies and movements of thought in the Roman Catholic Church about the beginning of this century. The word has also been used to describe movements in the Anglican Church. Parallel tendencies in Protestantism are usually termed 'liberal.'

But critical orthodoxy maintains a genuine dialectic between theology and the times, a process in which the times contribute to the theologian's intellectual equipment new concepts, analogies, and philosophical tools of analysis, which will enable him to achieve a profounder and more accurate articulation of the tradition, and the times themselves are purged by a critical and prophetic process which enables us to see what will live and what must die among the achievements of the modern age. For some of these achievements are indeed predestined to live, to survive as permanent elements in the Western tradition, while others, it is equally certain, are condemned to die, to be set on one side by the developing Western tradition as alien to its spirit and irrelevant to its vital needs.

Such a critical sifting through of contemporary intellectual culture is the theologian's vital concern. The very weight and extent of contemporary intellectual culture impose an immensely heavy burden on such a man. He must know something of the history of science and much of the present scientific trends; he must be quite as much a philosopher as a theologian; he cannot ignore politics and sociology; for the same reason, political and social history falls well within the sphere of his interests; art and the experience of the artist are for him fraught with immense significance; and yet at the same time his whole intellectual life must be deeply grounded in scripture and liturgy and the great traditions of the Christian Church. Classical and past theology is for him a daring and adventurous attempt to articulate the meaning of those traditions, an attempt richly rewarded and in part successful. Present theology, the intellectual venture in which he is himself actively engaged, is an attempt to articulate those traditions with even greater clarity of thought and language. He could not take part in the search for theological understanding if he did not believe it was possible to deepen and extend it. If there can be no development and progress in theology, there can be no honest theologian, and theology itself is a waste of time. Yet for him theology is also a criticism of life and culture, a prophetic as well as a merely scholarly task.

But perhaps the primary responsibility of the theologian here and now is to restore our culture's confidence in the integrity of theology as an honest and self-respecting intellectual enterprise. Clearly this is not the kind of question that can be discussed at length in a book such as this, dedicated to very different themes. Clearly also this is not the kind of question that can be fruitfully discussed otherwise than at length. Here I can say no more than this: theology will not regain either the respect of modern intellectual culture, or its own self-respect — and self-respect is very largely a reflection of the respect given to us by other men whom we ourselves respect; it is being respected by the sort of people whose respect we covet — unless and until the theological task is carried on within the Church in such a way that the genuine intellectual freedom and independence of the theologian in the pursuit of his task, comparable to that which other men now enjoy in other spheres of thought and research, are made quite manifest to the world. The suspicion that the theologian is the paid advocate of a cut-and-dried point of view has done more than anything else to damage the reputation of theology in the modern world, and the practice of not a few Christian Churches and communities has done much to foster and reinforce precisely this widespread misconception. Naturally the theologian is tied down to a certain initial subject matter. He can no more twist his data to suit his own theories than any other honest investigator in any other sphere of research, but in relation to his data he must insist on being as free as other men studying other sets of data are accustomed to insist on being free. He must not only insist on being free, he must manifest his freedom. The one tribunal to which he can and must refer is the tribunal of his peers, the theological community, other theologians as free-thinking and critical as he is himself.

Such a state of affairs does not mean the end of orthodoxy. On the contrary, it is only in such an atmosphere that orthodoxy can live and develop and display its vitality. We need have no fear for the future of theological orthodoxy if the world can see the critical intellects of free men developing it, articulating it freshly, bringing out of their treasury things new and old, displaying its prophetic vigor and force in a ruthless criticism of contemporary culture and the prevalent assumptions — a criticism that responds to and appreciates the real achievement of modern man by setting it free from those characteristic illusions which in the actual history of our culture have provided the earthen vessels that contain the treasures of modern discovery and science. The essence of modernity is a peculiar kind of vision which is a by-product of a peculiar kind of blindness. Since men have only two eyes, and those situated on the front of the face, to see anything clearly is necessarily not to see something else at all. This is one of the inescapable limitations inherent to the finitude of the human mind, and this is why tradition is so vitally important in preserving the balance of a culture, for tradition corrects the blindness of the present age by handing down to us an account of what our forefathers saw when they were looking in a different direction. Without tradition we are indeed imprisoned in modernity, the helpless slaves of the *zeitgeist*. But a tradition that no longer possesses the capacity to add present vision to past vision, and to construct from the two a unified world view and a harmonious philosophy of life, is a tradition that has lost its vitality. When tradition has lost its vitality, the days of the civilization of which the particular tradition is the motivating force are clearly numbered. Many people today suppose that the great Christian tradition that underlies our civilization has lost this genius for combining things new and old in a single life-giving vision, although few of them are prepared to go on from there and deduce from such a premise the inevitable conclusion that if this is indeed tragically so then our civilization must inevitably perish. Obviously, I do not believe that this is so, and I regard it as the peculiar and heavy responsibility of the theologian to demonstrate to the world that the many reports of the death of the Christian tradition, which have been issued at regular intervals ever since the eighteenth century, have in fact been, in Mark Twain's immortal words, 'greatly exaggerated.'

In his Gifford Lectures on *The Mystery of Being*[7] — one of the most valuable and memorable volumes in a valuable and memorable series — the contemporary French philosopher, Gabriel Marcel, speaks again and again of what he calls 'a broken world,' a world which, as he defines it, 'in striving after a certain type of unity . . . has lost its real unity.' This book might well have been entitled *The Broken World* and it might well have quoted Marcel's definition of a broken world on its title page. But I have preferred to use as my title a kindred phrase from one of the great sonnets of Gerard Manley Hopkins, 'the bent world.' The bent world suggests to me something that comes even closer to the truth than the phrase, 'a broken world.'

7. Henry Regnery Co., Chicago, 1951.

For I cannot see that there has yet been anywhere anything quite so clean and final as a definite break. What we see in the modern history of Western civilization is better described as a bending and a straining, a declining of Western civilization at a sharp angle, so that it has lost its proper stature and no longer points upward to the stars. The bent world slants away from its proper purposes; it is estranged from its nature, out of line with its past, astray from its destiny, but, being a resilient, strain-bearing creature, it has not lost all contact and connection with the roots that are the source of its vitality. The traditions of our civilization are still represented in the heart and center of our civilization; our modernity has never lacked its critics; there have always been those among us who knew that our illusions were illusions. Two great revolutions have swept over our civilization, each of them pledged to the destruction of what they have agreed in interpreting as the 'infamous thing,' and yet the 'infamous thing' still continues in being. History — with its tragic record of the way in which men have survived external horrors and internal treacheries, endured alike the consequences of their own sins and the sins of other men — is still the natural and proper nourishment of faith and hope. We cannot say that the bent world will be straightened; we can only labor, not altogether without confidence, to straighten out the crooked places, to stand it erect once more in the center of the stage of human history. My guess is that when at last this bent world of ours is made straight, when at last it stands erect among us once more, it will be seen, surprisingly enough to some, to embody the form of a cross, and that men will rejoice to sit in the shade of its wide, all-encompassing, all-comprehending boughs. 'The leaves of the tree of life were for the healing of the nations.'